Piety and Politics

Piety and Politics

Religion and the Rise of Absolutism in England, Württemberg and Prussia

MARY FULBROOK

Lecturer in German History,
University College, London

CAMBRIDGE UNIVERSITY PRESS

Cambridge
London   New York   New Rochelle
Melbourne   Sydney

Published by the Press Syndicate of the University of Cambridge
The Pitt Building, Trumpington Street, Cambridge CB2 1RP
32 East 57th Street, New York, NY 10022, USA
296 Beaconsfield Parade, Middle Park, Melbourne 3206, Australia

First published 1983

Printed in Great Britain at
the University Press, Cambridge

Library of Congress catalogue card number: 83-5316

British Library Cataloguing in Publication Data
Fulbrook, Mary
Piety and politics.
1. Protestantism
2. Great Britain – Politics and government – 1603–1714
3. Great Britain – Politics and government – 1714–1760
4. Germany – Politics and government – 1517–1648
5. Germany – Politics and government – 1648–1789
I. Title
280'.4'0942   BX4838

ISBN 0 521 25612 7 hard covers
ISBN 0 521 27633 0 paperback

Contents

Preface

The relationship of Protestant religious movements to social and political changes in early modern Europe has long intrigued historians and sociologists. Did religious ideas have an independent influence on the course of social and political development, or were they rather dependent on deeper, underlying socioeconomic changes? Marx, Weber, Tawney, and many others have sought to interpret the complex interrelationships among elements of cultural, political and socioeconomic changes in a formative period for the modern world.

In the context of continuing historical and theoretical controversies, this book undertakes a systematic comparative-historical analysis of religion and politics in three carefully selected cases. In England, Württemberg, and Prussia, at the times when the rulers were attempting to introduce the apparatus of absolutist rule, there were very similar religious movements for the further reform of the Protestant state churches: the Puritan and Pietist movements. Yet, while sharing similar religious aims and ethos, Puritans and Pietists developed very different attitudes and activities in relation to would-be absolutist rule in each case. These ranged from the activism and anti-absolutism of English Puritans, through the passive anti-absolutism of Pietists in Württemberg, to the activism and support of absolutism of the Prussian Pietists. Such surprisingly different patterns of political contribution to the success or failure of absolutism – with its fundamental historical consequences – represent promising terrain for the generation and testing of a coherent explanation.

In the course of examining these three cases, it became clear that approaches focussing on inherent characteristics of a religious movement, whether idealist or materialist in emphasis, were essentially inadequate. Neither religious ideas, nor social class bases, appeared to account for the different political stances developed by the Puritan and Pietist movements. Instead, it was only by examining the different sociopolitical environments in which Puritans and Pietists sought to establish the Kingdom of God upon earth that the different patterns of political attitude and alliance became comprehensible. There was a complex interplay of historically given aspirations and capacities, in the context of differing structural opportunities and constraints, which in combination explain the different paths of political development.

This work is one of historical sociology. Combining a structural analysis with an account of agency, it seeks to cut across the boundaries of the institutionally separated disciplines of history and sociology, in the interests of gaining a more adequate understanding of the patterns of the past as they appear to us today. As well as proposing a particular solution to a specific historical problem, the book is intended to contribute towards a more adequate theoretical approach to the study of ideas and sociopolitical change.

In an earlier incarnation, the argument was presented as a doctoral dissertation at Harvard University. I would like to thank my thesis advisers for their stimulation and advice: Daniel Bell, Theda Skocpol, and Ann Swidler. Hartmut Lehmann also provided help on Pietists at a very early stage. During the lengthy process of revising and rewriting the thesis into its present form, a number of individuals have been particularly helpful. I am most grateful to John Morrill for his challenging scepticism about the entire enterprise, combined with some excellent historical advice; and to Christopher Hill for his generous support of the project. Geoffrey Hawthorn, John Morrill, and Valerie Pearl very kindly took the trouble to read through the entire draft of the book, and made comments which helped me to reduce the historical inaccuracies and to clarify the presentation of the argument. Theda Skocpol assuaged my doubts about the concluding chapter, and was a constant source of stimulus and encouragement for the writing of both thesis and book. None of these, of course, bears any responsibility for the inadequacies which remain. The Fellowship of New Hall, Cambridge, where my rewriting was carried out, provided a congenial and lively atmosphere in which to work. My husband, Julian, sustained my endeavours throughout.

The work was supported by Harvard graduate scholarships; by a Harvard Center for European Studies Krupp Fellowship, held at the London School of Economics; and by a Lady Margaret Research Fellowship at New Hall, Cambridge. A small grant from the LSE staff research fund enabled me to spend some time working at Tübingen University Library. I am grateful not only for the financial support of these institutions, but also for the academic communities and environments which make work such as this both possible and pleasurable.

London
September 1982

MARY FULBROOK

1

Introduction: cases and controversies

In seeking to understand the patterns of the past, we are frequently confronted with questions of religion. Men and women assess the inequities of this world in the light of transcendent standards, and strive to bring about a better society. Sometimes religious movements have seemed merely expressive of intolerable conditions: momentary outbursts of inefficacious revolt. Sometimes they have appeared to render the intolerable more bearable: to interpret present sufferings in ways which make it possible to continue living with them. And sometimes religious movements have appeared to act as autonomous creative forces, with a capacity to transform the nature of the societies in which they arose.

One such movement, which has been credited with a powerful role in the making of the 'modern world', is English Puritanism. In the century prior to the 'Puritan Revolution', a set of religious ideas and orientations arose which has been linked, in a variety of ways, with aspects of innovation in early modern Europe: with the beginnings of modern rational capitalism, science, democratic liberalism, individualism.[1] This movement has been seen, in particular, as playing a crucial part in the overthrow of attempts at absolutist rule in England, thus laying the foundations of the parliamentary state in which capitalist and industrial development could flourish. Interpretations of the part played by Puritanism vary, from those allowing it an independent causal role, to those representing it as a dependent factor, reflecting more basic underlying socioeconomic conditions.

A movement inherently similar to Puritanism, considered in terms of its religious ethos and aspirations, arose also under conditions of attempted

---

[1] There is a vast literature on Puritanism and its supposed historical consequences. The classics include: Max Weber, *The Protestant Ethic and the Spirit of Capitalism* (London: George Allen and Unwin, 1930, transl. T. Parsons); R.K. Merton, *Science, Technology and Society in Seventeenth-Century England* (New York: Howard Fertig, 1970; orig. 1938); R.H. Tawney, *Religion and the Rise of Capitalism* (Harmondsworth: Penguin, 1938); and the controversies ensuing. In relation to the topic of this study, the various works of Christopher Hill are particularly relevant, as are: Michael Walzer, *The Revolution of the Saints* (New York: Atheneum, 1974) and Walzer, 'Puritanism as a Revolutionary Ideology' in S.N. Eisenstadt (ed.), *The Protestant Ethic and Modernization* (New York: Basic Books, 1968); and for a guide to approaches to the 'Puritan Revolution' from the seventeenth century onwards, see generally R.C. Richardson, *The Debate on the English Revolution* (London: Methuen, 1977).

absolutist rule in certain continental European states. This was Pietism: a variant, like Puritanism, of what may be termed a 'precisionist' religious orientation. Pietism too has been credited with the paternity of various aspects of the 'modern world'.[2] Yet it played a very different part in the development of the absolutist states in which it arose. In one state, Württemberg, Pietists generally shared the parliamentary sympathies of the English Puritans. Yet when, in the mid-eighteenth century, the Württemberg Estates found themselves embroiled in constitutional struggles with their ruler, attempting to defend the representative tradition against prerogative rule, Württemberg Pietists remained on the whole politically passive and quietistic. In another state, Brandenburg-Prussia, Pietists did make a major political contribution; but in this case, they positively supported the development of absolutist rule. Pietist institutions, ideology, and organisation were integral to the successful establishment of absolutism in Prussia.[3]

How can these different patterns of political attitude and activity be accounted for? What made three essentially similar religious movements make such different contributions to the politics of absolutism in early modern Europe? Some historians and sociologists have sought the answer in theological and social-psychological aspects of Puritanism and Pietism; others have focussed rather on material interests and class bases of the movements. The field is mined with theoretical controversies, as scholars with different assumptions and inclinations suggest different answers in each case. Marxists and anti-Marxists, Whigs and revisionists, neo-Weberians and 'a-theoretical' narrative historians have all, explicitly or implicitly, suggested different answers to the problem.

[2] See for example: Kurt Aland, *Pietismus und Moderne Welt* (Witten: Luther-Verlag, 1974); Koppel Pinson, *Pietism as a Factor in the Rise of German Nationalism* (New York: Columbia University Press, 1934); A. Lindt and K. Deppermann (eds.), *Pietismus und Neuzeit* (Bielefeld: Luther-Verlag, vol. 1, 1974, vol. 2, 1975); Martin Schmidt, 'Einleitung' to M. Schmidt and W. Jannasch (eds.), *Das Zeitalter des Pietismus* (Bremen: Carl Schünemann Verlag, 1965).
[3] The classic study of Pietism is Albrecht Ritschl, *Geschichte des Pietismus* (Bonn: Adolph Marcus, 3 vols., 1880–6); the most important recent studies, for present purposes, are: Hartmut Lehmann, *Pietismus und Weltliche Ordnung in Württemberg vom 17. bis zum 20. Jahrhundert* (Stuttgart: W. Kohlhammer Verlag, 1969); Klaus Deppermann, *Der Hallesche Pietismus und der Preussische Staat unter Friedrich III. (I.)* (Göttingen: Vandenhoek und Ruprecht, 1961); Carl Hinrichs, *Preussentum und Pietismus* (Göttingen: Vandenhoek und Ruprecht, 1971); and the series of articles on Puritanism, Jansenism, and Pietism, edited by Angermann under the title 'Religion – Politik – Gesellschaft im 17. und 18. Jahrhundert. Ein Versuch in Vergleichender Sozialgeschichte', *Historische Zeitschrift* 214 (1) (1972): 26–95.
  In this study, the terms 'Prussia' and 'Brandenburg-Prussia' are used interchangeably, to refer to the various territories over which the Hohenzollerns ruled during the period under study. The investigation is concerned particularly with Pietism in Halle, in the province of Magdeburg-Halberstadt; Berlin, in Brandenburg; and Königsberg, East Prussia. For the complexities of Prussian politics, see Chapter 3, below; and for the general historical background, see the dated but still useful book by W.H. Bruford, *Germany in the Eighteenth Century* (Cambridge: Cambridge University Press, 1935).

One notable feature of most approaches is that they have tended to explore aspects of each movement in isolation. Specialists in each field have concerned themselves with one or another of the three cases, and have sought explanations in features (whether 'ideal' or 'material') internal to the particular movement in question. Proffered solutions have not then been tested systematically against comparative evidence.

This study seeks, not to present new material hitherto unexplored, but rather to develop a new approach to the evidence which may help to provide a more adequate explanation. By a systematic comparative-historical analysis of three cases, which present certain suggestive and interesting similarities and differences, it is possible to cross-check and evaluate certain prevalent explanations. It is also possible to determine more clearly what features might be causally important in different patterns of development. Such comparative analysis can suggest a new answer to the historical problem of the different political contributions made by English Puritanism, Pietism in Württemberg, and Pietism in Prussia. It can also have wider, theoretical implications for approaches to the study of religion, politics, and social change.

In this introductory chapter, brief sketches are presented of the three movements under analysis, and the organization of the argument developed in subsequent chapters is previewed in the context of current controversies.

The cases

In England from the Elizabethan settlement of religion (1559) to the outbreak of the Civil War in the 1640s, there existed a broad, complex and varying set of religious, social and cultural concerns which were known as Puritanism. Similar concerns, collectively known as Pietism, arose in Germany in the 1680s and '90s. In Württemberg, a Pietist tradition has continued, through changes of form and substance, to the present day. In Prussia, after the mid-eighteenth century, Pietism generally dissolved and dissipated as a coherent movement. 'Puritan' and 'Pietist' were initially used (as were 'precisian', 'precisionist', and 'Präzisionismus') as terms of mockery and abuse. When used to refer specifically to religious orientations, they denoted, broadly, attitudes of particular piety and unusual moral earnestness, or 'preciseness'; and, more narrowly, particular and varying programmes for the further reformation of the Protestant state church. The terms tended to denote a position on a spectrum, rather than a completely specifiable viewpoint on a set of particular issues. In Chapter 2, problems of definition will be considered in more detail; here, the external histories of each movement will be introduced.

The word 'Puritanism' first came into use in England in the so-called vestiarian controversies of the 1560s: in the disputes over the continued wearing of popish vestments in the Protestant Church of England. These disputes were the direct consequence of the incomplete nature of the Elizabethan Settlement of 1559 – a settlement which, while reversing the Catholicism of Mary's reign, failed to bring about a complete doctrinal and ceremonial reformation which would have brought the English church into line with the 'best reformed churches' of the continent. Elizabethan Puritans may be characterised as those people, both clerical and lay, who urgently pressed for further reformation of the English church from within. Those who, on the other hand, urged a 'reformation without tarrying for anye' and became separatists, abandoning the concept of one Holy Commonwealth of church and state, have usually been excluded from the concept of Puritanism. Puritans decried the fact that the Elizabethan church was 'but halfly reformed'; they were not prepared to accept uncritically the status quo; but yet they felt that the church remained a viable vehicle within which to work for further reform. Specific programmes for change ranged from moderate proposals for the encouragement of a 'godly, preaching ministry' within an episcopalian framework, to the more radical presbyterian movement led by Field, Travers, and Cartwright.[4]

These agitations for further reform experienced varying fortunes in the Elizabethan period. In a time of leniency, under Archbishop Grindal, the cause of moderate reformers appeared hopeful; in a time of reaction, in 1583 and subsequently, the persecutions of Whitgift and Bancroft drove Puritans to more extremist measures and underground organisation. By the 1590s the – largely clerical – presbyterian movement had been harried into disarray. It was the more moderate Puritan orientation to the conduct of life and the quality of worship which survived into seventeenth-century England.

Puritan hopes for further reform on the accession of James I were dashed in the aftermath of the Hampton Court Conference; and in the following two decades Puritanism remained a largely quiescent orientation of piety within a relatively tolerant broad church. But with the ascendance of the Laudian party in the 1620s and '30s, Puritans were roused into active opposition. 'Puritanism' now came to include, not only those desiring further reform, but also a large proportion of English men

---

[4] The classic studies of Elizabethan Puritanism are: M.M. Knappen, *Tudor Puritanism* (Chicago: University of Chicago Press, 1939); and Patrick Collinson, *The Elizabethan Puritan Movement* (London: Jonathan Cape, 1967); for the background, see A.G. Dickens, *The English Reformation* (New York: Schocken Books, 1964). On problems of definition, see for example, Basil Hall, 'Puritanism: The Problem of Definition' in G.J. Cuming (ed.), *Studies in Church History*, vol. 2 (London: Nelson, 1965); and Christopher Hill, *Society and Puritanism in Pre-revolutionary England* (New York: Schocken Books, 1967), ch. 1; and Chapter 2, below.

and women concerned to defend the settlement of the Church of England against the catholicising innovations, as they saw them, of the Arminians and Laud. Furthermore, these religious positions were intertwined with social and political controversies in such a way that the contemporary meaning of 'Puritan' broadened to embrace a diversity of themes and positions, leading into what has become known as the 'Puritan Revolution'.[5]

During the period of the Civil Wars and Interregnum, the varying alliances making up the initial opposition to Charles I and Archbishop Laud fell apart. In the sphere of religion, there was a proliferation of different parties and sects – Presbyterian, Independent, Leveller, Ranter, Digger, Fifth Monarchist, Baptist, Quaker, and so on. By the time of the Restoration, specific labels for varying religious groups were used, in preference to the vague, all-embracing term 'Puritan'. Particularly after the Act of Toleration, 1689, 'Dissenters' and 'Nonconformists' are those whose piety, now outside the established church, might earlier have been directed towards the more protestant reformation of the Church of England.[6]

Thus English Puritanism, from the 1560s to the 1640s, was a broad, and changing, cultural force in England. As distinct from perennial attitudes of piety recurring in the history of the English church, it was also a movement for the reform of a church which was coterminous with a godly nation – or a nation that needed to be roused, educated, and disciplined into godliness. It found its expression both through organised movements – pressures in Parliament; ministerial *classes*, exercises, and prophesyings; research and propaganda, parish surveys, petitions, and pamphlets; publishing of tracts and literature; associations for the support of a preaching ministry and lectureships – and through more diffuse channels of cultural influence, ranging from Puritan preaching and education through to the lay piety cultivated in small circles of the godly. In all these ways, both diffuse and specific, Puritanism developed as a powerful force within Elizabethan and early Stuart England. When, for whatever other reasons, the English state experienced a crisis eventuating in Civil War and constitutional experiment, Puritanism was seen by

---

5 See, for example: Mark Curtis, 'Hampton Court Conference and its Aftermath', *History* 46 (156) (1961): 1–16; William Haller, *The Rise of Puritanism* (Philadelphia: University of Pennsylvania Press, 1972); N. Tyacke, 'Puritanism, Arminianism and Counter-Revolution' in C. Russell (ed.), *The Origins of the English Civil War* (London: Macmillan, 1973); H.R. Trevor-Roper, *Archbishop Laud, 1573–1645* (London: Macmillan and Co., 1940).

6 See for example: Christopher Hill, *The World Turned Upside Down* (Harmondsworth: Penguin, 1975); A.L. Morton, *The World of the Ranters* (London: Lawrence and Wishart, 1970). The term 'Puritan' is still used by some scholars for the post-Restoration period, as in Whiting's *Studies in English Puritanism, 1660–1688* (London: SPCK, 1931), and Hugh Barbour, *The Quakers in Puritan England* (New Haven: Yale University Press, 1964).

many to have played a central role in the parliamentary opposition to would-be absolutist rule. That absolutism never succeeded in England, setting it on a different historical path from many of its European neighbours, was determined partly by the political conflagration of the mid-seventeenth century. And historians of diverse theoretical perspectives would agree with the assertion of Lawrence Stone that

It is as safe as any broad generalization of history can be to say that without the ideas, the organization and the leadership supplied by Puritanism there would have been no revolution at all.[7]

Or, in the words of Christopher Hill:

the English Revolution could not have succeeded even to the limited extent it did without the power of Puritanism to awaken and organize and discipline large masses of people who knew what they fought for and loved what they knew.[8]

Pietism in Germany originated, as did English Puritanism, as a movement for the reform of the church from within. Yet in the case of Lutheran Germany, it was not a recent and 'but halfly reformed' Protestant church, but rather an orthodoxy with over a century of institutionalisation, characterised to some extent by scholasticism, dogmatic dispute, and irrelevance to the daily life of most people. Despite the endeavours of a few progressive, reforming individuals, in the years during and following the Thirty Years War religious life was at a low ebb. German churches were open to criticism, as those concerned to bring about an active Christianity saw the need for a missionary effort to awaken the people to a living and genuine faith.[9]

The individual generally regarded as the father-figure of Pietism, Philipp Jakob Spener, developed a coherent intellectual synthesis of a number of ideas tending to go beyond the doctrinal reformation started by Luther. Spener's *Pia Desideria*, published in 1675, presented a theologically respectable programme for reform. At the same time, his support of the idea of conventicles, one of which he had supervised in Frankfurt since 1670, provided a model for the institutional vehicle for fostering a pious life. Spener's institution of small groups within the established church, for Bible reading, repetition of the sermon, prayer and discussion, and Spener's exhortations to the personal practice of piety in all aspects of everyday life, formed the basis and pattern of the Pietist movement.[10]

---

[7] Lawrence Stone, *The Causes of the English Revolution, 1529–1642* (London: Routledge and Kegan Paul, 1972), p. 103.

[8] Christopher Hill, *Economic Problems of the Church* (Oxford: Clarendon Press, 1956; 1963 edn), p. 352.

[9] See generally: Hans Leube, *Die Reformideen in der Deutschen Lutherischen Kirche zur Zeit der Orthodoxie* (Leipzig: Verlag von Dörffling und Franke, 1924); Ritschl, *Pietismus*; Martin Schmidt, *Pietismus* (Stuttgart: W. Kohlhammer Verlag, 1972).

[10] On Spener, see particularly: Johannes Wallmann, *Philipp Jakob Spener und die Anfänge des Pietismus* (Tübingen: J.C.B. Mohr (Paul Siebeck), 1970); Paul Grünberg, *Philipp Jakob Spener* (Göttingen: Vandenhoek und Ruprecht, 3 vols., 1893–1906).

The Pietist emphasis on the reformation of life as well as doctrine built both on existing religious traditions in Germany and on the influence of Dutch Reformed Pietism and English Puritanism. Lutheran orthodoxy even accused Pietists of dissolving the Lutheran purity of doctrine in their interest in achieving a genuine experience of faith and regeneration. The Pietist movement experienced different fortunes in different German states. In some areas, established secular and religious authorities opposed the movement to such an extent that committed Pietists were forced to leave, incapable of gaining any sort of foothold from which to work. Hamburg in the 1690s is a notable example of such persecution. In other areas, Pietists found some sort of base from which to attempt to reform the religious life of church and people. It would, in principle, be possible to undertake a detailed comparative analysis of the fates of the Pietist movements in a number of German towns and states. But this study is concerned only with two in particular, in which Pietism became a historically important force. In both Württemberg, a small Duchy in the south-western corner of what we now know as Germany, and Brandenburg-Prussia, a sprawling mass of territories largely in the more recently colonised areas of the north-east, Pietists were able to establish themselves. And, as indicated in the opening remarks of this chapter, in these two areas the Pietist movements developed in interestingly different ways.

In Württemberg, in the late seventeenth and early eighteenth centuries, Pietist attitudes became widespread in critical response to a combination of social and natural disasters at a time when the ruler was introducing baroque, hedonistic culture in imitation of French absolutism and the Versailles court. Württemberg Pietists interpreted the various devastations as signs of God's wrath, and in the manner of Old Testament prophets inveighed against the sins of an iniquitous court and an ungodly people. Culturally, Pietism echoed English Puritanism's stance of 'country' criticisms of the debauchery and immorality of the court. Politically, Pietists worked to uphold the old Estates traditions of co-operation with the ruler in a representative system.[11]

After the Treaty of Utrecht in 1713, Württemberg experienced a period of increasing prosperity and peace. The character of Pietism began to change. Moral, political and social criticism gave way to a quietistic period of theological study and doctrinal elaboration, as Pietist concerns were in practice incorporated into the Württemberg state church. The peace of the church was briefly disturbed in the reign of the Catholic Duke Karl Alexander; but following his sudden death, Pietist activities were able to continue. The figure dominating the Pietist movement for

---

[11] See generally: Heinrich Hermelink, *Geschichte der Evangelischen Kirche in Württemberg* (Stuttgart and Tübingen: Rainer Wunderlich Verlag Hermann Leins, 1949); Lehmann, *Pietismus und Weltliche Ordnung*.

decades, through his teaching and writings, was Johann Albrecht Bengel, whose Biblical and mathematical labours suggested 1836 as the year of the Second Coming.[12]

Troubles erupted again in the 1750s and '60s, as the Seven Years War posed again the problems of raising unconstitutional revenues, making policy decisions without the Estates' consent, and the ruler's control of the army. In many ways, the issues at stake were similar to those of the 1640s in England, as the Württemberg Estates struggled to retain what they considered to be their inherited constitutional rights and privileges against the aspirations of the ruler for prerogative rule. These struggles did not, as in England, lead to Civil War; and they were partially resolved in the *Erbvergleich* of 1770. But, despite their earlier political activism in the cause of the Estates, Pietists in the mid-eighteenth century remained largely passive and quietistic: they played no active role in political life comparable to that of the Puritans. The one major exception, Johann Jacob Moser, who was imprisoned by the Duke in 1759, commanded little general support and sympathy among Württemberg Pietists. On the whole, Württemberg Pietists tended in principle to support the cause of the Estates. But in practice they did little to contribute to the political struggles. Millennial beliefs in Württemberg tended, not towards political activism, but rather to a certain passivity, as Pietists suffered the rule of Anti-Christ on the assumption that God knew best in determining the course of history.[13]

Pietism in Prussia was introduced partly through the work of Spener, who moved to Berlin in 1691, and partly through the activities of his young friend and admirer, August Hermann Francke, in Halle. Francke, ejected from Saxony for his Pietist activities, set about establishing a firm foundation for religious, moral and social reform in his pastorate of Glaucha on the outskirts of Halle. Having experienced a profoundly affecting personal conversion, Francke sought to bring to others a living, active Christianity through a variety of institutional means. He was not prepared, in old-Lutheran fashion, to remain a 'vessel' of the divine, withdrawing into emotional and contemplative mysticism; rather, Francke saw himself as God's 'tool' for transforming the world and establishing God's Kingdom on earth. Relying on God's beneficence, as providentially expressed through the generosity of his fellow men, Francke founded a series of institutions (still known as the *Franckesche Stiftungen*), starting with his renowned orphanage and ranging from Biblical translation, publishing and promotion works to worldwide missionary, manufacturing and trading concerns. Pietism as insti-

[12] See Gottfried Mälzer, *Johann Albrecht Bengel: Leben und Werk* (Stuttgart: Calwer Verlag, 1970).
[13] Lehmann, *Pietismus und Weltliche Ordnung*; Reinhard Rürup, *Johann Jacob Moser: Pietismus und Reform* (Wiesbaden: Franz Steiner Verlag, 1965).

tuted in Prussia was initially conceived as a missionary movement with universalistic aims and ideals.[14]

Gradually however Prussian Pietism became absorbed into the workings of the Prussian state. Initially under Elector Friedrich III (who crowned himself King Friedrich I in Königsberg, East Prussia, in 1701), and more particularly under his successor Friedrich Wilhelm I, the 'soldier King', Pietism was transformed into an ideological and organisational support of Prussian absolutism. Pietists rethought their attitudes towards absolutist court life, as they made use of the legal, political and financial support of the state in furtherance of their religious projects. Prussian rulers, on investigating Pietist activities, saw their potential usefulness for purely secular purposes. A partnership developed, asymmetrically biassed in the interests of the more powerful partner, the state, which used Pietist organisational ability and activism for its own ends. An orphanage for soldiers' children was founded at Potsdam, designed and staffed by Halle-trained Pietists; the Berliner Kadettenhaus, a military analogy of the Halle Pädagogium, was similarly founded and run on Pietist lines; Pietist preachers were employed to minister to the needs of the army, and to spread literacy, piety, and obedience among the soldiers; and Pietists were sent to fill key positions in the provinces. By the late 1730s, a Pietist education and a personal profession of Pietism (however cynical) were essential prerequisites for those aspiring to state service. As Carl Hinrichs has put it, Pietism in Prussia had been transformed from an ecumenical movement with universal aims into a servant of the Prussian state.[15]

In the mid- and late eighteenth century, Pietism lost its hard-won position of dominance in Prussia. Political, cultural and intellectual developments under Friedrich II ('Frederick the Great') pushed Pietism once more into a marginal and passive position. But in the crucial period of the establishment of Prussian militaristic absolutism, and the conversion of the provincial, feudal aristocracy into a court-oriented service nobility, Pietism played a vital, positive political role. In ideology and organisation, it was perhaps as central to the successful establishment of absolutist rule in Prussia as Puritanism was to its defeat in England.

English Puritanism, Württemberg Pietism, and Pietism in Prussia were movements with similar religious aims and ideals. Chapter 2 will consider the common elements in their religious profiles: in their attempts to purify the established church; to renew the religious life of the people

---

[14] See for example: Schmidt, *Pietismus*; Deppermann, *Der Hallesche Pietismus*; Hinrichs, *Preussentum und Pietismus*; Grünberg, *Spener*; Erich Beyreuther, *August Hermann Francke, 1663–1727* (Marburg an der Lahn: Verlag der Francke-Buchhandlung GmbH, 1956); Beyreuther, *August Hermann Francke und die Anfänge der Ökumenischen Bewegung* (Leipzig: Koehler und Amelang, 1957); Beyreuther, *Geschichte des Pietismus* (Stuttgart: J.F. Steinkopf Verlag, 1978).

[15] Hinrichs, *Preussentum und Pietismus*, pp. 254ff., and p. 173.

through preaching, Bible-reading, arousing souls to fear of damnation and experience of conversion; and to erect a holy community on earth, through improved social and moral discipline. Yet these religious aspirations had very different political implications in each case. In England, a movement originally concerned with issues of doctrine and ceremonial broadened out to become a cultural orientation arousing the emotions of large numbers of people: an orientation capable eventually of motivating and justifying the abolition of monarchy and the judicial execution of the King. In Württemberg, a similar movement for religious reform expressed similar attitudes and made similar criticisms of attempted absolutism. Yet when the Württemberg Estates, like the English Parliamentarians, defended inherited rights against absolutist innovation, Pietists remained politically passive. In Prussia, Pietism was perhaps as important to the course of political development as was Puritanism in England. Yet it worked its effects in a diametrically opposite substantive direction. Prussian Pietists, in pursuing their religious goals, made a positive contribution to the successful establishment of absolutist rule in Prussia.

Schematically, these positions may be represented as follows. Three similar movements for religious reform in early modern European Protestant states developed different degrees of politicisation, and different responses to absolutist rule, as is shown in the table below. This study will seek to explain, both why there were different degrees of activity across cases, and why the political attitudes and contributions of the Puritan and Pietist movements developed in such different directions.

Puritan and Pietist politics	England 1560–1640	Württemberg 1680–1780	Prussia 1690–1740
Degree	Active	Passive	Active
Direction	Anti-absolutist	Anti-absolutist	Pro-absolutist

Controversies

The first question which might be raised, even before considering substantive controversies over explanation, is the methodological question of whether the comparisons are indeed warranted. English Puritanism was, after all, a century earlier than its Pietist counterparts. What justification can there be in comparing a religious movement in late sixteenth- to mid-seventeenth-century England with movements in late seventeenth- to mid- and late eighteenth-century German states? Furthermore, how can one compare an essentially Calvinist movement with movements in a Lutheran context? And was not the structure of the early modern English state so different from the German states that there is really no sensible basis from which to begin to compare?

These are serious questions. It is hoped that in the course of this study the rationale for comparison will be justified; but some preliminary remarks explicitly clarifying the selection of cases and dates must be made here. The broadest question prompting this investigation is that of the relationships between religion and social change: of the conditions under which religious movements appear to be capable of transforming the course of history in one direction or another. The more specific historical question is that concerning religious contributions, of a precisionist nature, to the defeat or success of attempts to institute absolutist rule in early modern European states, with the fundamental implications this had for the course of subsequent political history. The particular cases analysed here have been selected for two basic reasons. First, as will be argued in Chapter 2, despite the different Reformation backgrounds, Puritanism and Pietism in fact converged into a very similar form of religiosity. Secondly, the periods chosen for study in each case are the periods which cover the emergence of the precisionist movements, and the time of their greatest impact on attempts to institute absolutist rule. It can be argued (and has been, frequently) that the development of England was in some way 'precocious' as compared with its European neighbours. Eastern Europe, including Prussia, was supposedly particularly 'backward' as compared to the West. This sort of argument, and the language of precocity and backwardness, generally implies an evolutionist vision of social change. But if one discards the intellectual framework of evolutionism, and operates with a purely typological and comparative approach, one can appropriate the element of truth in these characterisations. European political history is characterised by the emergence of centralised nation states out of the complex patch-work of dispersed sovereignty and overlapping jurisdictions known as feudalism. In many areas, out of the late-mediaeval *Ständestaat* there developed, through a series of struggles between Estates and ruler, a form of absolutist state. These struggles, and the development of absolutism, took place in different ways and at different times, according to the particular dynamics of different socioeconomic and political configurations in varying historical circumstances. Retrospectively, we may characterise certain periods as crucial turning-points, times when the fate of absolutism was in one way or another effectively sealed. Such periods can be found in mid-seventeenth-century England; in late seventeenth- to mid-eighteenth-century Prussia; and in late seventeenth- to late eighteenth-century Württemberg.[16]

---

[16] On patterns of early modern political developments, see for example: Perry Anderson, *Lineages of the Absolutist State* (London: New Left Books, 1974); and Gianfranco

This is not to suggest that the actual social and political structures of these three states were similar in these periods. They were in fact very different, as will be described in Chapter 3, below. It is however to suggest that the policies of the rulers in these cases at these times were tending in similar directions: towards centralisation of sovereignty and rule without the genuine partnership of the Estates. Issues in each case were similar: they revolved on questions of whether the ruler could achieve financial autonomy, an effective state administrative apparatus with control of local government (and revenue extraction), and the means for an independent foreign policy, generally through maintenance of a standing army which also had domestic uses. Whether or not rulers could succeed in their projects depended not only on their own personalities and degrees of political competence, but vitally on particular sets of circumstances both at home and abroad.

Different resolutions of conflicts between Estates and rulers, and different historical outcomes concerning would-be absolutist rule, constitute historical problems in their own right. No attempt is made to solve these wider problems here. The present concern is solely with the different ways in which the Puritan and Pietist movements became embroiled in these complex developments, contributing rather differently to their eventual outcomes. The periods in a sense select themselves: they are the periods when there was an inner-churchly precisionist movement for the further reform of a Protestant state church, at a time when the ruler was attempting to dispense with the co-rulership of the Estates and develop the apparatus of absolutist rule. Analytically, given this framework for investigation, each case must be viewed in its own terms. In many ways, for example, one can see greater similarities between early seventeenth-century England and early eighteenth-century Württemberg (socio-economically, politically, and culturally) than one can between the latter and the chronologically contemporaneous Prussia.

Of course we do not have perfect comparisons. The interest of history is partly in its diversity, its individuality. But that should not blind us to certain general patterns and regularities, and to certain systematic variations in particular relationships. It is with these regularities and patterns that this study is concerned. Macro-societal analysts neither have the control over all relevant variables possible in laboratory experiments, nor the statistical advantages of large numbers of cases possible where the unit of analysis is the individual rather than the state. (There are of course other problems associated with these types of approach.) Nevertheless, macro-societal comparisons can be an illuminating means of developing and testing systematic hypotheses, in the interests of more adequate historical explanations. It will be for the reader to judge, at the end, whether the effort has been worthwhile.

What sorts of substantive explanation of the political attitudes and activities of the Puritan and Pietist movements in each case are available? Two main sorts of approach to Puritanism and Pietism – and to the analysis of the role of ideas and religion in history generally – may be distinguished. Some scholars focus on the consequences of ideas, or psychological ethos fostered by ideas, for personal conduct and hence social change. Other scholars focus rather on the social carriers of ideas, on the material bases which determine what ideas are likely to be accepted and historically effective. Such a distinction of course vastly oversimplifies the variety of debates, the diversity of theoretical approaches in this area; but it serves to group approaches according to the fundamental thrust of the assumptions involved in explanation. A further, partly cross-cutting, distinction has to do with the focus of analysis. Most explanations refer to features of the religious movement itself, whether these features are to do with religious ideas, or with social bases. But some approaches adopt a more holistic approach, and appeal to concepts such as 'mode of production' or 'society as a whole'; such approaches are generally implicitly or explicitly functionalist, explaining phenomena in terms of the needs they fulfil in a given stage of development within a particular evolutionary schema.

The classic analysis of the historical consequences of certain Protestant orientations for secular conduct is of course Max Weber's *The Protestant Ethic and the Spirit of Capitalism*. This work aroused a continuing spate of historical and theoretical controversy; the only clear conclusion to emerge so far is that the status of Weber's argument is at least ambiguous.[17] Located in the context of Weber's more wide-ranging comparative-historical investigations, it seems that in this case he was concerned to analyse the relatively autonomous impact on social action of the psychological consequences of certain ideas, given a particular set of historical circumstances, and to reflect on the cultural descendants of these ideas in altered conditions.[18] Adopting what might in principle be termed a 'Weberian approach' would require consideration of Weber's wider opus, with the rather different emphases evident in his other works; but generally scholars interested in early modern Europe have

---

[17] Weber, *Protestant Ethic*. For the most recent lucid analyses of Weber's work in the light of continuing controversies, see Frank Parkin, *Max Weber* (London: Tavistock Publications, 1982), and Gordon Marshall, *In Search of the Spirit of Capitalism* (London: Hutchinson, 1982).

[18] See more generally my interpretation of Weber, in Fulbrook, 'Max Weber's "Interpretive Sociology": A Comparison of Conception and Practice', *British Journal of Sociology* 29 (1) (1978): 71–82.

been most inspired by the Protestant Ethic thesis alone, and have located their own work in relation to one particular hypothesis assumed to be present in this. Some historians have focussed on the supposed consequences of the doctrine of predestination, for example. Carl Hinrichs, historian of Prussian Pietism, asserts that Puritans would be 'individualistic' and work only for their own benefit, whereas Pietists, who believed in the possibility of salvation for all, would be 'socialistic' and work for the benefit of others. For Hinrichs, a specialist in the German sources, the predestinarian beliefs of Calvinists must lead to fatalism and a lack of concern with the community. Almost precisely the opposite is assumed by a specialist on Puritanism, William Haller, who contrasts the 'mere pietism' of Lutherans with the 'activism' of Puritans. A similar stress on activism and world-mastery among Puritans is found in the work of Walzer, who suggests that the Calvinist striving for discipline, mastery, and control over the social environment prepared Puritanism to become the first truly revolutionary movement in modern Europe.[19] These scholars, and others, have tended to consider the rational or the psychological consequences of certain theological doctrines for conduct and hence social change, refining or varying particular substantive hypotheses within what is in effect an essentially idealist position.[20]

Other approaches have tended to reduce the relative independence of religious ideas as a factor in social change. Tawney, for example, while supporting Weber's thesis concerning the close relationship between Puritanism and early capitalism, yet undermines it to some extent in his stress on the emergence of a bourgeois class to whom Puritan religious ideas might appeal. Christopher Hill's theoretical approach is vastly more complex than some of his detractors suggest, but a similar undermining of the autonomy of religious beliefs is evident in Hill's emphasis on the 'non-religious reasons' why people might be attracted to Puritan ideas and attitudes. While Hill explicitly denies any desire to 'reduce' religious ideas to necessary orientations of their class carriers, his work generally explores the 'tightness of fit' between the two. (In some ways, this is very much in the spirit of Weber's analyses in his discussion of religion in *Economy and Society*.) By making it easier for us to comprehend the beliefs of another age, Hill makes these beliefs appear almost inevitable, given the social conditions in which they were

[19] Hinrichs, *Preussentum und Pietismus*, pp. 12, 74, 342–4; also Carl Hinrichs, *Friedrich Wilhelm I. König in Preussen* (Hamburg: Hanseatische Verlagsanstalt, 1941), pp. 561, 581; Haller, *Rise of Puritanism*, p. 124; Walzer, *Revolution of the Saints*.
[20] Walzer is less of an idealist than the other two, and it is perhaps misleading to classify him with them, since he considers both the implications of the social experience of particular groups for their religious attitudes, and the consequences of these attitudes for modes of action. But his general emphasis is more on the consequences of ideas and attitudes, conceived as intellectually autonomous responses to experience of rapid social change, than on the conditions or causes of these ideas – as with the theorists mentioned in the following paragraph.

held.[21] Trautwein has similarly attempted to see affinities between forms of land tenure in Württemberg and Pietist attitudes in the area; while Scharfe has interpreted Pietism in terms of its social-psychological functions in an era of industrialisation.[22]

Some approaches appealing to social bases are interested, not so much in the relationships (whether as 'reflection' or 'elective affinity') between class base and religious ideas, but rather in the consequences of class capacities for action. Thus, for example, Puritanism was capable of strong political action only because it was carried by an 'independent bourgeoisie', in contrast to Prussian Pietism. Sometimes this sort of approach characterises the movement in terms of historical outcomes: thus Württemberg Pietism was 'conservative' because it attempted to *defend* the inherited privileges of the Estates, whereas English Puritanism was 'revolutionary' (despite the fact that Puritans, too, considered themselves to be defending inherited rights) because it was carried by a 'rising bourgeoisie', or because English parliamentarianism, as established by the Puritan Revolution, is conceived to be 'modern'. On the other hand, others classify Prussian Pietists as 'progressive' because the absolutist state with which they joined forces represented 'innovation' and 'modernisation' against the 'reactionary' feudalism of the Estates.[23]

Many works on Puritanism and Pietism do not link religious ideas to social conduct in any way at all; rather, they are conceived in the more ethereal framework of the history of ideas as such. Pinson's work on Pietism and the rise of German nationalism simply points to affinities between the two clusters of orientation, suggesting that the latter is in some way a 'secularised' version of the former, but failing to specify any detailed historical links between the two. The volume in the German series of *Arbeiten zur Geschichte des Pietismus* which is devoted to the theme of *Pietismus und Moderne Welt* similarly contains a number of essays discussing Pietist ideas in relation to modern notions of ecumenicism, toleration, pedagogy, the 'social question', and so on, with little serious examination of the ways in which these ideas might (or might

---

[21] Tawney, *Religion and the Rise of Capitalism*; Hill, *Economic Problems of the Church and Society and Puritanism.* But see also Hill's 'Introduction' to his *Intellectual Origins of the English Revolution* (Oxford: Clarendon Press, 1965), for a discussion of the relationship between ideas and historical context. Hill's work cannot be simply categorised. See also Max Weber, 'Religious Groups (The Sociology of Religion)' in M. Weber, *Economy and Society*, ed. by Guenther Roth and Claus Wittich (New York: Bedminster Press, 1968), vol. 2, ch. 6, pp. 399–634.

[22] Joachim Trautwein, *Religiosität und Sozialstruktur* (Stuttgart: Calwer Verlag, 1972); Martin Scharfe, *Die Religion des Volkes* (Gütersloh: Gütersloher Verlagshaus Gerd Mohn, 1980); Scharfe, 'Pietistische Moral im Industrialisierungsprozess' in Burkhard Gladigow (ed.), *Religion und Moral* (Düsseldorf: Patmos Verlag, 1976).

[23] For example: Helen P. Liebel, 'The Bourgeoisie in Southwestern Germany, 1500–1789: A Rising Class?' *International Review of Social History* 10 (2) (1965): 283–307, p. 307; Lehmann, *Pietismus und Weltliche Ordnung*, p. 34; Hinrichs, *Preussentum und Pietismus*, p. 175.

not) have been used in practice, or whether they have any genuine historical relationships with the twentieth-century notions to which they are assumed to be linked.[24] Much of the German work on Pietism is explicitly theological in intent, attempting to interpret and locate Pietism within the development of the Protestant tradition. Despite the beginnings made by Weber and Troeltsch, far less work of a sociologically relevant nature has been done on Pietism than on Puritanism.

This brief sketch of the varieties of prevalent approach is intended to locate the nature of the present study. An introductory chapter is not the place for a detailed theoretical analysis of a range of other works, which make serious contributions in their own right. But in the context of the question central to this investigation, none of the approaches mentioned above provides entirely adequate answers. Approaches which focus centrally on the differences, theological and psychological, between Puritanism (with a Calvinist background) and Pietism (Lutheran in heritage) cannot account for the differences between Pietists in Württemberg and Pietists in Prussia. Approaches which focus mainly on the social bases of the movements run into difficulties when empirical analysis suggests that in all three cases the movements were socially relatively broadly based, and cannot sensibly be interpreted as class movements in any narrow sense having obvious political implications. The present investigation, therefore, attempts to develop a rather different approach.

First, the focus of explanation is shifted away from analysis of ideas, or material factors, viewed in isolation. Rather, it is on the structural contexts of action. The argument is, that it was not anything inherent in the religious or social characteristics of the Puritan and Pietist movements themselves which determined their political responses to absolutist rule; what did influence their different trajectories of development was the different obstacles they faced in pursuit of their specifically religious goals. It was because of the different features of their sociopolitical environments that Pietists and Puritans developed different political strategies and alliances. What needs analysis, then, are different patterns of relationships among church, state, and crucial social groups in each case.

Secondly, the approach developed here attempts to do justice to the reality of religious ideas and motivations for believers without disregarding the fundamental importance of political, social and economic conditions. It seeks to avoid both the determinism implied by some forms of structuralist Marxism and functionalism, as well as the voluntarism inherent in many approaches seeking to understand the importance of ideas and culture (both non-Marxist and within the neo-Marxist tradition). An attempt is made to develop a precise account of the relationships among the variables under analysis, without doing an injustice

[24] Pinson, *Rise of German Nationalism*; Aland (ed.), *Pietismus und Moderne Welt*.

either to human individuality and capacity for innovation or to the limiting conditions of structural circumstances of action.

Let me briefly preview the substantive argument developed below. What determined whether or not a precisionist religious movement became politically active was the degree to which it was tolerated or opposed. If it was opposed, it was more likely to be politically active; if it was tolerated, it was more likely to be politically passive. But it needed some degree of support from some quarter to have a sufficient base from which to fight opposition. If the religious movement *was* politicised in the fight to achieve its goals, then the direction of its political sympathies and alliances would depend on who was doing the opposing, and who else was fighting against the opposers. This was determined, not by anything to do with the precisionist movement itself, but rather by the social, economic, and political location of the established church which the precisionists sought to reform. The state church in each case was related in very different ways to the ruler and to crucial social groups. It was the different state/society/church relations in each case which determined the specifically political implications of a religious movement for reform of the church, and hence the different patterns of alliance and opposition. These relationships determined the field of opportunities and constraints for ardent Protestants seeking to establish the Holy Commonwealth on earth. They also determined the possible strategies and alliances of would-be absolutist rulers. Together, they help to explain how precisionists came to develop different relationships with absolutism in each case. But the structural analysis of interrelationships among church, state, and society only maps the different terrains in which the battles were to take place. It must be supplemented with historical accounts of the actual skills and fortunes of particular actors as they seized or missed particular opportunities, as they made better or worse use of particular resources.

The study is organised as follows. Chapter 2 seeks to establish the nature of the Puritan and Pietist movements: their essential comparability as movements for further religious reform, with similar aspirations and ethos, which cannot be interpreted as class ideologies, and which may be subsumed under the common generic term of 'precisionism'. Chapter 3 turns to the dynamics of absolutism in each case: the relations between state and society, as these affected rulers' attempts to introduce absolutist rule. In Chapter 4, the social, economic and political location of the established church is examined, and the consequences for degrees and sources of religious toleration assessed. Together, Chapters 3 and 4 establish the crucial variables and relationships which influence the different precisionist responses to absolutist rule in each case. Chapters 5, 6, and 7 re-examine the three movements in the light of the structural analysis, showing how the different patterns of political development can be more readily understood in terms of the framework established.

18 *Piety and politics*

Chapter 8, the final chapter, summarises the substantive conclusions, the hypothesis which appears to account for the problem posed in this introduction, and discusses the wider theoretical implications of the study.

2

In pursuit of further reformation

How can Puritanism best be defined? What were the Puritan and Pietist movements? How can Puritans and Pietists be distinguished from other early modern English and German Protestants? What makes Puritanism and Pietism inherently comparable phenomena?

Scholars have hotly debated these questions. A part of the problem lies in the fact that there were no very consistent definitions, even among contemporaries. Used as terms of abuse, part of the art of application was, as Henry Parker put it, to 'so stretch and extend the same, that scarce any civill honest Protestant... can avoid the aspersion of it, and [then to]... so shrink it into a narrow sense, that it shal seem to be aimed at none but monstrous abominable Heretickes and miscreants. Thus by its latitude it strikes generally, by its contraction it pierces deeply, by its confused application it deceives invisibly.'[1] Puritanism and Pietism began as movements, within Protestant state churches, to achieve further reform of these churches, or to complete what was perceived as an incomplete reformation. Early Puritans and Pietists in each case did not perceive themselves as different, in any fundamental sense, from other members of the church. They were merely more energetic in their positive criticisms of present deficiencies in the institutional church, and more active in the attempt to bring about changes. But, over time, Puritanism and Pietism developed into distinctive sociocultural phenomena, partly formed by the reactions of ecclesiastical and secular authorities and the responses of different groups in society. They emerged as movements for further reform; they developed into complex, politically charged, social as well as religious phenomena.

This chapter will attempt to establish the inherent comparability of the Puritan and Pietist movements in the light of controversies surrounding definition. It is the contention of this study that Puritanism and Pietism represent essentially similar types of precisionist movement for religious reform. In origins, they had similar aspirations and goals concerning the further reform of the institutional church. In development, they had very similar forms of religious experience and ethos. And in each case, these aspirations and experiences appealed across a relatively broad social range: Puritanism and Pietism were not class ideologies in any simple

[1] Henry Parker, *A Discourse Concerning Puritans* (London, 1641), p. 11.

19

sense. It is because of these overall similarities of the movements that the comparison of their very different political developments is warranted. First, we shall look at the origins of the movements; then, their religiosity; and finally their social bases.

Movements for further reform

That Puritanism was a movement for the completion of the Reformation is very obviously the case. Henry VIII had undertaken a largely political reformation, removing the supremacy of the church from the pope in Rome to the monarch in England, but, particularly in the later years of his reign, remaining doctrinally conservative and as unwilling to tolerate 'Protestant heresy' as 'Romish Papistry' – symbolised by his simultaneous execution of dissenters of both left and right on the same day.[2] Under the Protestant protectorate of Edward VI's minority, the doctrinal reformation made more progress, and it was hoped that with the Protestant inclinations of the young King himself the process of reforming creeds, rites and ceremonies would proceed smoothly during his reign. However, with his early death and the ascent of Mary to the throne, such hopes were frustrated. Some Protestants, such as Elizabeth's future Archbishop of Canterbury, Parker, retired into the safety of obscurity in England; others, more prominent or less compromising of conscience, fled to the continent. These so-called Marian exiles settled largely in areas of Reformed theology – Frankfurt, Strassburg, Basel, and Geneva itself – and it is in the disputes among the exiles that the beginnings of English Puritanism may be found.

Differences can be seen already in the troubles at Frankfurt. The English exiles had been allowed the use of a church, shared with, but used at different times from, another congregation, on condition that their manner of service and discipline conformed adequately with established local custom. Their call to English exiles elsewhere to join their project of establishing an ideal church occasioned a major controversy between two sorts of approach: between those exiles who wished to push forward the process of reformation and adopt a continental form of worship and church discipline more advanced than what was envisaged in the Edwardian reforms; and those more insular English Protestants who wished to retain the forms of a national church, preserving and protecting the heritage of the – admittedly incomplete – English Reformation in a time of adversity. The squabbles over specific, in themselves

[2] For the Henrician Reformation, see particularly A.G. Dickens, *The English Reformation* (New York: Schocken Books, 1964); and as it relates to the origins of Puritanism: M.M. Knappen, *Tudor Puritanism* (Chicago: University of Chicago Press, 1939; pbk edn, 1970); Patrick Collinson, *The Elizabethan Puritan Movement* (London: Jonathan Cape, 1967), Part One.

seemingly trivial, organisational and ceremonial issues raised also the question of pluralism and separatism: how far could different English congregations in exile agree to differ without making nonsense of the concept of a national church? In practice, the controversies were only partially resolved, through tactical manoeuvres and power politics, before the accession of Elizabeth to the English throne brought the exiles home to establish the Protestant Church of England in earnest.[3]

As Professor Haller has pointed out, 'English Puritanism, that spiritual outlook, way of life and mode of expression which eventually flowered so variously and so magnificently in Milton, Bunyan, and Defoe, was in the first instance the result of the conditions imposed by Elizabeth upon the reform movement within the English church.'[4] Or, as the author of Elizabeth's scheme for reformation – probably Cecil – put it, the Elizabethan settlement would be seen by some as but 'a cloaked papistry or mingle-mangle'.[5] While the returning exiles' hopes for a speedy and thorough reformation were frustrated, Elizabeth's policy of attempting to alienate no major section of her subjects, and no major power abroad, for too long a period of time – a policy of ambiguity and politic wavering – allowed a degree of freedom for the perpetuation of reformist aspirations and organisation. The Puritan movement of Elizabethan times was the active body of Protestants who continued, in one way or another, the pressure for further reformation. Those whom some later scholars have anachronistically termed Anglicans were, by and large, those English Protestants relatively content with the structure and orientation of the English church as established in Elizabeth's reign. There was a tendency for those with an internationalist outlook and experience of the continental reformed churches to be less satisfied with the Elizabethan settlement than those who had stayed at home and had greater attachment to 'the face of an English church'.[6]

The thrust of the English Puritan movement, in its sixteenth-century origins, was to try to remove from the Church of England all hated remnants of popery, and to bring it into line with the 'best reformed churches' of the continent. Specific elements in the Puritan programme for removing the 'Popishe abuses yet remaining in the Englishe Church'

[3] Dickens, *English Reformation*, pp. 289–94; Knappen, *Tudor Puritanism*, ch. 6.
[4] William Haller, *The Rise of Puritanism* (Philadelphia: University of Philadelphia Press, 1972; orig. 1938), p. 9.
[5] Knappen, *Tudor Puritanism*, p. 169.
[6] On Elizabeth's religious policies and the Elizabethan settlement, see: J.E. Neale, 'The Elizabethan Acts of Supremacy and Uniformity', *English Historical Review* 65 (1950): 304–32; Neale, 'Parliament and the Articles of Religion, 1571', *English Historical Review* 67 (1952): 510–21; Neale, *Elizabeth I and her Parliaments*, 2 vols. (London: Jonathan Cape, 1953, 1957); Neale, *Queen Elizabeth I: A Biography* (New York: Doubleday Anchor, 1957; orig. 1934). Neale's views have been questioned recently by historians such as Geoffrey Elton (Neale Lecture, 1978); but on Elizabeth's ambiguous conservatism there seems little doubt.

varied over time and between individuals. But, just as one can identify the 'left wing' of the late twentieth-century Labour movement in England, despite differences over particular issues such as disarmament or the European Economic Community, so it is possible to identify the broad aspirations and characteristics which distinguish early Puritanism. Many Puritans would have disagreed with the presbyterian ecclesiology of Field and Wilcox, but they shared the underlying motivation expressed in the 1571 *Admonition to Parliament*: 'You may not do as heretofore you have done, patch and peece, nay rather goe backeward, and never labour or contend to perfection. But altogether remove whole Antichrist, both head body and branch, and perfectly plant that puritie of the word, that simplicitie of the sacraments, and severitie of discipline, which Christ hath commanded, and commended to his church.'[7] As the Elizabethan reign proceeded, Puritanism became both a specific movement for the weeding out of 'Popishe abuses', and a more general movement attempting to bring a living religious faith based on the Bible to the general populace of England.

Both the more radical and the moderate forms of Puritanism found resonances in Elizabethan sociocultural conditions. The emphasis on the scriptures, the Word of the Lord, was well received in an era of expanding literacy, educational opportunity, and availability of the printed word. A Jesuit priest, observing a Puritan gathering from Wisbech Castle, at the height of the *classis* movement in the 1580s, gave this description:

Each of them had his own Bible, and sedulously turned the pages and looked up the texts cited by the preachers, discussing the passages among themselves to see whether they had quoted them to the point, and accurately, and in harmony with their tenets. Also they would start arguing among themselves about the meaning of passages from the Scriptures – men, women, boys, girls, rustics, labourers and idiots...[8]

The Puritan concern was to translate the doctrinal insights of the few into the way of life of the masses: to bring a living Christianity into every corner of the land. In Perkins' words, it was important to 'understand the meaning of the words, and be able to make a right use of the Commandments, of the Creeds, of the Lords Prayer, by applying them inwardly to your hearts and consciences, and outwardly to your lives and conversations'.[9] These endeavours were made easier for preachers and pamph-

---

[7] W.H. Frere and C.E. Douglas (eds.), *Puritan Manifestoes* (London: S.P.C.K., 1954), p. 19.

[8] Quoted in M. Spufford, *Contrasting Communities: English Villagers in the Sixteenth and Seventeenth Centuries* (Cambridge: Cambridge University Press, 1974), p. 263. Cf. also Keith Wrightson, *English Society, 1580–1680* (London: Hutchinson, 1982), ch. 7.

[9] William Perkins, 'The Foundation of Christian Religion: Gathered into Fixe Principles' in Perkins, *A Golden Chaine: Or, the Description of Theologie, containing the Order of the Causes of Saluation and Damnation, according to God's Word* (Printed by John Legat, Printer to the Universitie of Cambridge, 1600), p. 1028.

leteers in the quickening intellectual and cultural life of larger numbers of people in Shakespeare's England.

Pietism in Germany arose a good century after the reformation. Yet it too, like English Puritanism, originated as a movement for the further reform of what were considered to be incompletely reformed Protestant state churches. Pietists argued that while Luther had initiated a revolution in doctrine, there had not been a corresponding reformation of life: the *Reformation der Lehre* required completion with a *Reformation des Lebens*. The institutional reforms proposed by Pietists arose out of the compelling desire to produce a stronger church, bringing a living faith to the people, achieving improved religious knowledge, moral and social discipline. Pietist aims and aspirations echoed those of the Puritans.

Why did Pietism arise in Germany in the late seventeenth, rather than the sixteenth, century? In many ways, individuals earlier may be perceived to have had 'Pietist' concerns, ideas, and traits; but as a coherent intellectual, social and cultural movement of historical importance, Pietism did not emerge until the decades after the Thirty Years War. The answer has to do partly with the history of the Reformation itself in different German states, and partly with social conditions in Germany in the latter part of the seventeenth century. And, unlike English Puritanism, Pietism can point to the crucial impetus given by one particular individual, whose theological and organisational work gave shape and coherence to widespread concerns: Philipp Jakob Spener.[10]

There has been some dispute among German scholars as to the degree of scholasticism and theological aridity in seventeenth-century Lutheran orthodoxy. The older image of sterile disputatiousness has been revised, but more recent attempts to identify a clearly defined pre-Pietist 'Reform Orthodoxy' have gained few adherents. It seems clear that while there were a number of Lutherans concerned about religious life in a more practical sense than was implied by current dogmatic squabbles, there was in the early seventeenth century no coherent movement for reform. And once embroiled in the extensive turmoils known to history as the Thirty Years War, German Lutheranism was generally at a low ebb. One

---

[10] On the German Reformation, see for example: A.G. Dickens, *The German Nation and Martin Luther* (Glasgow: Collins, 1974; Fontana edn, 1976); Dickens, *Martin Luther and the Reformation* (London: Hodder and Stoughton, 1967); Dickens, *Reformation and Society in Sixteenth-Century Europe* (London: Thames and Hudson, 1966); G.R. Elton, *Reformation Europe* (Glasgow: Collins, Fontana edn, 1963); A.L. Drummond, *German Protestantism since Luther* (London: The Epworth Press, 1951); Roland Bainton, *The Reformation of the Sixteenth Century* (Boston: Beacon Press, 1952). On the background to the Pietist movement, see for example: Drummond, *German Protestantism*; Hans Leube, *Die Reformideen in der Deutschen Lutherischen Kirche zur Zeit der Orthodoxie* (Leipzig: Verlag von Dörffling und Franke, 1924); F. Ernest Stoeffler, *The Rise of Evangelical Pietism* (Leiden: E.J. Brill, 1965). On Spener, see particularly: Johannes Wallmann, *Philipp Jakob Spener und die Anfänge des Pietismus* (Tübingen: J.C.B. Mohr (Paul Siebeck), 1970); and Paul Grünberg, *Philipp Jakob Spener*, 3 vols. (Göttingen: Vandenhoek und Ruprecht, 1893–1906).

description of conditions after the end of the War, in the Maulbronn area of Württemberg, tells of the numbers of beggars, vagabonds, 'herrenlose Gesindel', the depopulation, the need for rebuilding of houses, churches and schools, and the general culture of hedonism and loose morality. It was complained that officials and magistrates in the towns and villages 'waren um kein Haar besser, als das gewöhnliche Volk'. Religious ignorance was almost complete: old and young knew so little of conventional Christianity, 'dass sie fast nicht mehr wussten, wer Christus oder der Teufel sei'.[11] Similar reports elsewhere, even allowing for some righteous exaggeration on the part of the observers, suggest that orthodox Lutheranism was having little general impact. At the same time, however, millenarian and chiliastic ideas were enjoying considerable appeal, as wandering prophets and prophetesses interpreted the signs of the times and diagnosed the fate of the world.[12] It is clear that there was considerable scope for an evangelical movement on the part of the established church.

In south-western Germany, troubles continued with the French wars of the later seventeenth century. At this time, a new political and cultural development took place: the emergence of baroque court culture and princely absolutism. The new aspirations of grandeur, expressed in architectural extravagance and conspicuous consumption, and associated with increased centralisation of sovereignty, stood in stark contrast to the poverty and misery of those of the populace who had survived the ravages of preceding decades. And it stood in some tension with the concerns and moral standards of the re-emerging burgher classes, the merchants and manufacturers re-establishing trade and industry as best they could.[13]

It was in these general conditions that Spener's message was received: a message which, in important respects, went beyond anything envisaged by

---

[11] They 'were not a hair's breadth better than the common people'; ... 'so that they almost no longer knew who Christ or the Devil were'. Bassler, 'Die Ersten Jahre nach dem Dreissigjährigen Krieg im Bezirk Maulbronn', *Blätter für Württembergische Kirchengeschichte* 2 (1898): 119–28 and 166–73, p. 128, p. 168.

[12] On the disputes over reform orthodoxy, see: Leube, *Reformideen*; the essays by Leube in D. Blaufuss (ed.), *Orthodoxie und Pietismus* (Bielefeld: Luther-Verlag, 1975); Stoeffler, *Evangelical Pietism*; Drummond, *German Protestantism*; Johannes Wallmann, 'Pietismus und Orthodoxie. Überlegungen und Fragen zur Pietismusforschung' in H. Liebing and K. Scholder (eds.), *Geist und Geschichte der Reformation* (Berlin: Walter de Gruyter, 1966); Lowell C. Green, 'Duke Ernest the Pious of Saxe-Gotha and his relationship to Pietism' in H. Bornkamm, F. Heyer, and A. Schindler (eds.), *Der Pietismus in Gestalten und Wirkungen* (Bielefeld: Luther-Verlag, 1975). On the general political background as it relates to religion, see for example: Hartmut Lehmann, *Das Zeitalter des Absolutismus* (Stuttgart: W. Kohlhammer Verlag, 1980); and Lehmann, *Pietismus und Weltliche Ordnung in Württemberg vom 17. bis zum 20. Jahrhundert* (Stuttgart: W. Kohlhammer Verlag, 1969), Part One, 'Französenkriege und Barockkultur'.

[13] Lehmann, *Pietismus und Weltliche Ordnung*, and *Zeitalter des Absolutismus*; Werner Fleischhauer, *Barock im Herzogtum Württemberg* (Stuttgart: W. Kohlhammer Verlag, 1958); Helen P. Liebel, 'The Bourgeoisie in Southwestern Germany, 1500–1789: A Rising Class?', *International Review of Social History* 10 (2) (1965): 283–307.

Luther. Spener was born in 1635 at Rappoltsweiler in Alsace, and studied at his local university of Strassburg. Strassburg, on the Rhine, was a major centre for the introduction and distribution of foreign literature, including a considerable quantity of English Puritan writings in German translation. Its church had an indigenous reforming tradition: already in 1636, one year after Spener's birth, Johann Schmidt had in the *Strassburger Gutachten* presented elements of a programme for practical religious reform. On his student travels Spener came into contact with the preaching of Jean de Labadie. He was later directly influenced by Johann Jakob Schütz, and, through Schütz, by English chiliastic speculations, and the Labadistic circles in Frankfurt. In Frankfurt, where Spener took up a post in 1666, he found that there were already lay individuals wishing to meet in small circles for religious discussion and edification. Perhaps to forestall the possibility of separatism, and because he sympathised with their concerns, Spener in 1670 agreed to supervise what became known as the first Pietist conventicle; from this he developed his ideas about *ecclesiola in ecclesia*. At the same time, Spener engaged intellectually with the original works of Luther, finding a fresh message and spirit not present in the interpretations of contemporary orthodoxy. Out of this variety of influences Spener produced – initially in his *Pia Desideria*, published in 1675 as an introduction to Johann Arndt's *Postille* – the intellectual and practical programme which became the basis for the Pietist movement. The most important points in which Spener broke with his Lutheran heritage were in the idea of conventicles, or a church within the church, and in his optimistic eschatology, his hope of better times to come. Unlike the increasingly pessimistic and quietistic Luther, Pietists believed in the possibility of the active transformation of this world, the achievement of the Kingdom of God on earth; and they believed, as did Calvinists, that it was their duty towards God, for the greater glory of God, to attempt to change conditions in the here and now.[14]

Spener was an intellectually and socially respectable theologian, and his ideas fell on receptive ground in a number of areas. Elsewhere in Germany, others too were troubled by the conditions of the times. People were seeking advice and solace in the writings of English Puritans (works by William Perkins, Lewis Bayly, Daniel Dyke, Joseph Hall, Richard Baxter, Emmanuel Sonthomb), in pious writings in the German tradition (Johann Arndt was particularly popular), and in mystic works such as those of Boehme. Others too sought to understand their location in

---

[14] On Spener, see particularly Wallmann, *Spener*; Grünberg, *Spener*; Kurt Aland, 'Philipp Jakob Spener' in Aland, *Kirchengeschichtliche Entwurfe* (Gütersloh: Gütersloher Verlagshaus Gerd Mohn, 1960); Martin Kruse, *Speners Kritik am Landesherrlichen Kirchenregiment und ihre Vorgeschichte* (Witten: Luther-Verlag, 1971); Spener, *Pia Desideria, oder Herzliches Verlangen / Nach Gottgefälliger Besserung der wahren Evangelischen Kirchen / Sampt einigen dahin einfältig abzweckenden Christlichen Vorschlägen...* (Franckfurt am Mayn / In Verlegung Johann David Zunners, 1676).

God's plan for humanity, and to achieve a practical reformation of religious life.[15]

In Württemberg in particular, where Spener stayed and made close friends during his travels of 1662, there was a receptive tradition for reformist ideas. Of particular importance was the work of Johann Valentin Andreae, whose early thinking, as sketched in his vision of an ideal society in *Christianopolis*, was purely Utopian. But when in 1634 war came to the town of Calw, deep in the Nagold valley on the edge of the Black Forest, where he was *Spezialsuperintendent*, Andreae was forced into more practical schemes for 'active Christianity'. On being called to Württemberg's capital Stuttgart as *Hofprediger* and *Konsistorialrat* in 1638, when Duke Eberhard III returned from a four-year exile after the battle of Nördlingen, Andreae worked for the reconstruction of order, discipline, and morality, and for the rebuilding of functioning schools and churches. Andreae was much influenced by Genevan ideas of moral and social discipline. In 1642–4 *Kirchenkonvente* were introduced, a form of church assembly on the Reformed Church model, combining secular and religious authorities in disciplinary functions, and introducing Calvinist elements into Württemberg Lutheranism. One of Andreae's pupils, Johann Andreas Hochstetter, later became particularly friendly with Spener. Hochstetter was to become one of the leading churchmen of Württemberg, following Andreae's path to become eventually Bishop and *Generalsuperintendent* of the beautiful abbey of Bebenhausen, near the university town of Tübingen. From the 1680s, many individuals in the Württemberg church were increasingly interested in Spener's ideas for religious reform. Educated at the abbey schools and in Tübingen, theologians, bishops (such as Osiander) and even the two lawyers on the Synod (Kulpis and Ruhle) engaged with Spener's ideas in the light of their own tradition.[16]

[15] On the translation and reception of English Puritan writings in Germany, see Leube, *Reformideen*, Part Three, ch. 5. Leube stresses the way in which German Lutherans were particularly impressed by the general religious *ideals* of English Puritans, however much they may have differed over specific *policies*, particularly over the question of *adiaphora*. See also: Martin Hasselhorn, *Der Altwürttembergische Pfarrstand im 18. Jahrhundert* (Stuttgart: W. Kohlhammer Verlag, 1958), ch. 4, p. 54; Carl Hinrichs, *Preussentum und Pietismus* (Göttingen: Vandenhoek und Ruprecht, 1971), p. 10 (for evidence that the bookshops were 'full' of English Puritan writings); and on the growth of book-ownership, largely devotional, F. Breining, 'Die Hausbibliothek des gemeinen Mannes vor 100 und mehr Jahren', *Blätter für Württembergische Kirchengeschichte* 13 (1909): 48–63.

[16] Heinrich Fausel, 'Von Altlutherischer Orthodoxie zum Frühpietismus in Württemberg', *Zeitschrift für Württembergische Landesgeschichte* 24 (1965): 309–28; Martin Brecht, 'Philipp Jakob Spener und die Württembergische Kirche' in Liebing and Scholder (eds.), *Geist und Geschichte*; Brecht, *Kirchenordnung und Kirchenzucht in Württemberg vom 16. bis zum 18. Jahrhundert* (Stuttgart: Calwer Verlag, 1967), ch. 2; Friedrich Fritz, *Altwürttembergische Pietisten* (Stuttgart: Im Quell-Verlag der Evangelischen Gesellschaft, 1950), ch. 1. On Andreae's *Christianopolis*, and its relations with English thinking, see for example K. Firth, *The Apocalyptic Tradition in Reformation Britain, 1530–1645* (Oxford: Oxford University Press, 1979), pp. 206–8.

Elsewhere in Germany too, concerned individuals were attracted to Spener's ideas. In Hamburg, Giessen, Mecklenburg, Saxony, even Königsberg in East Prussia, and a diversity of other towns and states, people warmed to the call for further reformation. The movement which came to be known as Pietism, given impetus by Spener, evidently was experienced as timely by large numbers of people in late seventeenth-century Germany. But conditions in different states varied, determining different receptions for Pietists in each area. The particular differences between Württemberg and Prussia will be explored in Chapters 3 and 4 of this study.

Thus both Puritanism and Pietism originated as movements for further reformation of Protestant state churches which were considered to be in some way inadequate. What then was the nature of the religious impulse, in the light of which further reformation was desired?

Puritan and Pietist religious profiles

It is easier to state how *not* to define Puritanism and Pietism than it is to present an acceptable positive characterisation. This is so for a number of reasons. First, inevitably, because the movements developed over time, there were changes in emphasis, orientation, and programme over specific policies. Secondly, because neither Puritans nor Pietists considered themselves heterodox, but rather to be working within their respective orthodox Protestant traditions, there are few clear and consistent lines of firm demarcation between 'precisionist' and 'orthodox' in each case. A cluster of variables located on a changing spectrum (for orthodoxy was as changeable as precisionism, over time) is the best that can be managed on this point; and this sort of complexity always permits anomalies and inconsistencies of classification. Thirdly, it must be borne in mind that Puritans and Pietists did not choose these labels for themselves. They became labelled, as part of a social process of mockery and abuse, and as part of a set of political processes. As contemporary labels, the terms could be put to a variety of uses, sometimes – as indicated by Henry Parker's observation quoted at the start of this chapter – widening their scope almost beyond any hope of precise definition. These problems have led certain scholars, such as the Georges on Puritanism, Dieter Narr and Michel Godfroid on Pietism, to abandon any attempt at characterisation. C.H. George even asserts that Puritanism is 'a bad concept... [which] should be abandoned'.[17] Other scholars, however, have gone to

[17] C.H. George, 'Puritanism as History and Historiography', *Past and Present* 41 (1968): 77–104, p. 104. See also: C.H. and K. George, *The Protestant Mind of the English Reformation* (Princeton, N.J.: Princeton University Press, 1961); Dieter Narr, 'Zur Stellung des Pietismus in der Volkskultur Württembergs', *Württembergisches Jahrbuch für Volkskunde* 3 (1957/8): 9–33; Michel Godfroid, 'Gab es den deutschen Pietismus?' in M. Greschat (ed.), *Zur Neueren Pietismusforschung* (Darmstadt: Wis-

the opposite extreme, constructing detailed definitions of enduring differences between 'Puritans' and 'Anglicans', or 'Pietists' and 'Orthodoxy'. Thus J.F.H. New asserts that 'two unities of principle existed at
the [Elizabethan] settlement and lasted to the Civil War, and ... they
were very different entities throughout'.[18] Schmidt and other German
historians and theologians have developed lists of contrasts differentiat-
ing Pietism from Orthodoxy, on similar assumptions.[19] A third sort of
solution has been attempted in terms of degree rather than substance:
Collinson, for example, speaks of 'the hotter sort of Protestant', Seaver
talks of 'holy violence' in pursuit of religious goals; though such
approaches implicitly adduce substantive criteria to distinguish such
piety from equally earnest and committed opponents (such as
Archbishop Laud, whose diary provoked unexpected public sympathy
when published for other purposes by Prynne).[20]

The problems of definition should not be overlooked, or argued
away. They are of the very essence of the historical development of
Puritanism and Pietism, as social, political and cultural phenomena as
well as purely religious movements. Part of the interest of analysing
Puritanism and Pietism is the very way in which particular traditions,
the reality of which was quite clear to contemporaries, shifted and
changed in meaning and emphasis over time. In this section, some of the
negative points will be briefly discussed, posing problems for neat classification; then the positive case will be put for certain common themes
for identification. No exhaustive or exclusive characterisations are
intended. Rather, certain aspects are highlighted to give an initial indication of the nature of the diffuse phenomena forming the subject of
investigation.

senschaftliche Buchgesellschaft, 1977); and for general problems of definition, see: Basil
Hall, 'Puritanism: The Problem of Definition' in G.J. Cuming (ed.), *Studies in Church
History*, vol. 2 (London: Nelson, 1965); Lehmann, *Pietismus und Weltliche Ordnung*,
'Einleitung'; and the articles in the discussion of 'Religion – Politik – Gesellschaft im 17.
und 18. Jahrhundert', *Historische Zeitschrift* 214 (1) (1972): 26–95.

[18] J.F.H. New, *Anglican and Puritan: The Basis of their Opposition* (London: Adam and
Charles Black, 1964), pp. 110–11.

[19] See for example Godfroid, 'Gab es den deutschen Pietismus?'; Wallmann, in Liebing and
Scholder (eds.), *Geist und Geschichte*; Martin Schmidt, *Pietismus* (Stuttgart: W. Kohlhammer Verlag, 1972); M. Greschat, 'Einleitung' to Greschat (ed.), *Zur Neueren Pietismusforschung*. Much of the German debate has revolved around problems of theological interpretation, such as whether Pietism represents a 'throwback' to mediaeval
Catholic mysticism, a heterodox deviation from Lutheran Protestantism, or rather a
'progressive' movement in the development of Lutheranism towards 'modernity'.
Ritschl, in his classic *Geschichte des Pietismus* (Bonn: Adolph Marcus, 3 vols., 1880–6),
contended that Pietism was 'eine Frömmigkeit von unlutherischem Gepräge, genauer
gesagt, [eine] spontane Wiedererzeugung mittelaltrigmönchischer Bestrebungen ausser-
halb des Klosters' (vol. 2, p. 417).

[20] Collinson, *Elizabethan Puritan Movement*; Paul Seaver, *The Puritan Lectureships:
The Politics of Religious Dissent, 1560–1662* (Stanford: Stanford University Press,
1970).

Neither Puritanism nor Pietism can be defined, in contrast to ortho-doxy, in terms of points of theology. As Heylyn put it, struggling to define Puritanism, 'Nor am I of the opinion, that Puritan and Calvinian are terms convertible. For though all Puritans are Calvinians both in doctrine and practice, yet all Calvinians are not to be counted as Puritans also; whose practices many of them abhor, and whose inconformities they detest.'[21] Archbishop Whitgift, tenacious harrier of Puritans, and argumentative opponent of Thomas Cartwright, was a staunch Calvinist; as were most members of the Church of England, both laity and eccle-siastical hierarchy, until the rise of Arminianism in the 1620s and '30s. Even so, the nature of English Calvinism itself was not fixed; many seventeenth-century Puritans, such as the congregationalist Hugh Peters, departed somewhat from Calvin's teachings. English Protestants were not dogmatic adherents of any earthly individual's doctrines; as John Smith, a member of the Plumbers Hall group, said under interrogation in 1567: 'Yes, we reverence the learned in Geneva, or in other places wheresoever they be; yet we build not on them our faith and religion.'[22] Richard Greenham nicely puts the position in his discussion of the authority of men, provoked by the problem of whether or not to sub-scribe:

But one may say: *Mai. Luther*, the father of religion thought it was good that such thinges should be retayned, I would aunswere, that Maister *Luther* was an elect vessell and chosen instrument of God. But yet without any iust disprayse to him I might say: ... *Luther* did not see all things. I reverence more the revealed wisedome of God in teaching Maister *Luther* so many necessarie thinges to salvation, then I search his secret iudgements in keeping backe from his know-ledge other matters of lesser importance. Yea but howe is it likelie (may it be obiected) that you should see that which he could not? whereto I say, that a meane sighted man may see that, when the Sunne shineth bright and cleare, which a sharpe sighted could not have espied in the dawning of the day. As it is the benefite of time to bring *Trueth* first to the light, so is it to cause it to be easier nowe to see, that abuses of ceremonies, than it was at the first, to espie the errours of doctrine.[23]

God's word, as they interpreted it, was the most important foundation of their faith for Puritans; and in general, it was not over issues of theo-

---

[21] Heylyn, *Cyprianus Anglicanus* (London, 1671), quoted in Seaver, *Puritan Lectureships*, p. 30. But Collinson, *Elizabethan Puritan Movement*, pp. 37–8, suggests that theological differences may have had considerable practical importance at the parish level.

[22] H.C. Porter (ed.), *Puritanism in Tudor England* (London: Macmillan, 1970), p. 87. L.J. Trinterud, 'The Origins of Puritanism', *Church History* 20 (1) (1951): 37–57, sees a greater influence of the Rhineland than Geneva on the indigenous English Puritan tradition.

[23] Richard Greenham, 'The Apologie or aunswere of Maister Greenham, Minister of Dreaton, unto the Bishop of Ely, being commaunded to subscribe, and to use the Romish habite, with allowance of the Com. booke' in *A Parte of a register, contayninge sundrie memorable matters, written by divers godly and learned in our time, which stande for,*

logical doctrine, or specifically Calvinist tenets, that Puritans differed with non-Puritan Protestants in England up till the time of the Arminian ascendance. Similarly, Pietists cannot easily be distinguished from non-Pietist Lutherans on the grounds of theology. Most Pietists regarded themselves as working firmly within the Lutheran tradition. Orthodoxy accused Pietists of dissolving 'purity of doctrine' in their stress on experience, the importance of genuine faith and *Herzensfrömmigkeit*. It is in fact possible that one unintended consequence of Pietist activities was to render Lutheran doctrines less central to religious experience, but this was not so at the start, and certainly did not form the grounds of their differences.[24] Theological analysis and interpretation were developing among all participants in the periods under investigation, in all cases departing in various ways from sixteenth-century foundations.

Nor can Puritanism and Pietism be clearly distinguished from orthodoxy in terms of ideas about church polity. The English presbyterian movement of the sixteenth century was supported only by a minority of those ardent Protestants seeking further reformation of the English church. It was effectively extinguished in the 1590s, and there was no serious re-emergence of presbyterianism on any scale until the late 1630s and '40s. Many of those who became known as Puritans, such as Edward Dering, were not even initially very interested in questions of church polity as such. Most would have been quite happy with the current episcopal structure, if only the church were to do its job properly, according to their criteria. One of the interesting features of the development of Puritanism is the way in which anti-episcopal ideas gained great support again in the Laudian period, for reasons which will be discussed in later chapters. Although it is possible to discern, in the decades preceding the Civil War, such tendencies as 'latent presbyterians', 'prewar Independents', 'non-separating congregationalists', and the like, Puritanism cannot narrowly be defined in terms of a specific ecclesiology: it was wider than any one of these positions. Nor can Pietists be said to have had serious and consistent differences with Lutheran orthodoxy over matters of church polity. The idea of conventicles, or the gathering of small groups of the reborn, is however a distinctive (if not sufficient) feature of Pietism. Religious gatherings, additional to public worship services, are characteristic of both Puritan and Pietist religious organisa-

---

and desire the reformation of our Church, in Discipline and Ceremonies, according to the pure Worde of God, and the Lawes of our Lande (1593), p. 89.

[24] See for example Ritschl, *Pietismus*; Mälzer, 'Bengels Theologie im Spiegel der Auseinandersetzung mit Zinzendorf' in M. Greschat (ed.), *Zur Neueren Pietismusforschung* (Darmstadt: Wissenschaftliche Buchgesellschaft, 1977), and Mälzer, *Johann Albrecht Bengel: Leben und Werk* (Stuttgart: Calwer Verlag, 1970); Reinhard Rürup, *Johann Jacob Moser: Pietismus und Reform* (Wiesbaden: Franz Steiner Verlag, 1965); Martin Greschat, *Zwischen Tradition und neuem Anfang: Valentin Ernst Löscher und der Ausgang der Lutherischen Orthodoxie* (Witten: Luther-Verlag, 1971).

tion, as these earnest Christians sought further religious edification in Bible-reading, prayer, repetition of the sermon, and discussion of pious literature together. As we shall see in subsequent chapters, an important question in each case concerns the ways in which these religious gatherings were perceived and treated by authorities: whether they were seen as permissible and harmless supplements to the public religious provisions, or as dangerous and seditious vehicles for subversive ends. Conventicles could potentially develop into separatist cells, or oppositional organisations. Whether they did so or not depended very much on the reactions of others, under particular circumstances, to the felt need of Puritans and Pietists to gather together and sustain their faith in additional private worship.

If ecclesiology and theology will not do, how then can Puritanism and Pietism be defined? And in what ways is their religiosity comparable? The important features include certain specific religious aims and emphases, as well as more general social-psychological aspects concerning ethos and style of life.

First, Pietists and Puritans shared a fundamental biblicism, which was expressed in a number of ways. They placed an overwhelming emphasis on the scriptures as the source of religious authority and guide to conduct in everyday life. This biblicism helps to distinguish Puritans from non-Puritan members of the Church of England, for example. Puritans wanted to erect a church according to the Word of God as revealed in the Bible; they sought scriptural authority for all their positions and practices (even though they might disagree among themselves over what the scriptures actually meant on any particular point); and the Word of God was the centre of any religious service. Non-Puritan members of the English Church tended to give more freedom to secular authorities to decide matters of ecclesiastical policy, where not directly contradicted by the Word of God; and, in worship, they tended to give greater weight to the role of the sacraments. These differences are differences of emphasis only. But in a number of early disputes, those not satisfied with the religious settlement sought positive biblical authority for all practices and organisational features, whereas those prepared to accept the settlement merely argued lack of explicit biblical prohibition of what the secular authorities had decided.[25] The question of the sacraments was somewhat separate; but again, those who most ardently sought to reform the Church of England were most interested in ensuring a sufficiency of preaching and exposition of the Word of the Lord; whereas others were

---

[25] Horton Davies, *The Worship of the English Puritans* (Glasgow: The University Press, 1948), ch. 1, suggests that for 'Anglicans' the Bible was the authority in doctrine, but not in government or worship, whereas for Puritans the Bible was the authority in all things. The differences in practice were evident from the vestiarian controversies onwards. (See Chapter 5, below.)

relatively satisfied if the church could fulfil its sacramental role. (There were also specific differences of opinion over the sacraments themselves.) Similarly, Pietists were profoundly biblicist in orientation. A considerable amount of Pietist energy, time and money was spent on the production and distribution of vernacular editions of the Bible, with appropriate introductions and commentaries, for the benefit of wider audiences. University courses influenced by Pietists emphasised biblical studies, as compared with the scholastic theology of orthodox Lutheranism. Sermons were to be not dogmatic, but rather biblical, in content. Bible-reading at home and in small circles of true believers was stressed as much by Pietists as by Puritans. Uses of the Bible by Pietists ranged from simple edificatory reading, through the practice of *Däumeln* (opening at random to discern God's wishes as revealed in the texts chanced upon), to Bengel's view of the Bible as the *Lagerbuch Gottes*, the *Geschichte des Gottesreiches*, providing the basis for eschatological speculation as well as federal theology.[26]

Related to this biblicism was the great emphasis put by Puritans and Pietists on a certain form of preaching. The aim of preaching was to bring the message of faith, regeneration, and salvation, as revealed in God's Word, to the people. Haller indeed sees this as the essence of Puritanism:

What distinguished the Puritan preachers... was the manner and purpose of their preaching... They asserted, as did others, that man could be saved by faith alone. They endeavoured to do this, however, in terms that common men might understand, in expressive images that would move men to repent, believe and begin the new life at once...[27]

As Thomas Cartwright put it, preaching 'is the excellentest and most ordinary means to work in the heart of hearers'.[28] Both Pietists and Puritans sought to arouse in the souls of others the living experience of conversion to an active faith and a new life as one of God's elect; and to maintain in the regenerate the sense of overcoming sin and temptation, to sustain the battle for living the Christian life. Pietist and Puritan preaching, in contrast to the dull doctrinal elaboration of orthodox Lutheranism and the 'witty', literary style of 'Anglican' sermons, was plain, immediate, and piercing in intent. That it frequently aroused people to a very lively fear of damnation, sense of frailty and sinfulness, is attested to in numerous autobiographies of individuals searching their souls and

---

[26] See, for example: Hinrichs, *Preussentum und Pietismus*, ch. 1; Heinrich Hermelink, *Geschichte der Evangelischen Kirche in Württemberg* (Stuttgart and Tübingen: Rainer Wunderlich Verlag Hermann Leins, 1949), ch. 22; Mälzer, *Bengel*; Martin Scharfe, *Die Religion des Volkes* (Gütersloh: Gütersloher Verlagshaus Gerd Mohn, 1980), pp. 92–7; Ritschl, *Pietismus*, vol. 3, pp. 107–9, tells the tale of the unfortunate Pfeil, who got married on the basis of a *Däumeln* exercise, an act he later was to regret.

[27] Haller, *Rise of Puritanism*, p. 19.

[28] Quoted in Mervyn James, *Family, Lineage, and Civil Society* (Oxford: Clarendon Press, 1974), p. 129.

struggling for eternal salvation. The Puritan preachers of Elizabethan England, vying with the flourishing popular drama, achieved considerable art in their 'plain' preaching; and August Hermann Francke in Halle consciously modelled his sermons on those of the English Puritans, aiming at similar effects. In practice, it seems, Puritan preachers disregarded the implications of Calvin's doctrine of predestination, and gave their audiences the benefit of the doubt: a clerical proverb of the time observed that 'we are all Calvinists when we pray, but all Arminians when we preach'. The seriousness of Puritan preaching was profound: Baxter tells us that he spoke 'as a dying man to dying men...'.[29]

Preaching was intended to bring the message of salvation to those who heard. Puritans and Pietists were particularly marked also by their emphasis on the sense of regeneration, a conversion experience which marked a great stage of transition from the old life in sin to the new life in Christ. Not all believed in, or experienced, the occurrence of rebirth at one particular moment; but it was a fairly widespread characteristic.[30] Weighed down with oppression and despair at their personal inadequacies, Puritans and Pietists would, in a moment of utter darkness of the soul, suddenly experience an overwhelming sense of God's forgiveness and grace. From this moment, their lives could start anew. The new life was not an easy one: it required a perpetual watchfulness, a guarding

[29] Clerical proverb quoted in Knappen, *Tudor Puritanism*, p. 392; Baxter, *Autobiography*, ed. J.M.L. Thomas (London: J.M. Dent and Sons Ltd, 1931), p. 79; on Francke's sermons, F. Ernest Stoeffler, *German Pietism during the Eighteenth Century* (Leiden: E.J. Brill, 1973), pp. 33–4; see also A.H. Francke, 'A Letter to a Friend Concerning the most useful Way of Preaching' (25 May 1725) in John Jennings, *Two Discourses: The First, of Preaching Christ; the Second, of Particular and Experimental Preaching*, with Preface by Isaac Watts (4th edn, Boston, 1740); and Spener, *Pia Desideria*. Spener stresses the need for simple preaching, 'weil die Kanzel nicht derjenige Ort ist / da man seine kunst mit pracht sehen lassen / sondern das Wort des HERRN einfältig / aber gewaltig predigen / und dieses das Göttliche mittel seyn sollte / die Leute selig zu machen...' (p. 150); also: 'Das vornehmste aber achte Ich dieses zu seyn / weil ja unser ganzes Christenthum bestehet in dem *innern oder neuen Menschen* / dessen Seele der Glaube und seine Würckungen die Früchten des Lebens sind: Das dann die Predigten insgesampt dahin gerichtet solten werden' (pp. 151–2).

[30] For Francke's conversion experience, see Francke, 'Anfang und Fortgang der Bekehrung A.H. Franckes von ihm selbst beschrieben' in G. Kramer (ed.), *Beiträge zur Geschichte August Hermann Franckes* (Halle: Verlag der Buchhandlung des Waisenhauses, 1861), pp. 28–55; see more generally for the implications of the emphasis on conversion, Friedrich de Boor, 'Erfahrung gegen Vernunft. Das Bekehrungserlebnis A.H. Franckes als Grundlage für den Kampf des Hallischen Pietismus gegen die Aufklärung' in Bornkamm, Heyer and Schindler (eds.), *Pietismus in Gestalten*. Baxter was somewhat troubled by his own lack of a particular experience of conversion: 'And as for those doubts of my own salvation, which exercised me many years, the chiefest causes of them were these...[First] Because I could not distinctly trace the workings of the Spirit upon my heart in that method which Mr. Bolton, Mr. Hooker, Mr. Rogers and other divines describe, nor knew the time of my conversion, being wrought upon by the forementioned degrees. But since then I understood that the soul is in too dark and passionate a plight at first to be able to keep an exact account of the order of its own operations...' (Baxter, *Autobiography*, p. 10).

against backsliding, a method to maintain oneself on the straight and narrow path, treading warily through the temptations, evils, and besetting doubts of the world. Puritans and Pietists were inclined to try to systematise such experiences, to record and analyse the mysterious ways in which God worked his purposes out for men. Halle Pietists, in particular, almost routinised a fixed series of stages through which the paradigmatic conversion experience must progress (a routinisation with grotesque consequences when Pietist credentials became a prerequisite for Prussian state service). The 'methodism' of Prussian Pietists was regarded with distaste by many Pietists in Württemberg; and nothing quite so formal ever developed among English Puritans. But for Pietists and Puritans generally, there was a considerable degree of introspection associated with the concern of the state of one's soul. The emotionalism of the German Pietists – predecessors of the romantic 'Gefühl ist alles!' – has frequently been pointed out. The experiential nature of Puritanism was perhaps different in many ways, but it was nevertheless as central, amply demonstrated in the outpourings of Puritan diaries.[31]

Puritans and Pietists, concerned as they were with leading the godly life, frequently developed precise rules according to which they could order their lives. The day could be carefully arranged, limits could be set to possible secular indulgence. But twentieth-century associations with the adjective 'puritanical' are misplaced. Puritans and Pietists were not, in general, the self-denying, ascetic bigots suggested by the term. As Thomas Cartwright asserted:

We eat and drink as other men, we live as other men, we are apparelled as other men, we lie as other men, we use those honest recreations as other men do; and we think there is no good thing or commodity of life in the world, but that in sobriety we may be partakers of it, so far as our degree and calling will suffer us, and as God maketh us able to have it.[32]

August Hermann Francke, in his _Schrifftmässige Lebensregeln_ (an insightful Pietist guide on how to win friends and influence people as a good Christian), speaks of the Christian's duty to look afer his body with temperance and balance, as God's gift, and not to mortify the flesh: 'Weil dir GOtt auch den Leib gegeben / so siehe zu / dass du ihn nach GOttes

---

[31] Cf. M.M. Knappen (ed.), _Two Tudor Puritan Diaries_ (Chicago: American Society of Church History, 1933). In his Introduction, Knappen stresses the experiential, pietistic nature of Puritanism. And in his study of Tudor Puritanism, Knappen suggests that 'for all his theology the Puritan, like the Pietist, lived each day for the joy of religion there and then' (Knappen, _Tudor Puritanism_, p. 351). On Pietist emotionalism and its cultural consequences, see for example Koppel Pinson, _Pietism as a Factor in the Rise of German Nationalism_ (New York: Columbia University Press, 1934). On attempts to record and systematise, see for example R.P. Stearns, _The Strenuous Puritan: Hugh Peter, 1598–1660_ (Urbana: University of Illinois, 1954), p. 51. See also, more generally, Owen C. Watkins, _The Puritan Experience_ (London: Routledge and Kegan Paul, 1972).

[32] Quoted in Porter, (ed.), _Puritanism_, p. 4.

Ordnung erhaltest'; and 'Darumb hält er auch sein gantzes Wesen / Leib und Seele in gebührender Ordnung / dass eines dem andern die Hand biethe / GOTT zu Ehren und Preis.'[33] Simplicity, moderation, and order in matters of daily life – dress, food and drink, behaviour – should be observed. In later Pietism, particularly in Prussia, a greater degree of asceticism for its own sake may have developed; but such asceticism was not integral to the original Puritan and Pietist impulse to achieve further religious reform. And many of those concerned with the practices of the state church were not in the least bit interested in restraining their personal habits of indulgence in a variety of worldly pleasures. The yearning for sobriety was by no means general.

Millenarian and eschatological beliefs were central to certain Puritans and Pietists, as indeed they were to many of their contemporaries. But millennial beliefs and expectations varied among Pietists and Puritans, both in content and in salience for action. To a large extent, circumstances influenced the way in which the practical implications of certain beliefs were interpreted. Millenarian beliefs could lead either to frenzied political activity, or to a passive waiting upon the ways of the Lord. Some Pietists rejected apocalyptic beliefs altogether: Hedinger, for example, left Giessen an apparently convinced defender of orthodoxy because he could not stand the chiliasm prevalent among Giessen Pietists. Bengel's eschatology, given an aura of scientific precision with its foundation in biblical scholarship and advanced mathematics, caused some embarrassment among many Württemberg Pietists.[34]

The central features rendering Puritanism and Pietism comparable have to do with their aims in attempting to complete an inadequate reformation. They sought to establish a holy community of Christian individuals leading a genuinely godly life, based on the Word of the Lord as revealed in the Bible, sustained by pure church services and an active preaching ministry, and supplemented by individual, household, and small group sessions for devotion and edification. They were not, in inception, separatist: they wanted to transform, not leave, the state church. Despite numerous differences and variations in specific points of doctrine, policy, and ecclesiology, these overriding aspirations characterise the broad tenor of the Puritan and Pietist movements.

[33] 'Because God also gave you your body, so take care that you look after it according to God's order', and 'Therefore let him maintain his whole being, body and soul, in proper order, so that the one gives the other a helping hand in honour and glory of God.' A.H. Francke, *Schrifftmässige Lebens-Regeln. Wie man so wohl bey als ausser der Gesellschaft die Liebe und Freundligkeit gegen den Nechsten / und Freudigkeit eines guten Gewissens fur Gott bewahren / und im Christenthum zunehmen soll* (Bremen: Bey Joh. Wesseln / Raths Buchdr., 1696), p. 73, p. 74.
[34] See, for example: Wallmann, *Spener*; Fritz, *Altwürttembergische Pietisten*; Mälzer, *Bengel*; William Lamont, *Godly Rule* (London: Macmillan, 1969); Christopher Hill, *Antichrist in Seventeenth-Century England* (London: Oxford University Press, 1971); Firth, *Apocalyptic Tradition*.

It may be noted that this general characterisation is in terms of emphases and aspirations. Yet 'movements' are commonly defined, not only in terms of programme and ideals, but also in terms of organisation and structure. This has not been done here for two reasons. The first has to do with the nature of the phenomena under study. It was only at specific periods, under particular sets of circumstances, that Puritans and Pietists organised into what might be called movements in the strong sense. An example would of course be the sixteenth-century English presbyterian movement. At other times, Puritanism and Pietism were more in the nature of diffuse cultural orientations, broad historical movements in the weak sense. As such, Puritan or Pietist attitudes could be held by individuals far apart in social status, political activity, network of organisation or pattern of action. Part of the interest of analysing Puritanism and Pietism lies in the question of the differing determination of organisational forms and alliances in differing conditions. The other reason is historiographical and theoretical. Most of the arguments about the supposed historical consequences of Puritanism and Pietism have focussed on these aspects of their religiosity and ethos: on the individualistic, biblicist, experiential form of religiosity which they represented. Therefore, to present a new case, arguing a different explanation, it is well to highlight those aspects which are frequently suggested to be causally crucial: to be discussing the same, and not some other, historical animal. Let me turn now to a related problem in this connection: the social bases of Puritanism and Pietism.

The carriers of Puritanism and Pietism

Who were the Puritans and Pietists? Who was attracted by the forms of religious aspiration and ethos sketched above? The question is almost more controversial than the primary question of identification. For it is bound up with fundamentally different modes of historical approach, different metatheoretical assumptions about patterns of social change. Can Puritanism be reduced to a form of class ideology? Did Pietism in Prussia bend to state service because there was no 'strong' and 'rising' bourgeoisie? Can one even analyse religion and society in early modern Europe in class terms?

These questions serve to locate the argument presented here. It is essentially this: Puritanism and Pietism cannot be interpreted as 'class ideologies' in any sensible way; in each case, Puritan and Pietist ideas appealed across a relatively broad social range, different aspects appealing to different groups; and while some form of class analysis is integral to an adequate understanding of early modern European politics, religion must be treated as an analytically independent variable related to other factors in ways which require empirical investigation rather than *a priori* assumption. Analysis of the class bases of Puritanism and Pietism alone is not sufficient to explain the different patterns of political development in each case, whether the proposed explanation be couched in terms of rationalisation of underlying material interests, or in terms of class capacities for action (strength or weakness in relation to other social groups).

There is a further problem in analysing social bases. As the movements developed over time, they became involved in particular social and political controversies which coloured and changed their meanings. As they developed particular associations, in particular circumstances, so the social groups which were particularly attracted to them changed. Changing social profiles – as in the attraction of the service nobility to Pietism in Prussia – might be more the consequence than the cause of particular political positions. These complexities must be borne in mind when disentangling the problem of the class carriers of Puritanism and Pietism.

Two main sorts of strong social interpretation have been presented of English Puritanism. The first, represented by Walzer, sees Puritanism as an overwhelmingly clerical movement, its leadership being supplied by ministers throughout the period until the 1630s. Walzer suggests that this clerical leadership underwent a change in social composition, corresponding to a shift in ideological emphasis, from the sixteenth to the seventeenth centuries. Earlier Puritan ministers, according to Walzer, came from generally lower social backgrounds than those of a later period. He relates this to the shift from the 'disciplinarian' period of Cartwright and Field, with its stress on clerical domination, towards the 'independent' positions of the early seventeenth century: the former was the 'ideology of a clergy almost entirely made up of commoners, socially and intellectually isolated in their native land'; the latter, 'the natural doctrine of a clergy which was growing into closer and closer rapport with the lesser gentry and the upper urban classes, and which included members of both in its ranks. There was much less in it of the anxiety and compulsive over-organisation that characterised Presbyterianism.'[35] The other strong sort of social interpretation focusses rather on the laity: on the middling groups of society, 'the industrious sort of people', whom Christopher Hill defines as 'the economically independent men, householders, to the exclusion both of the propertyless and the privileged classes'.[36] Brian Manning, for example, agrees with Hill in locating Puritanism firmly among the 'middle sort of people' whom 'Puritanism

[35] Michael Walzer, *The Revolution of the Saints* (New York: Atheneum, 1974), p. 137, p. 138. But see R. O.'Day, *The English Clergy: The Emergence and Consolidation of a Profession, 1558–1642* (Leicester: Leicester University Press, 1979), for evidence of changes in the status and composition of the clergy generally over this period.

[36] Christopher Hill, *Society and Puritanism in Pre-revolutionary England* (New York: Schocken Books, 1967), pp. 133–4.

taught... to think for themselves and to assert their independence against king, lords and bishops. Godliness gave them status and the ability to express their identity as a separate class; and it enabled them to formulate and dignify their hostility towards the ruling class.'[37] A rather different variant of this approach is found in Wrightson's and Levine's analysis of Puritanism as a 'cultural wedge' emerging between an increasingly polarised village elite and the lower orders of village society. Here, Puritans looked downwards, at the popular culture which they sought to control, rather than upwards, at the powers of a ruling class which they sought to question.[38]

These interpretations obviously not only suggest which social groups were supposedly the most important carriers of Puritanism, but also propose explanations of why this should have been so. These are of course separate issues; and whatever one may think of the general theoretical approaches of these authors, it would seem that the rather narrow substantive focus of their analyses is not entirely acceptable. Against Walzer's interpretation, the research of Patrick Collinson on Elizabethan Puritanism suggests that right from the start there were strong lay pressures on Puritan ministers, pushing them and sustaining them in nonconformity. This impression is confirmed by the work of local historians, such as Spufford, who emphasises the importance of 'grass roots' dissent and the keen interest of the laity in religious affairs.[39] In the light of such research, it now seems difficult to accept an interpretation of Puritanism as the ideology of alienated intellectuals seeking to impose order and discipline in a period of experienced social chaos. And any cursory glance at the history of Puritanism will show, *pace* Hill, that there were many supporters of Puritanism among the upper ranks of society: the aristocratic patrons of Elizabethan England such as Leicester, the Russells, the Cookes and other powerful families. They supplied political protection, both centrally and in the localities; they provided financial support and indeed 'investment' in the movement, such as in Sir Walter Mildmay's foundation of Emmanuel College, Cambridge; they provided social centres for the spread of lay piety and Puritan lifestyles, as in the circle around Lady Margaret Hoby in Hackness. Nor was Puritanism, for many of its adherents and a good part of its history, necessarily an anti-episcopal movement. Puritans certainly did develop a widespread antagonism to bishops in the late 1620s and '30s, but this antagonism arose as a result of specific circumstances of the time, which will be examined in later chapters.

[37] Brian Manning, *The English People and the English Revolution* (Harmondsworth: Penguin, 1978), p. 180.

[38] Keith Wrightson and David Levine, *Poverty and Piety in an English Village: Terling, 1525–1700* (New York: Academic Press, 1979).

[39] Collinson, *Elizabethan Puritan Movement*; Spufford, *Contrasting Communities*, chs. 9, 10, 12, 13. On the 'alienated intellectuals' notion, see Mark Curtis, 'The Alienated Intellectuals of Early Stuart England', *Past and Present* 23 (1962): 25–43.

It is in fact possible that the only class of English society among which Puritanism was not represented, at least in any coherent way that has survived in the historical record, was that of the very poor. Perhaps they had more immediate concerns on their minds than the state of their salvation; perhaps Puritanism was a form of religious endeavour which required a certain minimal level of education to be sustained over time. At any rate, the spiritual strivings of the poorest members of English society have not left an appreciable mark in the records of Puritanism, except perhaps in a diffuse anticlericalism which became important in the Civil War period.[40]

The relatively broad range of social support for Puritan aspirations suggests that Puritanism cannot be interpreted in any simple way as a 'class ideology'.[41] For a number of reasons it is difficult to see it as in some way a rationalisation, in a religious metaphor, of specific material interests – and particularly not of consciously revolutionary aspirations. Social revolution was far from most Puritans' minds right up to the period of political and intellectual ferment occasioned by the collapse of government in the 1640s. In the strong, pejorative sense, Puritanism was not an ideological cover-up. It is difficult also – although less so – to interpret it as a class ideology in the weaker sense, as reflecting in certain ways the social experience of the groups involved: as having, in Max Weber's term, an 'elective affinity' with certain forms of social position. For it is not at all clear why only a minority of people in any social position were attracted to Puritanism: it has had a historical importance far outweighing its numerical strength. Puritanism never became the lifestyle and outlook of the majority of any social group.[42]

The social distribution of Puritanism does however seem to have been skewed disproportionately in favour of certain groups. This suggests, on closer analysis, that rather than conceptualising it in terms of rationali-sation or reflection of class interests or experience, it is more helpful to consider its social basis in terms of enabling conditions. Some groups were better placed than others, in a variety of ways, to be exposed to

---

[40] Cf. for example, Wallace Notestein, *The English People on the Eve of Colonisation, 1603–1630* (London: Hamish Hamilton, 1954), p. 85, p. 162; Christopher Hill, *The World Turned Upside Down* (Harmondsworth: Penguin, 1975); A.L. Morton, *The World of the Ranters* (London: Lawrence and Wishart, 1970); James Fulton MacLear, 'Popular Anticlericalism in the Puritan Revolution', *Journal of the History of Ideas* 18 (4) (1956): 443–70.

[41] 'Ideology' is a concept enjoying a variety of meanings and uses. See for a recent lucid discussion of certain approaches, Raymond Geuss, *The Idea of a Critical Theory* (Cambridge: Cambridge University Press, 1981), ch. 1; see also Jorge Larrain, *The Concept of Ideology* (London: Hutchinson, 1979).

[42] Knappen, *Tudor Puritanism*, pp. 333–4, n. 24, attempts an estimate of the proportion of Puritans in the population. He suggests that perhaps 75% of the English were 'either religiously indifferent or without any opinions on religious questions'; and guesses that about 15% were Puritans by the middle of Elizabeth's reign (far more than Usher's estimate of 2%, but still not overwhelming).

and influenced by Puritan ideas. The enablement might be social, as illustrated in Baxter's well-known comment:

it was a great Advantage to me, that my Neighbours were of such a trade as allowed them time enough to read or talk of holy Things. For the town liveth upon the weaving of Kidderminster Stuffs; and as they stand in their Loom they can set a Book before them, or edifie one another: whereas Plowmen, and many others, are so wearied or continually employed, either in the Labours or the Cares of their Callings, that it is a great Impediment to their Salvation.[43]

But it might also be geographical. In Lancashire, for example, Puritanism took hold in the south-eastern region which had trading links with the West Riding, East Anglia, and London, and was exposed to radical ideas; but Puritanism had little success among the linen-weavers elsewhere in Lancashire, whose trading links were with Catholic Ireland.[44] Social, economic, and geographic elements are frequently hard to disentangle: Richardson found in his study of north-west England that Puritanism 'took firmest root in the most economically developed areas of the diocese, in the clothing towns, in marketing centres and in the "industrialising" pastoral regions in the east of the diocese'; Puritanism was also strong in those pastoral and woodland areas which were weakly manorialised, with partible inheritance and the family unit most important in farming.[45] In Yorkshire, Cliffe found that among gentry families, Puritanism cross-cut all levels of income and ancientness of gentility; but there were more Puritan gentry in towns and clothing regions than elsewhere.[46] Enablement might also be cultural, as in the question of education and literacy. Wrightson and Levine, who found Puritans disproportionately among the 'upper and middling ranks of village society' in Terling, stress the importance of the educational revolution of the time, serving culturally to crystallise the increasing social differentiation.[47] (It should not be forgotten, of course, that expanding literacy was enabling for people of other persuasions also, and the explosion of tracts and pamphlets was indicative of a thinking public in general.) It was, quite obviously, in places where Puritan ideas were available, and people were able to hear, read, and discuss these ideas, that Puritanism would achieve greatest strength. But, while Puritanism was of course refracted through the social experience of its adherents and necessarily implied

[43] Baxter, *Reliquiae Baxterianae*, p. 89, quoted in Alan Simpson, *Puritanism in Old and New England* (Chicago: University of Chicago Press, 1955), pp. 116–17, n. 13; see also pp. 11–12.

[44] Christopher Haigh, *Reformation and Resistance in Tudor Lancashire* (Cambridge: Cambridge University Press, 1975), chapters 18 and 19; partic. p. 325.

[45] R.C. Richardson, *Puritanism in North-West England* (Manchester: University of Manchester Press, 1972), pp. 14–15, p. 94.

[46] J.T. Cliffe, *The Yorkshire Gentry from the Reformation to the Civil War* (London: Athlone Press, 1969), p. 262.

[47] Wrightson and Levine, *Poverty and Piety*, p. 161; see also pp. 166–7.

certain secular orientations, the politics of Puritans cannot easily be derived from their social profile.

Similar comments can be made about Pietism. In Württemberg, on a far smaller scale, there has been a similar debate about the respective importance of clerical leadership and the socioeconomic background of lay Pietists.[48] Certainly there was strong clerical leadership of Württemberg Pietism; but there is also considerable evidence of lay pressures, at all social levels, which were potentially separatist in nature if not harnessed and contained in the practices of the established church. This tension gave a certain dynamism to the early development of Pietism in this area. Pietist ideas appear to have appealed across a variety of social categories, ranging from the solid, upper and middle ranks of Calw society – where leading Pietists were prominent members of the Calw manufacturing and trading company, wealthy and respectable pillars of the social order – to the motley collection of artisans, tradesmen, apprentices, and servants who belonged to the Stuttgart group.[49] Even this group, however, met in the house of a respectable teacher, and included members of the court community among its participants. One was the widow of a privy councillor, and there were relatives of other court officials; the group was also visited by somewhat unorthodox clergymen. The Tübingen *Stunde* of 1703 was started by the request of certain common *Weingärtner* for further religious education, responded to by advanced graduate students (*Repetenten*) at the theological seminary. Later Tübingen Pietist groups were led by a Professor, Reuchlin, and a lawyer, Moser.[50] Part of the complexity of the situation, making it difficult for the church to determine an unambiguous response, was the lack of clear social implications of Pietism. In villages and towns, among the small independent peasantry, the artisans, traders, and solid burghers, Pietism appears to have cut across social distinctions in ways which cannot be simply explained. Nor can any class analysis explain why Pietism appealed only to a minority of any social group in Württemberg. The social profile of Württemberg Pietism may have changed somewhat, with changes in its social meaning over time – clergy and

---

[48] See, for example: Lehmann, *Pietismus und Weltliche Ordnung*; Joachim Trautwein, *Religiosität und Sozialstruktur* (Stuttgart: Calwer Verlag, 1972); Lehmann, 'Probleme einer Sozialgeschichte des Württembergischen Pietismus', *Blätter für Württembergische Kirchengeschichte* 75 (1975): 166–81.

[49] Hartmut Lehmann, 'Pietismus und Wirtschaft in Calw am Anfang des 18. Jahrhunderts', *Zeitschrift für Württembergische Landesgeschichte* 31 (1972): 249–77; Christoph Kolb, 'Die Anfänge des Pietismus und Separatismus in Württemberg', *Württembergische Vierteljahresheft für Landesgeschichte* 9 (1900): 368–412, p. 403; and 10 (1901): 201–51, pp. 201–19; Hermelink, *Geschichte der Evangelischen Kirche*, ch. 23.

[50] Martin Leube, *Die Geschichte des Tübinger Stifts*, vol. 2 (Stuttgart: Verlag Chr. Scheufele, 1930), ch. 12; F. Fritz, 'Konventikel in Württemberg von der Reformationszeit bis zum Edikt von 1743', *Blätter für Württembergische Kirchengeschichte* 51 (1951): 78–137; Johann Jacob Moser, *Lebensgeschichte von ihme selbst beschriben* (1768), pp. 55–6, and on his later Stuttgart *Erbauungsstunden*, p. 63.

schoolmasters gaining the initiative from the laity, and providing the leadership in the middle years of the eighteenth century, new lower-class and potentially separatist groups emerging in the latter part of the century – but these changes resulted from a combination of factors analysed further below. They do not in any immediate way explain the political responses of Württemberg Pietism, considered in isolation.

Halle Pietism has perhaps a slightly more distinctive social location. The economic enterprises of Pietists, under the dynamic and entrepreneurial organisation of Francke, antagonised local guilds and trading associations, who felt their livelihood to be threatened. Francke's political activities aroused the antipathy of the local Estates and their representatives. Thus Halle Pietism found its initial support among groups not involved in the established economic and political organisations, those who had least to lose from disruptions of the traditional order. This appears to have been the case also in Berlin, where in the controversies of the 1690s orthodoxy was supported by 'Exponenten der landständischen Ordnung und des städtischen Zunftbürgertums' while the Pietist cause found adherents who were 'Angehörige der sozial und gesellschaftlich benachteiligten Schichten der Vorstädte,...Tagelöhner, Handwerkgesellen, kleine Gewerbetreibende, u. a.', allied with 'den aufgeklärten Vertretern des sich herausbildenden Grossbürgertums'.[51] Similar alignments were evident in later controversies in Königsberg, in East Prussia.[52] Among the aristocracy, it appears to have been the small independent nobles, and the newly ennobled court aristocrats who were initially most attracted to Pietism; the old, landed provincial aristocracy were in general opposed, although as they became co-opted into state service, over time, this changed to a remarkable degree.[53] Pietism in Prussia in general appears to have gained most adherents among groups outside traditional feudal structures, whether these were lord–serf relationships on the land or guild and political organisations in the towns.

A number of suggestions have been made as to why this should have

---

[51] 'Spokesmen of the provincial estates' order and urban guild bourgeoisie'; 'members of the socially disadvantaged strata of the suburbs.... day labourers, journeymen, small tradesmen, etc.' and 'the enlightened representatives of the developing big bourgeoisie.' Klaus Deppermann, *Der Hallesche Pietismus und der Preussische Staat unter Friedrich III. (I.)* (Göttingen: Vandenhoek und Ruprecht, 1961); E. Selbmann, 'Die Gesellschaftlichen Erscheinungsformen des Pietismus Hallischer Prägung' in *450 Jahre Martin-Luther-Universität Halle–Wittenberg*, vol. 2 (Halle–Wittenberg: Selbst-Verlag der Martin-Luther-Universität Halle–Wittenberg, 1952); Hinrichs, *Preussentum und Pietismus*; Helmut Obst, *Der Berliner Beichtstuhlstreit* (Witten: Luther-Verlag, 1972), p. 147.

[52] Cf. Erich Riedesel, *Pietismus und Orthodoxie in Ostpreussen* (Königsberg und Berlin: Ost-Europa-Verlag, 1937), pp. 29–30.

[53] Cf. Hinrichs, *Preussentum und Pietismus*; Ritschl, *Pietismus*, vol. 2, ch. 39; Deppermann, *Hallesche Pietismus*, pp. 29–31; also D.P. Walker, *The Decline of Hell* (London: Routledge and Kegan Paul, 1964), chapters 13 and 14, on the influence of the Petersens and Jane Leade on Berlin court society.

been so, and what implications it might have had. Some have sought affinities between elements of Pietist ideals and the social experience of these various groups. Ritschl, for example, saw a useful correspondence between Pietist asceticism and the limited means and weak status and power positions of the petty independent nobles, such as the various Grafen Reuss. Greschat has suggested that Pietist activism and optimism corresponded with new bourgeois experience of entrepreneurial striving for secular transformation, while at the same time Pietist morality coincided with bourgeois reaction against the wasteful hedonism of absolutist court life. Obst proposes that the lower-class lay Pietists were interested in personal emancipation from the constraints imposed by estates-society social and political structure. Lutheran orthodoxy at the time insisted that 'the common man' would get ideas above his station in the atmosphere of religious brotherhood fostered in Pietist conventicles, although in fact Pietists were careful to preserve the conventions of the social hierarchy.[54] Pietism was evidently a quite flexible ideology, capable of representing many different things to different social groups, and certainly not reducible to any particular one of them. Moreover, the reasons for the strong opposition of particular groups have to do with certain structural features of church and state in Brandenburg-Prussia, and hence the sociopolitical implications of the Pietist movement, rather than with the social experience as such of these groups. These features will be outlined in the following chapters. In terms of the implications of the social basis of Prussian Pietism, it seems difficult to argue that it was inherently politically committed to any particular position. It was not necessarily socially weak, with a foothold in court society (including also among its ranks a few members of the old aristocracy, such as Georg Rudolf von Schweinitz), and it was distributed across social groups in a manner which renders its political implications at least ambiguous.

What then can be concluded from this cursory, preliminary survey of the social location of the Puritan and Pietist movements? It is possible that the patterns of distribution lend some support to interpretations appealing to the notion of 'transitional ideologies'. Innovatory in themselves, seeking for religious, moral and social transformation, Pietism and Puritanism appear to have commanded slightly less support among certain established groups than among others involved in new enterprises and activities. But this does not seem to me to carry the analysis very far, and is certainly inadequate to the task of explaining the very different political contributions made by Puritans and Pietists in the three cases under analysis. The social bases of Puritanism and Pietism in England,

[54] Ritschl, *Pietismus*, vol. 2, ch. 41; Martin Greschat, 'Simon Philipp Klettwig – Bürger und Pietist' in Bornkamm, Heyer and Schindler (eds.), *Pietismus in Gestalten*, partic. pp. 203–8; K. Deppermann, 'Pietismus und moderne Staat' and K. Aland, 'Der Pietismus und die soziale Frage' in K. Aland (ed.), *Pietismus und Moderne Welt* (Witten: Luther-Verlag, 1974); Obst, *Beichtstuhlstreit*, p. 147.

Württemberg and Prussia tell us more about the different general socio-economic structures of these states than they do about the likely 'revolutionary' or 'conservative' implications of the religious movements. Moreover, the social profiles of the movements, as they developed in different situations, are the result more of external factors to do with sociopolitical location and emergent social meanings than they are of inherent aspects of Puritan and Pietist religiosity as such. At the very least, the social profiles of Puritanism and Pietism suggest that any adequate explanation of their different politics must press beyond any simple class analysis, to probe other factors in each situation.

It cannot be suggested that Puritanism in England, Pietism in Württemberg, and Pietism in Prussia, in the varying periods between the mid-sixteenth and late eighteenth centuries, were in some way 'identical' phenomena. Of course they were not. But their specifically religious aims, aspirations and activities were remarkably similar; their forms of religious organisation, conventicles and preaching, were fundamentally comparable; their ethos, or social-psychology, was strikingly convergent, given their different theological backgrounds. Puritanism and Pietism represented, not class ideologies, but autonomous impulses to achieve religious regeneration and reform, along lines which were essentially similar. It is a legitimate sociological question to ask why such inherently similar movements should work themselves out so differently in each case.[55] And the answer does not seem to lie in 'internal' features of the movements. It is the argument of this study that the differences can be adequately explained only in terms of certain structural features of the different configurations in which Pietists and Puritans set about erecting the holy community. Let us turn then to look in more detail at the nature of the different states and societies in which Puritans and Pietists sought to achieve their specifically religious aims.

[55] Readers who are still not convinced of the legitimacy of the comparison between earlier English Puritanism and later German Pietism might like to focus their minds particularly on the comparison between Pietists in Württemberg and Pietists in Prussia, where there were no such differences of Reformation background or temporal context, yet still striking differences in politics.

3

State and society: the attempts at absolutism

Puritans and Pietists were aiming at similar ends: the spread of a living, active Christian faith based on the Word of the Lord as expressed in the Scriptures; and the reformation of this world in the light of God's Word. The ways in which they became involved with the political conflicts of their times have much to do with certain differing features of the socio-political landscapes in which Puritans and Pietists sought to establish God's Kingdom on Earth. In this and the following chapter we shall examine those aspects of the contexts of the three movements which together help to explain why similar religious movements should make such different political contributions. It will then be possible to examine more closely the divergent patterns of development of the movements, showing how in each case Puritans and Pietists faced varying obstacles to achievement of their religious aims and developed different strategies of political action, attitude, and alliance.

Common to each of the three cases was the incipient trend towards absolutist rule: the attempts being made by rulers to centralise power, to reduce the role of the Estates in the tradition of the late mediaeval *Ständestaat*.[1] This trend was not a later invention of systematising historians, unnoticed by contemporaries. As certain members of the English Parliament put it in the 1604 *Apology of the Commons*, expressing their disquiets in the light of continental European developments:

What cause we your poor Commons have to watch over our privileges is manifest in itself to all men. The prerogatives of princes may easily and do daily grow; the privileges of the subject are for the most part at an everlasting stand. They may be by good providence and care preserved, but being once lost are not recovered but with much disquiet.[2]

The outcomes of the rulers' attempts were rather different, however, and their strategies varied in accordance with the dynamics of the socio-

---

[1] On the *Ständestaat* and absolutism, see generally: Gianfranco Poggi, *The Development of the Modern State* (London: Hutchinson, 1978); H.G. Koenigsberger, *Estates and Revolutions* (Ithaca: Cornell University Press, 1971); Perry Anderson, *Lineages of the Absolutist State* (London: New Left Books, 1974).

[2] Quoted in Conrad Russell, *The Crisis of Parliaments* (London: Oxford University Press, 1971), p. 270.

economic and political structures they had inherited. Absolutism succeeded to the greatest extent in the militarised bureaucratic state of eighteenth-century Prussia; it was expressed, in limited and ineffective form, in the splendours of court culture, court architecture, the tiny standing army and the incessant aspirations of the Württemberg Dukes, to be finally truncated after constitutional struggles in the mid- and later eighteenth century; and the attempt of Charles I in England culminated, notoriously, in the loss of his head and the series of constitutional experiments which finally made way for the establishment of the foundations for parliamentary rule and constitutional monarchy.

Historians have reached no consensus on explanations of the success or failure of absolutism in different states; indeed, there is no agreement even on the very meaning of the term.[3] Arguments on how absolutism is to be defined range from those seeking to resurrect the (changing) meanings of 'absolute' for contemporaries to those suggesting characterisations in terms of aspects of political structures, constitutional theories, or functional class interests. Explanations show an equally wide range of variation, such that absolutism – within the terms of one theoretical tradition alone – has been variously interpreted as the last carapace of a threatened feudal nobility, a transitional state in an era of feudal/capitalist balance, and the harbinger of the new era of capitalism itself. In this chapter, the term 'absolutism' is used as an ideal-typical concept, a tool for comparative analysis, to refer to a political form in which the ruler, through the use of state bureaucratic and repressive apparatuses, is able to raise revenues and undertake independent domestic and foreign policy decisions without the co-determination of the Estates as represented in Parliaments or Diets. Sovereignty is not dualistic, shared with the Estates, but is the ruler's alone. The successful establishment of such a structure, and the decline in power of Estates in relation to ruler, cannot be explained simply in terms of its functionality for a given class; rather, it must be viewed as the outcome of a process of political struggle, negotiation, and resistance, among ruler, nobles, peasants, and burghers, in an international context of military aggression and economic change. The

[3] See for example: James Daly, 'The Idea of Absolute Monarchy in Seventeenth-Century England', *The Historical Journal* 21 (2) (1978): 227–50; Fritz Hartung and Roland Mousnier, 'Quelques Problèmes concernant la Monarchie Absolue', *X. Congresso Internazionale di Scienze Storiche, Relazione*, vol. 4, Storia Moderna (Rome, 1955); Brian Manning, 'The Nobles, the People, and the Constitution', *Past and Present* 9 (1956): 42–64; J.P. Cooper, 'Differences between English and Continental Governments in the Early Seventeenth Century' in J.S. Bromley and E.H. Kossmann (eds.), *Britain and the Netherlands* (London: Chatto and Windus, 1960); H.G. Koenigsberger, *Estates and Revolutions*, 'Introduction'; Koenigsberger, 'Dominium Regale or Dominium Politicum et Regale?' in Karl Bosl and Karl Möckl (eds.), *Der Moderne Parlamentarismus und seine Grundlagen in der Ständischen Repräsentation* (Berlin: Duncker und Humblot, 1977); Koenigsberger, 'Revolutionary Conclusions', *History* 57 (191) (1972): 394–8; Anderson, *Lineages*.

following sketches, based on these conceptual and explanatory assumptions, are intended to highlight the tasks and strategies of would-be absolutist rulers in England, Württemberg and Prussia, and to delineate crucial features of the differing sociopolitical contexts of the Puritan and Pietist movements.[4] We shall begin with the case of most successful absolutism: Brandenburg-Prussia.

Prussia: the rise of a militaristic absolutist state

The eighteenth-century Prussian state, with its unlikely origins and its profound historical consequences, has long presented an intriguing case for historians. Scholars have seen it as a paradigm case, an 'exemplary absolutism', illustrating to the full the central features of a militaristic bureaucratic form of political organisation.[5] Yet this fully fledged absolutism arose in the sandy wastes of the north-eastern colonial backwater of Europe. In the early decades of the seventeenth century, the disparate possessions of the Hohenzollerns, with their poor soil, declining trade, and sparse population, can scarcely have seemed promising material on which to build a great European state. Yet little over a century later, in the reign of Friedrich II, 'Frederick the Great', Prussia had developed into a European power of foremost importance; and it was this strong Prussian state, as it developed in the nineteenth century, which was eventually to control the unification of a national Germany excluding the Hapsburg Austria. What then were the dynamics of this development? With what forces and constraints did the early Hohenzollern state-builders have to contend?

The first point of importance is that seventeenth- and eighteenth-century Brandenburg-Prussia was a 'composite state'.[6] The Hohenzollern rulers, originating in south-western Germany, had acquired, through the haphazard processes of marriage, diplomacy, and conquest, a disparate set of territories, held under an astonishing diversity of legal titles, ranging from the Rhenish and Westphalian provinces in the west to the province of East Prussia in the east. The central territory, in which the Hohenzollerns based their operations, was Brandenburg, bestowing on the ruler the title of Elector of the Holy Roman Empire. It was in East

---

[4] It should be made clear at the outset that the following sketches are not intended as comprehensive analyses or explanations of the political histories of each case. They are rather intended to highlight selected features of the sociopolitical structures and developments of England, Württemberg, and Prussia, insofar as these are important for understanding the nature of the ruler's position and the context of Pietist and Puritan responses to attempted abolutism.

[5] As in Poggi, *Modern State*; and an exemplary 'Eastern Absolutism' in Anderson, *Lineages*; see also Hans Rosenberg, *Bureaucracy, Aristocracy and Autocracy* (Boston: Beacon Press, 1966).

[6] Cf. Koenigsberger, 'Dominium regale', for the importance of composite states.

Prussia, outside the boundaries of the Empire, that the Elector Friedrich III was able in 1701 to crown himself 'King *in* Prussia', thus becoming King Friedrich I. Francke, in addressing the King at the beginning of his *Erneuertes und vermehrtes Privilegium des Wäysen-hauses*, starts out:

...Friederich... König in Preussen, Marggraf zu Brandenburg, des Heil. Röm. Reichs Ertz-Cämmerer und Churfürst, Souverainer Printz von Oranien, zu Magdeburg, Cleve, Jülich, Berge, Stettin, Pommern, der Cassuben und Wenden, auch in Schlesien, zu Crossen Herzog, Burggraf zu Nürnberg, Fürst zu Halberstadt, Minden und Camin, Graf zu Hohenzollern, der March, Ravensberg, Lingen, Moerss, Bühren und Lehrdam, Marquis zu der Vehre und Blisslingen, Herr zu Ravenstein, wie auch der Lande Lauenberg und Bütow, Arlay und Breda...[7]

The scattered provinces of the Hohenzollerns had different historical traditions, different social and economic structures, different patterns of political organisation. A major task thus had to be the reduction of provincial autonomy and the centralisation of political power. But the converse of this problem was the disunity and diversity of the Estates, rendering possible a strategy of divide and rule.

Socioeconomically, there were great differences between the western and eastern provinces.[8] In the east, large areas of land were organised under the system of *Gutsherrschaft*, in which the once relatively free colonising peasants were increasingly brought under the control of noble landlords, until they were finally repressed into serfdom. On their own estates, Junkers possessed patrimonial rights of political and juridical domination over their unfree peasants, as well as purely economic mastery. With the sixteenth- and early seventeenth-century reorientation of European trade to the Atlantic seaboard, the towns in the east were in decline; and the effects of the Thirty Years War were such as to devastate trade and production as well as agriculture. Vast areas were ravaged and depopulated. In the western provinces, the social structure was freer: peasants retained their rights, towns continued to be of importance politically and economically.

[7] 'Friedrich... King in Prussia, Margrave of Brandenburg, Lord Chamberlain and Elector of the Holy Roman Empire, Sovereign Prince of Orange, Magdeburg, Cleve, Jülich, Berg, Stettin, Pommern, Cassuben and Wenden, also in Silesia, Duke of Crossen, Baron of Nürnberg, Prince of Halberstadt, Minden and Camin, Count of Hohenzollern, March, Ravensberg, Lingen, Moerss, Bühren and Lehrdam, Marquis of Vehre and Blisslingen, Lord of Ravenstein, as also of Launberg and Bütow, Arlay and Breda...' August Hermann Francke, *Segens-Volle Fußstapfen des noch Liebenden und Waltenden Liebreichen und Getreuen Gottes...* (Halle: in Verlegung des Waysen-hauses, 1709), p. 121. For a modern account of the Hohenzollern titles, see R.A. Dorwart, *The Administrative Reforms of Frederick William I of Prussia* (Cambridge, Mass.: Harvard University Press, 1953), p. 1.

[8] See generally: F.L. Carsten, *The Origins of Prussia* (Oxford: Clarendon Press, 1954); Friedrich Lütge, *Deutsche Sozial- und Wirtschaftsgeschichte* (Berlin: Springer Verlag, 2nd edn, 1960); Lütge, *Geschichte der deutschen Agrarverfassung* (Stuttgart: Verlag Eugen Ulmer, 2nd edn, 1967); Heinrich Bechtel, *Wirtschafts- und Sozialgeschichte Deutschlands* (München: Verlag Georg D.W. Callwey, 1967); Bechtel, *Wirtschaftsgeschichte Deutschlands*, vol. 2 (München: Verlag Georg D.W. Callwey, 1952).

Hohenzollern strategies of rule varied according to local conditions. The more prosperous western provinces were treated largely as a source of income, and were never as fully subjugated to central political authority as were those of the east. Yet at the beginning of the seventeenth century, Estates and landowners enjoyed great powers across all the provinces of what was to become a unitary Prussian state. F.L. Carsten speaks of the predominance of Estates and Junkers in Brandenburg and Prussia not only in the economic and social but also in the political and constitutional fields. Nevertheless, he continues:

By the end of the seventeenth century a powerful Hohenzollern state had arisen in north-eastern Germany in which the Estates no longer were an important political factor. They had lost their influence over civil and military appointments, were not consulted in foreign affairs and hardly in internal matters; above all, they no longer wielded the power of the purse, but the elector had become independent of their financial grants.[9]

This astonishing transformation was brought about through the conversion of the political power of the nobility, from being independent feudal magnates exercising their collective powers through the Estates to being a new service nobility oriented to central state power. The first crucial steps in this transformation were taken in the reign of the Great Elector, Friedrich Wilhelm (1640–88).

Following the economic devastations and political and military exigencies of the Thirty Years War, the general Brandenburg Diet of 1652 (the last of its type), adjourned into the *Recess* of 1653, renegotiated the relations between Elector and Estates. In return for economic and political concessions to the nobility – including confirmation of the *leibeigen* status of peasants, and the rights of noble church patronage and judicial and policing functions in the *Gutsherrschaft* – the Elector was granted sufficient money for the maintenance of a small standing army in peacetime.[10] The Swedish–Polish War of 1655–60 saw the foundations for the *Generalkriegskommissariat*, later to become a central institution of Prussian military bureaucracy; and at the termination of the war in 1660, the Great Elector failed to dissolve the army, appealing in subsequent decades to what Rosenberg terms a somewhat fictional 'permanent state of war'.[11] The deputation Diet of 1667 led to further advances in the ruler's power: for, after confusions and negotiations, a reorganisation of taxation into two distinct systems was confirmed. An indirect excise tax was introduced for the towns; the direct 'contribution' tax was levied in the country. This served to separate the interests of towns and nobles,

---

[9] F.L. Carsten, 'The Great Elector and the Foundation of the Hohenzollern Despotism', *English Historical Review* 65 (1950): 175–202, pp. 176–7.
[10] Ibid.; see also Sidney Fay and Klaus Epstein, *The Rise of Brandenburg-Prussia to 1786* (New York: Holt, Rinehart and Winston, 1964).
[11] Rosenberg, *Bureaucracy*, p. 36.

leaving the towns without political allies. It also gave the Elector an excuse not to summon the towns to Diets, which he considered to be concerned with the assignment and repartition of the contribution tax, and the administration of the country's debts and loans; and since these functions could in any case be performed by the *Kreistage* of local nobles, there was no need for Diets at all.[12] The 1670s saw the destruction of the self-government of the towns, which were now subordinated to a body of officials appointed by, and responsible to, the Elector; this system gradually spread from Brandenburg to more outlying provinces. While the Estates were thus weakened, the founding of the *Offizierkorps* served to attract the nobility into central state service via the prestigious higher ranks of the army hierarchy.[13]

Elector Friedrich III, from 1701 King Friedrich I, while personally a weaker ruler than his predecessor, made important advances on the cultural and symbolic front in the development of absolutism. It was he who aspired to, and achieved, the title of King; it was he who founded the University of Halle and the Berlin Academy of Sciences, early centres of the German Enlightenment through the influence of Wolff and Leibniz respectively; it was he who supported the architect Schlüter and commissioned the royal palaces and state buildings symbolic of royal power at its height. The court of Friedrich I was as frivolous as any in Western Europe; the court nobility were able to glory in the cultural appurtenances of absolutist rule.[14]

The frivolity, at least, terminated abruptly with the accession of the so-called 'Soldier King', Friedrich Wilhelm I, in 1713. The symbolic aspects of absolutism gave way to the administrative and repressive features, which were refined and developed to an unparalleled degree. The centre-point of Friedrich Wilhelm's state was the army; the keynote was central organisation of power. After nearly a decade of active reorganisation and development, Friedrich Wilhelm set out the main themes of his rule in his 1722 'Instructions for his Successor'.[15] In this 'Sparta of the North', the king should beware of operas, comedies, ballets, masquerades, mistresses, drinking and feasting, and other scandalous pursuits of the devil.[16] The ruler should take personal control of

---

[12] Carsten, 'Great Elector'.

[13] F.L. Carsten, 'Die Ursachen des Niedergangs der deutschen Landstände', *Historische Zeitschrift* 192 (2) (1961): 273–81.

[14] See generally: H.W. Koch, *A History of Prussia* (London: Longman, 1978), chapter 4; Jürgen von Kruedener, *Die Rolle des Hofes im Absolutismus* (Stuttgart: Gustav Fischer Verlag, 1973); Hajo Holborn, *A History of Modern Germany*, vol. 2 (New York: Alfred Knopf, 1964); Walter Henry Nelson, *The Soldier Kings* (London: J.M. Dent and Sons Ltd, 1971).

[15] 'Instruktion König Friedrich Wilhelms I. für seinen Nachfolger', *Acta Borussica. Die Behördenorganisation und die allgemeine Staatsverwaltung Preussens im 18. Jahrhundert*, vol. 3 (Jan. 1718–Jan. 1723) (Berlin: Verlag von Paul Parey, 1901), pp. 441–70.

[16] Ibid., pp. 442–3. It should be noted that the puritanical nature of the Prussian court

government, keeping his officials on low basic salaries and rewarding them for good work, such that they are directly dependent on his goodwill and not on the patronage of others; and the ruler must ensure personal control over the army and state finances. Ministers will say the expense of the army is impossible; they will seek to make difficulties for the king at every turn and indulge in all manner of intrigues; but the ruler must stand firm and not allow his ministers to 'lead him by the nose'. Friedrich Wilhelm I continues his 'Instructions' by discussing the state of his various provinces and the characters of the different provincial nobilities: he makes it clear that to retain central control and make the best use of each set of aristocrats, firm and differentiated handling is required. It is useful to employ the higher nobility in the army, and to recruit their children into the cadets. The nobility of certain provinces – in particular Alt Mark and Magdeburg – are under no circumstances to become officials in their own localities; they must be sent elsewhere in local government service, to break their independence and political disobedience.[17] In practice, Friedrich Wilhelm had an eye for merit regardless of birth; while it may not have been a conscious policy, during the course of his reign a large number of commoners came to achieve high ranks in government service and to attain finally new noble status.[18]

More than with many other rulers' intentions, Friedrich Wilhelm's theories of rulership corresponded with his practice. It was during the first decade of his reign, before and immediately after writing these 'Instructions' of 1722, that Friedrich Wilhelm I made crucial advances in the organisation of the Prussian state. As Dorwart puts it:

Between 1713 and 1723 Brandenburg-Prussia experienced a reforming activity, of which the king was the moving spirit, which was almost unequalled in its achievement by any other decade in Prussian history. Only the decade 1651–1661 and the era of the Stein-Hardenberg reforms achieve an equal significance in institutional development... This was a decade of construction, of integration, of reducing the administrative machinery to order – and of establishing complete absolutism.[19]

Building on the administrative organisation initiated by the Great Elec-

made it distinctively different from other absolutisms, as pointed out by Kruedener, *Rolle des Hofes*; a difference which had important consequences for the Pietist response.

[17] 'Instruktion', pp. 452–3. Cf. also Otto Hintze, 'The Hohenzollern and the Nobility' in Felix Gilbert (ed.), *The Historical Essays of Otto Hintze* (New York: Oxford University Press, 1975).

[18] F.L. Carsten, 'Prussian Despotism at its Height', *History* 40 (1955): 42–67, takes issue with the interpretations of Dorn, Schmoller, Hintze, Dorwart and others as to whether or not this was a conscious policy on the part of the King.

[19] Dorwart, *Administrative Reforms*, p. 34. See also for the background, Gustav Schmoller, 'Einleitung. Über Behördenorganisation, Amtswesen und Beamtenthum im Allgemeinen und speciell in Deutschland und Preussen bis zum Jahre 1713' in G. Schmoller and D. Krauske (eds.), *Acta Borussica. Die Behördenorganisation und die allgemeine Staatsverwaltung Preussens im 18. Jahrhundert*, vol. 1 (June 1701–June 1714) (Berlin: Verlag von Paul Parey, 1894).

tor, Friedrich Wilhelm I institutionalised the central administration of war and taxes by consolidating the organisation of the *Generalkriegs-kommissariat* and creating the General Finance Directory; these two were combined in 1723 in an important body under the King's personal control, the 'General Superior Finance War and Domain Directory' (*General-Ober-Finanz-Kriegs-und-Domainen-Direktorium*). With this, Dorwart comments, 'financial, military, police and domain administration were completely emancipated from the privy council, and were focussed in a new supreme body subordinate only to the king, who himself presided over it'.[20] In practice, officials serving on the body simply ratified the King's decisions. From 1723 until his death in 1740, Friedrich Wilhelm I employed the General Directory as his central administrative organ of absolutist rule. At the same time, he concentrated on building up his army; by the end of his reign, as much as eighty per cent of state revenues was devoted to support of the army.[21]

Friedrich II – 'Frederick the Great' – was able to build on this legacy. Contemporaries might have laughed at the 'Soldier King's' troop of giant soldiers, and his obsession with things military; it was realistic fear that was inspired by the uses made by Friedrich II of the streamlined military police state which he inherited. In the course of his reign, Prussia achieved international recognition as a major European power with a mighty and well-trained army; by the end of the century, Minister von Schrötter aptly remarked that Prussia was 'not a country with an army, but an army with a country...'.[22] The administrative rationalisation of the state bureaucracy was continued, with, at the head of it all, the unremitting energies of the King himself, directing from his cabinet in Potsdam or riding around his domains to oversee in person the execution of his orders.[23] To the General Directory Friedrich II added a series of specialised ministries; while during his reign these remained under his personal control, they paved the way for the domination of bureaucracy in the later Prussian state. There were seventeen Provincial Chambers overseeing financial, commercial and economic activities; a series of subaltern officials and civil servants – employed in areas other than their native provinces; and royal spies to report on the conduct of members of the chambers and local commissaries. Nevertheless, local nobles retained certain degrees of freedom in their local powers: apart from their juridi-

---

[20] Dorwart, *Administrative Reforms*, p. 178.
[21] Von Kruedener, *Rolle des Hofes*, p. 17. See more generally Gordon Craig, *The Politics of the Prussian Army 1640–1945* (Oxford: Clarendon Press, 1964), chapter 1.
[22] Quoted in Rosenberg, *Bureaucracy*, p. 40.
[23] See particularly Walter L. Dorn, 'The Prussian Bureaucracy in the Eighteenth Century', *Political Science Quarterly*, 46 (3) (1931): 403–23 (Part One); 47 (1) (1932): 75–94 (Part Two); 47 (2) (1932): 259–73 (Part Three); and more generally, M.S. Anderson, *Europe in the Eighteenth Century* (London: Longman, 2nd edn, 1976); Ludwig Reiners, *Frederick the Great* (London: Oswald Wolff Ltd, English transl., 1960).

cal and repressive powers on their estates, supported by the ruler in the interests of social control and maintenance of the social hierarchy, Junkers were able to thwart the King's wishes over measures of agrarian reform which would have run counter to their immediate economic interests.[24]

The political and administrative transformations sketched above were intimately related to transformations of social life in eighteenth-century Brandenburg-Prussia. Otto Büsch opens his book on *Militärsystem und Sozialleben im alten Preussen 1713–1807* with this uncompromising assertion:

Das soziale System des preussischen Staates in der Epoche seiner Geschichte von den Reformen des 'Soldatenkönigs', Friedrich Wilhelm I., seit 1713 bis zur Zeit der Erneuerung durch den Freiherrn von Stein und den Staatskanzler Hardenberg nach 1807 ist... in hohem Masse ein Ergebnis der altpreussischen Heeresverfassung des 18. Jahrhunderts gewesen. Die preussische Armee war Anlass, Mittel und Basis zugleich für die Errichtung, Ausbildung und Aufrechterhaltung dieses sozialen Systems.[25]

While this might perhaps be overstating the case – and making excessive claims of causality – there can be no doubt that important social changes were associated with the development of Prussian absolutism. The most immediately evident of these was the changing nature of the nobility and its relationship to the state; but at the same time there were changes in agrarian class relations. The feudal nobility was attracted into central state service through two interrelated channels: the army and the bureaucracy. A major task of the latter was the administration of activities maintaining the army: revenue extraction and local organisation of billeting of troops, raising of recruits, ensuring food and fodder. The officer corps of the army gave the service nobility a new status ethic; the local officials of the bureaucracy aided the transformation of local power structures. Through the office of *Steuerrat*, centrally appointed and responsible to the Crown, the last vestiges of urban local government autonomy were abolished; and through the office of *Landrat*, filled by a local aristocrat serving as mediary between Crown and locality, responsible to both, links were strengthened between monarch and nobility.

[24] See Dorn, 'Prussian Bureaucracy', Part Three; Hintze, 'Hohenzollern and Nobility'; Rosenberg, *Bureaucracy*, pp. 42–3, on the dualistic nature of the Prussian state; and A. Goodwin, 'Prussia' in A. Goodwin (ed.), *The European Nobility in the Eighteenth Century* (London: Adam and Charles Black, 1953).

[25] 'The social system of the Prussian state in the historical era from the reforms of the "soldier king" Friedrich Wilhelm I, from 1713 till the time of renewal by Baron von Stein and Chancellor Hardenberg after 1807 is... to a great extent a product of the old Prussian military constitution of the eighteenth century. The Prussian army was at once the occasion, means, and basis for the establishment, development and maintenance of this social system.' Otto Büsch, *Militärsystem und Sozialleben im alten Preussen 1713–1807: Die Anfänge der Militarisierung der preussisch-deutschen Gesellschaft* (Berlin: Walter de Gruyter and Co., 1962), p. 1.

Agrarian sociopolitical structures were reorganised in the interests of
military efficiency: by 1733, Friedrich Wilhelm I had introduced 'can-
tons' for the organisation and enrolment of peasants for military training
and service, compromising between the needs of agriculture and the
needs of the army; in the mid- and later eighteenth century, the politics of
peasant protection and emancipation and the nature of civil justice and
administration were intimately affected by military considerations.[26] At
the same time as new policies to protect the peasantry were developed,
the recently transformed nobilities were strengthened in certain aspects
of their local powers in their estates, in order to sustain the relations of
deference and obedience which were to be repeated in the context of
different roles in the army. Thus while losing their wider political rights
in provincial government, nobles were sustained in their local patrimonial domination. Apart from in the western provinces, which continued to develop along different lines, an extremely high percentage of
nobles were active or retired officers: as many as sixty per cent or more,
depending on the province; and retired officers frequently continued in
state service in such offices as that of *Landrat*, having responsibility for
local military administration.[27]

These transformations did not take place without strains or resistance,
both between Crown and nobility and within the ranks of the agrarian
classes. The relationships between non-army aristocrats and the officer
corps could be distinctly ambivalent: landed nobles had many complaints
about certain aspects of military activities, such as recruiting methods,
pressures put on peasants, misuse of recruits for personal services on the
recruiting officer's estates – and some landowners concerned for the
productivity of their own estates went so far as to help their peasants to
evade conscription. Büsch comments that in the estates' *Gravamina* is
revealed 'der offenkundige Gegensatz zwischen dem Adel als Stand und
dem aus Adeligen gebildeten Offizierkorps als Berufsstand'.[28] There were
continuing tensions between Crown and nobility: the resistance by the
nobility to monarchical attempts at protection of the position of the
peasantry throughout the mid- and later eighteenth century is illustrative
of this, as are the perpetual problems with the East Prussian nobility. The
absolutism that developed in the eighteenth century reflected these tensions; nevertheless, it was a remarkable achievement.

It would be foolish, in the context of a brief sketch such as this, to
attempt to suggest causes of the success of absolutism in Prussia. But, for
the purposes of the limited comparisons with England and Württemberg,

[26] Ibid.; see also Lütge, *Agrarverfassung*, pp. 225ff., on the prehistory of the Stein-
Hardenberg reforms, which essentially codified developments of preceding decades.
[27] Büsch, *Militärsystem*, pp. 94–5; see also Dorwart, *Administrative Reforms*, ch. 6.
[28] 'The open opposition between the aristocracy as a class, and the aristocratic officer corps
as a professional group.' Büsch, *Militärsystem*, p. 90.

certain selected features may be reiterated. The rulers in Prussia had to deal with a large and disunited set of territories in which there were a variety of provincial Estates, and in which towns and country were divided. Once the separate tax systems had been introduced, with central control of revenue extraction, and once a standing army had been achieved, the foundations had been laid for independent policy determination by the ruler. It remained to strengthen the administrative, bureaucratic apparatus of the centralised state; to develop the army for internal and external purposes of defence and aggrandisement; and to reorientate class interests and loyalties. Rulers were aided in that they faced weak towns and nobilities which were prepared by and large to make compromises in which provincial autonomy was traded for more immediate political or economic advantages. The condition of the oppressed peasantry on the large *Gutsherrschaft* estates was such as to render potential peasant independence or political influence through resistance essentially nugatory. In this situation, the main political protagonists remained the King and the nobility; and in the compromise absolutism which developed, both could be said, with qualifications, to be the victors.

England: absolutism truncated

There are a few bare bones of English seventeenth-century history, as far as it is concerned with the explanation of the English Civil Wars, on which historians are agreed. Between 1629 and 1640 Charles I attempted to rule without Parliament; incapacity to deal with troubles in Scotland necessitated the calling of the Short and Long Parliaments in 1640; in 1642 Civil War broke out. In the following years of turmoil, tremendous political and ideological developments took place, eventuating in the execution of the King and the abolition of monarchy in 1649. Beyond these few facts – in themselves little more than dates – there is scant agreement on how best to interpret and explain the so-called English Revolution, a concept which is indeed itself contested.[29] The corollary of

---

[29] The literature is too extensive to be covered in a footnote. See generally R.C. Richardson, *The Debate on the English Revolution* (London: Methuen, 1977); and for some widely varying general interpretations: G.E. Aylmer, *A Short History of Seventeenth-Century England* (New York: Mentor Books, 1963; published in England under the title *The Struggle for the Constitution*); Robert Ashton, *The English Civil War* (London: Weidenfeld and Nicolson, 1978); J.P. Cooper 'The Fall of the Stuart Monarchy' in J.P. Cooper (ed.), *The New Cambridge Modern History*, vol. 4 (Cambridge: Cambridge University Press, 1970); Barry Coward, *The Stuart Age* (London: Longman, 1980); Christopher Hill, *The Century of Revolution 1603–1714* (New York: W.W. Norton, 1966 edn); Ivan Roots, *The Great Rebellion 1642–1660* (London: Batsford, 1966); Conrad Russell, *The Crisis of Parliaments 1509–1660* (London: Oxford University Press, 1971); Lawrence Stone, *The Causes of the English Revolution 1529–1642* (London: Routledge and Kegan Paul, 1972); Perez Zagorin, *The Court and the Country* (London: Routledge and Kegan Paul, 1969).

disagreement over the nature and causes of the Civil War or Revolution is disagreement over the most appropriate mode of characterising the developments of the previous century of English history. Older interpretations of the English Revolution (a label I shall continue to use) had traced deep-seated and long-standing conflicts in pre-revolutionary English society, culture and politics: conflicts between Parliament and Crown, between rising social classes and bastions of privilege, between new ideologies and old. Recent approaches have emphasised rather the stability and conservatism of pre-revolutionary England, the short-term and contingent nature of the events which led, between 1640 and 1642, from a united nation to one torn into opposing camps involved in fratricidal strife. In this section no comprehensive coverage of these controversies can be attempted; nor can a definitive statement be developed on the nature and causes of the English Revolution. Rather, within the context of the historiographical debates, a few of the salient features of pre-revolutionary English social and political structure will be outlined which help to explain why, in comparison with Prussia, England was an inherently unpromising location for the establishment of absolutist rule. This outline presupposes that it was the would-be absolutist monarch who was essentially the most innovative participant politically; and that the English Revolution, which originated in the resistance of much of the nation against absolutist innovations, can be adequately explained only with reference to long-term features of the English sociopolitical landscape, in addition to the short-term conjunctural factors precipitating the crisis of the 1640s.

It will be well to begin, very briefly, with a sketch of the state of debate. Recent historical research has been oriented towards testing and revising hypotheses derived from what have been termed the 'traditional' 'Whig', 'Marxist' and 'sociological' approaches. These 'traditional' approaches, it has been argued, share a focus on the long-run causes of the Civil War, and trace the progressive conflicts between classes, parties, or institutions.[30] The thrust of revisionist research has been to show that, first, there was no *intentional* revolution, pre-planned and consciously made by any coherent and organised party, class, or institution (such as an 'opposition', a 'rising bourgeoisie' or the gentry or some element thereof, or the House of Commons); and, secondly, that there are serious problems associated with any attempt to delineate simply the lines of conflict in the Civil Wars when they did in fact occur. The polarisations of 'traditional' interpretations have been dissolved; thus for example the meticulous researches of Conrad Russell on the Parliaments of the 1620s

---

[30] Conrad Russell, 'Introduction' to Russell (ed.), *The Origins of the English Civil War* (London: Macmillan, 1973); see also G.R. Elton, 'A High Road to Civil War?' in Charles Carter (ed.), *From the Renaissance to the Counter-Reformation: Essays in Honour of Garrett Mattingley* (London: Jonathan Cape, 1966).

in particular have shown that, far from being a strong and 'rising' institution seeking to appropriate more power to itself, and using its powers of the purse to withhold supply until it obtained redress of grievances, the House of Commons in the early seventeenth century was in fact merely a weak mediating body, representing the Crown to the provinces and the provinces to the Crown.[31] Furthermore, within the Parliaments of the 1620s no clear and consistent parties of 'government' and 'opposition', with alternative sets of principles and policies, can be discerned. The conflicts of the 1620s must be explained, in terms either of political mismanagement, or of conflict between rival factions adhering to different circles of patronage.[32] The 'Whig' interpretation of the rise of the House of Commons and its conflicts with the monarch is thus assumed to be demolished. Other revisionist studies have been oriented towards explanations in terms of social change, implicitly or explicitly arguing with older hypotheses concerning a putative 'rise of the gentry', 'crisis of the aristocracy', and so on.[33] Some studies have been devoted to resurrection of the peerage as powerful political actors; others have analysed the changing economic fortunes and political activities of the gentry in the localities.[34] Local studies in particular have shown the difficulties involved in any simple attempts at correlating obvious economic interests with opposing political sides in the Civil Wars and, in highlighting the importance of neutralism, have emphasised how little the mass of the English political nation wanted any sort of civil war.[35] Much useful empirical research has recently been carried out, stimulated

---

[31] Conrad Russell, 'Parliamentary History in Perspective, 1604–1629', *History* 61 (201) (1976): 1–27; Russell, *Parliaments and English Politics 1621–1629* (Oxford: Clarendon Press, 1979).

[32] Cf. Kevin Sharpe (ed.), *Faction and Parliament* (Oxford: Clarendon Press, 1978).

[33] For the older social interpretations, see Richardson, *Debate*; Stone, *Causes*, and Stone (ed.), *Social Change and Revolution in England, 1540–1640* (London: Longman, 1965), and *The Crisis of the Aristocracy, 1558–1641* (London: Oxford University Press, 1967 edn); J.H. Hexter, 'Storm over the Gentry' and 'The Myth of the Middle Class in Tudor England' in Hexter, *Reappraisals in History* (London: Longman, 1961); Christopher Hill, 'Recent Interpretations of the Civil War' in Hill, *Puritanism and Revolution* (London: Secker and Warburg, 1958).

[34] On the peerage, see: Sharpe (ed.), *Faction and Parliament*; Paul Christianson, 'The Causes of the English Revolution: A Reappraisal', *Journal of British Studies* 15 (2) (1976): 40–75; Christianson, 'The Peers, the People and Parliamentary Management in the First Six Months of the Long Parliament', *Journal of Modern History* 49 (1977): 575–99; Mark Kishlansky, 'The Emergence of Adversary Politics in the Long Parliament', *Journal of Modern History* 49 (1977): 614–40; but see also Derek Hirst, 'Unanimity in the Commons', *Journal of Modern History* 50 (1) (1978): 51–71.

[35] See, for example: B.G. Blackwood, *The Lancashire Gentry and the Great Rebellion 1640–1660* (Manchester: for the Chetham Society, 1978); J.T. Cliffe, *The Yorkshire Gentry from the Reformation to the Civil War* (London: Athlone Press, 1969); J.S. Morrill, *Cheshire 1630–1660: County Government and Society during the English Revolution* (London: Oxford University Press, 1974); Morrill, *The Revolt of the Provinces* (London: Longman, 1980 edn); Morrill, 'The Northern Gentry and the Great Rebellion', *Northern History* 15 (1979): 66–87; Anthony Fletcher, *A County Community in Peace and War: Sussex 1600–1660* (London: Longman, 1975); and more gener-

by the desire to revise 'traditional' approaches. But as yet this work has provided little by way of a coherent alternative explanatory framework. The wider aims and concerns of older historians remain essentially unassailed: the extension and revision of detail provided by recent research awaits assimilation.[36] In the context of this contested area of interpretation, what can be said about the sociopolitical structure and development of England in the century prior to the Revolution?

First, in comparison with Prussia, England enjoyed certain crucial geopolitical advantages in its development as a united nation state. There was of course the Scottish relation, posing a recurrent problem; but the island location of England helped to delimit national boundaries, protecting England from the ravages of land warfare that repeatedly dissolved and reshaped the states of continental Europe. Furthermore, England was unique in mediaeval Europe for having a relatively high degree of centralisation of rule at an early date. Thus late Tudor and early Stuart monarchs did not face to such an extent the crucial problems presented to the rulers of the Hohenzollern domains: the unification of disparate territories into one nation and the centralisation of rule. Nevertheless, associated with these advantages – viewed from the perspective of the monarch – were certain features of English governmental structure which were at least ambivalent in their consequences for rulers seeking greater independence of action.

Early modern English social structure and local government organisation presented at once strengths and weaknesses for the English Crown. In the late sixteenth and early seventeenth centuries, the English aristocracy was very different in strength and orientation from the aristocracy of late seventeenth-century Prussia. No longer the independent military

ally, Alan Everitt, *Change in the Provinces: the Seventeenth Century* (Leicester: Leicester University Press, 1969).

[36] Revisionist historians tend implicitly to suggest that by demolishing certain specific hypotheses (frequently rather in the nature of straw men) they have disposed of the wider theoretical concerns of the traditions from which the particular hypotheses derived: a mistaken assumption. And in overreacting against a variety of 'progressive' teleological approaches, they tend to celebrate excessively the more 'conservative' aspects of the past. The denial of conflicts of interest and of principle is also overdone: the fact that clearly organised revolutionary groups cannot, anachronistically, be found in the seventeenth century does not necessarily entail a form of politics based exclusively on issue-less factional struggles for power. Despite the efforts of recent revisionist historians, ideological and social conflicts were prevalent in seventeenth-century England and cannot be ignored in analyses of the causes of the Revolution, however inadequate particular older interpretations might be. For some comments on the revisionist historians, see: J.H. Hexter, 'Power Struggle, Parliament, and Liberty in Early Stuart England', *Journal of Modern History* 50 (1) (1978): 1–50; Hirst, 'Unanimity'; Christopher Hill, 'Parliament and People in Early Seventeenth-Century England', *Past and Present* 92 (1981): 100–24; the articles by T.K. Rabb, 'The Role of the Commons', and Derek Hirst, 'The Place of Principle', *Past and Present* 92 (1981): 55–78, 79–99; and Mary Fulbrook, 'The English Revolution and the Revisionist Revolt', *Social History*, 7 (3) (1982): 249–64.

magnates of mediaeval times, the English nobility was already a domesticated, court-oriented class, building fine, unfortified country houses
expressing wealth and status rather than military might.[37] A series of
economic and social changes in the sixteenth century, while perhaps
weakening certain individuals within that subsection of the aristocracy,
the peerage (as well as individuals in other sections of society), were in
general combining to make of the aristocracy as a whole a vital, commer-
cialised class interested in trade and production rather than predation
and warfare.[38] A consequence of this was that the Crown could reason-
ably hope to govern with the aid of court-oriented aristocrats, rather
than having to suppress their political pretensions in the localities and
build up a separate state bureaucracy, as was necessary in the provinces
of Brandenburg-Prussia.[39] Thus while England as a whole was a unified
nation state, the government of the localities could be remarkably
decentralised. The upper echelons of county society were responsible for
maintaining the peace, caring for the poor, organising taxation, super-
vising the upkeep of roads, and a multitude of other such activities,
organised through special and general commissions, the most important
of which was the Commission of the Peace. A large number of English
gentry were at one time or another involved with the latter, being
prepared to serve as unpaid Justices of the Peace, having administrative
as well as judicial functions. The lower social strata – those immediately
below the gentry – served in more minor offices of local government, as
parish constables, churchwardens, and the like.[40] The officials who were
directly officers of the Crown, the Lieutenants and their deputies, whose
importance increased in the late sixteenth and seventeenth centuries,
were frequently chosen from the greatest men of the county; but this was
not always the case, and when an outsider filled the office, tensions could
be observed between central policies and local considerations. These
were in any case likely to arise, for the duties of the Lieutenants were to
supervise the militia and organise the military preparedness of counties –
not a popular task. In general, the contrast with Prussia in the arena of
local government is marked; and particularly so in the question of the
assessment and raising of taxes, for which the local English gentry were

---

[37] Cf. W.G. Hoskins, *The Making of the English Landscape* (Harmondsworth: Pelican,
1970); Mark Girouard, *Life in the English Country House* (New Haven: Yale University
Press, 1978); W.T. Maccaffrey, 'England: The Crown and the New Aristocracy,
1540–1600', *Past and Present* 30 (1965): 52–64.

[38] Cf. Stone, *Crisis*; D.C. Coleman, *The Economy of England 1450–1750* (London:
Oxford University Press, 1977).

[39] Cf. D.M. Loades, *Politics and the Nation 1450–1660* (Glasgow: Fontana, 1979); R.
Bendix, 'Introduction' to Bendix (ed.), *State and Society* (Berkeley: University of California Press, 1968).

[40] Cf. G.R. Elton, *The Tudor Constitution* (Cambridge: Cambridge University Press,
1960), ch. 10; Carl Bridenbaugh, *Vexed and Troubled Englishmen 1590–1642* (Oxford:
Clarendon Press, 1968).

themselves responsible. English monarchs failed to develop the separate state officials so efficiently employed in Brandenburg-Prussia. Nor, given the lack of a standing army in England, did they have any very effective means of backing up and enforcing policies with which the leaders of local society did not feel inclined to comply.

Representative institutions in England also differed from those in Prussia. Unlike the various Estates in Prussia, the Houses of Parliament in England were relatively homogeneous in social composition and outlook.[41] Towns and country were not represented and treated separately, as in Prussia, but rather sat together in the House of Commons; and while the bishops in the Lords tended to act as government spokesmen, the temporal Lords were more closely related to the Commons than might initially be assumed, those in the Commons being related by ties of kinship and common interest to the Peers. Interestingly, however, the House of Commons was in the century prior to the Civil War becoming more representative of the nation as a whole: as the research of Derek Hirst has shown, the electorate of England was expanding for a variety of reasons, and the number of contested elections was increasing, such that Members of Parliament came increasingly to represent and take heed of the wishes of larger numbers of people.[42] If the monarch were prepared to rule in and through Parliament, this could be a source of strength; but, coupled with the fact that it was those who were represented in the House of Commons who were directly responsible for raising revenues, it made it exceedingly difficult for a ruler to achieve financial independence by raising supply which had not received parliamentary consent.

Financial and administrative problems were central in the period leading up to the breakdown of government in the 1640s. The financial position of the English monarchy worsened during the early decades of the seventeenth century, partly because of the effects of inflation, partly because of a reduced revenue base after the great resale of church lands indulged in by Elizabeth, and partly, although probably less importantly than has sometimes been suggested, because the early Stuarts were less parsimonious than their Tudor predecessor. Whatever the reasons, early Stuart income was increasingly inadequate for ordinary peace-time expenditure, let alone for the ever-increasing costs of the extraordinary expenditure of war. Between 1610 and 1629, parliamentary discussion of the status of taxation to support the ordinary expenditure of the King – whose estates should be sufficient to allow him to 'live of his own' – unintentionally raised fundamental issues concerning sovereignty.[43]

[41] Elton, *Tudor Constitution*, ch. 8; Russell, *Crisis of Parliaments*, p. 41.
[42] Derek Hirst, *The Representative of the People?* (Cambridge: Cambridge University Press, 1975).
[43] See G.L. Harriss, 'Mediaeval Doctrines in the Debates on Supply' in Sharpe (ed.), *Faction and Parliament*; Russell, 'Parliament and the King's Finances' in Russell (ed.), *Origins*.

These issues reappeared in another form in the later years of collection of Ship Money, despite the more mundane causes of initial resistance to it.[44] Associated with the lack of financial independence of the Crown were the administrative problems inherent in attempts to pursue unpopular policies.

One way of attempting to overcome the resistance of Parliaments and local governors was prerogative rule.[45] This is where the tendency towards the development of absolutism in England can most easily be located; and where the powers of the local governors become most apparent. The question of a court/country polarity has been hotly debated; but behind the historiographical controversies, a genuine problem can be seen to have been developing.[46] 'Court' and 'country' may have been interpenetrating entities, a man's standing at court depending on his standing in the country, and vice versa; and cultural and psychological conflicts between 'court' and 'country' might have been matters internal to the minds and loyalties of particular individuals rather than factors separating clearly delineated groups. Nevertheless, in another sense – the sense concerning the centralisation of rule, with which this chapter is particularly concerned – there was a salient tension in late Tudor and early Stuart England. The tensions aroused by central interference in local government are increasingly being revealed in local studies.

Already in Elizabethan Norfolk, as the research of Hassell Smith has shown, there were conflicts between local governors and Crown officials, patentees and licensees.[47] As Hassell Smith aptly remarks, 'masterly inactivity... was one of the characteristics of Elizabethan local government': at the lower levels, churchwardens, constables, and jurors were unwilling to offend peers and neighbours; and at the higher levels, Justices of the Peace would take seriously and implement only those conciliar directions and demands which accorded with locally felt needs or interests.[48] In the latter half of the sixteenth century, Norfolk gentry,

---

44 Cf. Morrill, *Revolt of Provinces*, p. 28.
45 A not entirely successful analysis along these lines has been started by R.W.K. Hinton, 'The Decline of Parliamentary Government under Elizabeth I and the Early Stuarts', *Cambridge Historical Journal* 13 (2) (1957): 116–32.
46 On 'court' and 'country', see Zagorin, *Court and Country*; Ashton, *Civil War*; P.W. Thomas, 'Two Cultures? Court and Country under Charles I' in Russell (ed.), *Origins*; Derek Hirst, 'Court, Country and politics before 1629' in Sharpe (ed.), *Faction and Parliament*. A related debate exists over the notion of a 'county community'; cf. Clive Holmes' review of Fletcher, *County Community*, in *American Historical Review* 82 (3) (1977): 632–3. My analysis of relations between local and central government is not directly parallel to either debate, dealing as it does with only one very limited aspect of the court/country question, and not presupposing the reality of a united and insular 'county community'.
47 A. Hassell Smith, *County and Court: Government and Politics in Norfolk, 1558–1603* (Oxford: Clarendon Press, 1974).
48 Ibid., ch. 6; the quotation is from p. 125.

Justices, and merchants were united in their opposition to Council restriction of exports and to the Crown's administrative, dispensing and monopoly patents. They were also unwilling to foot the bill for the militia. Opposition to patentees and licensees became overlaid, after the appointment of a permanent Lord Lieutenant in 1585 – a non-local agent of the Crown – with a more general opposition to prerogative instruments of government. Justices and common lawyers attacked patentees and central interference in local affairs, particularly at Quarter Sessions and in Parliament.[49]

In a number of ways, Elizabethan Norfolk may have been precocious, and even unique: Norfolk Members of Parliament appear to have been politically principled, in comparison with the early seventeenth-century Somerset M.P.s whose personal rivalries are depicted by Barnes; after the demise of Howard, there was no great resident nobleman; Lord Hunsdon, appointed Lord Lieutenant, was not a local man; there was a considerable amount of ad hoc taxation, and the militia was a great burden; and Norfolk had a tradition of political and religious dissent. Nevertheless, similar problems were to be found in other counties, developing at different times and in different ways, but indicative of similar conflicts and tensions. Clark's study of Kent, for example, has shown the alienation of the ordinary county gentry from the agents of the Crown under the impact of the crises of the 1590s, reappearing as a polarisation in the late 1620s and 1630s.[50] Barnes, whose study of Somerset under the personal rule of Charles I was seminal in dissolving simplistic Court/ Country oppositions and highlighting the mediating role of M.P.s, points up the problems arising from central interference in local government.[51] Barnes shows how the increasing conciliar direction of the local government of Somerset in the 1630s strained it almost beyond capacity. He comments that 'the fact was that by 1630 the justices were already working at very near their maximal capacity, unless they were to become full-time servants of the state'; yet with the publication of the Book of Orders in 1631 local government was required to stretch its efficiency further. In contrast to certain other counties, such as Sussex and Kent, Somerset actually succeeded in raising and sustaining the efficiency for execution of the Book of Orders.[52] It was Ship Money that finally focussed Somerset's opposition to central rule. The first writ, of 1634,

---

[49] Ibid., ch. 12.

[50] Peter Clark, *English Provincial Society from the Reformation to the Revolution: Religion, Politics and Society in Kent, 1500–1640* (Sussex: Harvester Press, 1977), chs. 8 and 12.

[51] T.G. Barnes, *Somerset 1625–1640: A County's Government during the 'Personal Rule'* (London: Oxford University Press, 1961).

[52] Ibid.; Fletcher, *County Community*; Clark, *English Provincial Society*; and more generally, L.M. Hill, 'County Government in Caroline England 1625–1640' in Russell (ed.), *Origins.*

moderate and apparently temporary, was accepted; rating disputes arose in 1635, and rising antagonism led to refusals to pay in 1637; Hampden's case in 1638 occasioned the defection of constables, and in 1639 the sheriff found himself isolated in attempting to collect Ship Money; in 1640 collection was simply impossible. In Sussex, where local governors were aware of the importance of the fleet to protect the coast, resistance was slower to emerge: haggling and refusing began in 1639.[53] With local variations, the same patterns can be traced all over England. As local government was increasingly overstrained by the effects of prerogative rule, breakdowns in local government elicited the resistance of local governors to the policies of the centre. As Morrill comments, the gentry 'were less concerned with the theoretical implications of Charles's use of his prerogative than with the unacceptable consequences of his actions'.[54]

The administrative and financial problems were reproduced and reflected in the military problems of the English state. England was justly proud of its naval capacity; but English monarchs, free from the perpetual ravages of land warfare of their continental counterparts, dispensed with the maintenance of a standing army. Instead, they relied on the local mustering of the militia. This had been dormant during the peaceful years of James' reign, but a concerted attempt was made under Charles to revive and develop a 'perfect and exact militia'. This attempt was hardly popular with local governors. As Fletcher sums up the situation:

The exact militia was an impracticable programme for a government which lacked agents other than independently minded gentry to enforce its will. Every aspect of the programme broke down, sooner or later, because men were not prepared to bear the charges that arose.[55]

The military weakness of the English state was a major contributory factor in the early and mid-seventeenth-century political crises. Conrad Russell attributes the problems of the Parliaments of the late 1620s, not to the change of ruler and the personality of Charles I as compared with his father, but rather to the problems aroused by the attempts to wage war.[56] And the crisis of 1640–2 was directly precipitated by the Crown's attempts to pursue an unpopular military policy, seeking to raise the resources and troops to wage a war against the Scots with which a large number of Englishmen had no sympathy whatsoever. Finding he was unable to proceed without the support of Parliament, Charles I twice called the latter in 1640; but support was the last thing Parliament was prepared to give at this time. In 1640, a relatively united country was ready to give expression to its mounting opposition to any attempt at absolutist rule in England. Monarchs of England would not be able to

[53] Fletcher, *County Community.*
[54] Morrill, *Revolt of Provinces*, p. 28.
[55] Fletcher, *County Community*, p. 200.
[56] Russell, *Parliaments and English Politics*, 'Conclusion'.

pursue their policies independently, without the consent of the representatives of the people.

Little has been said as yet on the vexed problem of social change and its relationship with political developments in England. Following the impetus given by the theses of Tawney, Stone, Trevor-Roper and others, much attention has been paid in recent research to the fortunes of the upper ranks of landowning society, the gentry. From local studies it appears clear that simple attempts to correlate economic fortunes with civil war allegiances produce little by way of positive illumination.[57] The allegiances of the gentry were determined by a wide variety of local and personal factors, of which the most important may have been pragmatic policies for self-preservation or the higher principles of religious commitment, considered further in later chapters.[58] However, to conclude from this narrow focus on the gentry that socioeconomic factors can be excluded from accounts of the English Revolution would be mistaken.

In the first place, the century prior to the Revolution was one of major socioeconomic changes which posed considerable problems for English government. Rapid demographic expansion took place, for reasons which are still unclear. In Coleman's summary of the question, he states:

> Over the three centuries 1450 to 1750, total numbers [of the population of England and Wales] roughly trebled, but most of that rise was probably compressed into the period between the mid-sixteenth and the mid-seventeenth centuries.[59]

London in particular saw a vast rise in population – much of it from immigration, as people left the land in search for work – increasing from a population of about 33,000 at the beginning of the sixteenth century to 400,000 by the mid-seventeenth century.[60] At the same time, there took place the notorious 'price revolution' of the 'long' sixteenth century; the most important aspect of this was perhaps the rise in the prices of foodstuffs, particularly cereals. Historians are still debating the causes and consequences of these changes, and their differential effects on different elements of the population, but a few facts seem to be accepted. While within the aristocracy different individuals and families were variously rising and falling, benefiting and losing, thus changing the specific composition but not the general standing of the group, more fundamental changes were taking place in the lower ranks of rural society.[61] The numbers and proportion of landless agricultural labourers,

---

[57] See the references given in note 35 above.

[58] Cf. the comments of Cliffe, *Yorkshire Gentry*, p. 360. Previous political alignments on local issues also seem to have been important; see for an example from urban politics Roger Howell, *Newcastle-upon-Tyne and the Puritan Revolution* (Oxford: Clarendon Press, 1967). And see below, Chapters 5 and 6.

[59] Coleman, *Economy of England*, p. 13.

[60] Ibid., p. 20.

[61] The importance of this is recognised by Russell (Russell (ed.), *Origins*, pp. 8–9), without

small peasants, beggars and 'masterless men' were rising, as the lesser yeomanry, minor husbandmen and smaller copyholders lost out in the processes of economic change; at the same time the upper ranks of the yeomanry were able to make gains in wealth and status, many becoming indistinguishable from the lesser gentry in all but armigerous status. The 'great rebuilding' of Elizabethan England still stands as testimony to the greater prosperity of many ordinary farmers in the late sixteenth century. And with increasing economic differentiation in the lower echelons of rural society came increasing political and cultural differentiation within the English peasantry: local studies such as that of Wrightson and Levine in Terling have documented the progressive dissociation of higher and lower levels of society, and the increasing concern of local elites with problems of political, moral and social control.[62] These developments had important consequences, both for the representation of local issues in Parliament and the strength and nature of local government in pre-revolutionary times, and for the actual course of developments in the 1640s, to which we shall return below.

Much debate has centred on the problem of the early stages of capitalist development and its relationship to the English Revolution.[63] In a purely formal sense, the increasing numbers of propertyless in early modern England constituted the origins of a proletarian class; at the same time, trade and industry in England were quickening. The economic decline experienced by Brandenburg-Prussia was not a feature of English society at the time when monarchs attempted absolutism. Historians have suggested that English monarchs had no very consistent economic policies one way or the other, concerning early capitalist development, except insofar as it was government policy to pursue anything that might be a source of profit to the Crown so long as it was not outweighed by considerations of preventing social unrest and maintaining the peace.[64] Nevertheless, the very inconsistencies and unpredictability of late Tudor and early Stuart economic policies could be a problem for merchants and manufacturers; and patents and monopolies were a continuing source of

any further positive suggestions. Recently Christopher Hill, in his 1980 Neale Lecture, has attempted to give an outline of an explanatory framework incorporating considerations on changes in the lower ranks of society. See Hill, 'Parliament and People'.

[62] Keith Wrightson and David Levine, *Poverty and Piety in an English Village: Terling 1525–1700* (New York: Academic Press, 1979); see also David Hey, *An English Rural Community: Myddle under the Tudors and Stuarts* (Leicester: Leicester University Press, 1974); Margaret Spufford, *Contrasting Communities: English Villagers in the Sixteenth and Seventeenth Centuries* (Cambridge: Cambridge University Press, 1974).

[63] For early Marxist statements on the theme, see: Christopher Hill, *The English Revolution 1640* (London: Lawrence and Wishart, 1940); Maurice Dobb, *Studies in the Development of Capitalism* (New York: International Publishers, 1947); Brian Manning, 'Nobles, People and Constitution'; see generally the discussions in the works referred to in note 29, above.

[64] Cf. Penelope Corfield, 'Economic Issues and Ideologies' and Michael Hawkins, 'The Government: Its Role and Its Aims' in Russell (ed.), *Origins*.

friction, except for those to whose benefit they operated. Perhaps more important than possible lines of conflict and opposition, however, was the simple fact of the very wealth and independence of significant sectors of English society at this time, and the interpenetration of landed and urban society. These factors contributed to the relative incapacity of the Crown to impose its will on unconvinced subjects.

None of the facets of early modern England touched upon above can be said to have 'caused' the English Revolution. But taken together they help to explain why, with the calling of Parliament in 1640, there was such strength of opposition to Stuart personal rule. (The nature of this opposition will be considered in more detail in later chapters, as it relates to the question of religion.) They also illuminate the course of events leading to the outbreak of civil war in 1642; for it seems likely that the intervention of popular forces at this time provoked, on the one hand, a conservative reaction of sections of the governing classes who by 1642 were prepared to rally to the King against the threat from below, and, on the other hand, a radicalisation of the Parliamentarian position in response to popular demands and with the aim of retaining and controlling popular support.[65] Furthermore, the split within the classes below the gentry helps to explain why the English Revolution remained a purely political, and not a social, revolution; for the lack of peasant solidarity in England contributed to the eventual success of the property-owning classes against more radical political movements.[66] The revolutionary crisis itself originated in the structural weaknesses of the English state as a machine for waging war: lacking independent military and financial strength, the English King found he could not pursue an unpopular war against the Scottish Protestant brethren of the English people; when the Irish troubles erupted, the would-be absolute monarch was constrained to confront his own alienated subjects as well.

Württemberg: constitutional oligarchy against absolutist rule

Württemberg, a small duchy in the south-western corner of what is today Germany, is hardly comparable in size or world-historical significance to England or Brandenburg-Prussia. Its population at the start of the eighteenth century was less than 350,000; in the closing decade of the century, with the acquisition of new territories as well as demographic expansion,

[65] See particularly Brian Manning, *The English People and the English Revolution* (Harmondsworth: Penguin, 1978); for further perspectives on the relation between popular and parliamentary politics, see J.H. Hexter, *The Reign of King Pym* (Cambridge, Mass.: Harvard University Press, 1941); Valerie Pearl, *London and the Outbreak of the Puritan Revolution* (London: Oxford University Press, 1961); Derek Hirst, 'The Defection of Sir Edward Dering, 1640–1641', *The Historical Journal* 15 (2) (1972): 193–208.
[66] For suggestions along these lines, see Theda Skocpol, *States and Social Revolutions* (Cambridge: Cambridge University Press, 1979), pp. 140–4.

it had reached 620,000.[67] England and Wales, by comparison, had a population of about 3 million in the mid-sixteenth century, which had risen to 5.2 million by 1695.[68] Württemberg never became an internationally significant power, as did, in their different ways, England and Prussia. Yet for the student of historical forms, this little-known corner of the German past reveals a fascinating pattern of social and political development. In many ways more similar to England than to the German-speaking lands east of the Elbe, Württemberg maintained a functioning parliamentary tradition right through from the late mediaeval *Ständestaat* to the emergence of a modern constitution in the nineteenth century. In the later eighteenth century, Charles James Fox remarked that there were only two constitutions in Europe: the British and that of Württemberg.[69] The preservation of the parliamentary tradition in Württemberg was based on certain unique features of its socioeconomic and political structure, and was supported at crucial times by particular international configurations favourable to the cause of the Estates rather than the prince.[70]

The pattern for 'Alt-Wirtemberg' – the old core state, prior to the Napoleonic expansion and reorganisation – was set by the *Tübinger Vertrag* of 1514. This has been dubbed the 'Magna Carta' of Württemberg.[71] In exchange for the taking on of ducal debts, the Württemberg Estates obtained certain political rights and privileges, including co-determination of foreign policy and the granting or withholding of revenues, collectively known as 'das Alte Recht' in later times, to which they clung tenaciously against ducal attacks for most of the next three centuries. At the same time, the composition of the Württemberg Estates was crystallised, which, although developing and changing in certain respects, remained fundamentally the basis of the Estates' continuing

---

67 Arthur Schott, 'Wirtschaftliches Leben' in (hrsg.) Württembergische Geschichts- und Altertumsverein, *Herzog Karl Eugen von Württemberg und seine Zeit* (Esslingen a. N.: Paul Neff Verlag (Max Schreiber), vol. 1, 1907, vol. 2, 1909), vol. 1, p. 314; Joachim Mantel, *Wildberg. Eine Studie zur wirtschaftlichen und sozialen Entwicklung der Stadt von der Mitte des sechzehnten bis zur Mitte des achtzehnten Jahrhunderts* (Stuttgart: W. Kohlhammer Verlag, 1974), p. 5.
68 Coleman, *Economy of England*, p. 12.
69 Cited in F.L. Carsten, *Princes and Parliaments in Germany* (Oxford: Clarendon Press, 1959), p. 5.
70 Württemberg history is less controversial than that of seventeenth-century England. The following account is largely based on: Carsten, *Princes and Parliaments*; Walter Grube, *Der Stuttgarter Landtag 1457–1957* (Stuttgart: Ernst Klett Verlag, 1957); Hartmut Lehmann, 'Die Württembergischen Landstände im 17. und 18. Jahrhundert' in Dietrich Gerhard (ed.), *Ständische Vertretungen in Europa im 17. und 18. Jahrhundert* (Göttingen: Vandenhoek und Ruprecht, 1969); Eugen Schneider, *Württembergische Geschichte* (Stuttgart: J.B. Metzlersche Verlag, 1896); Karl Weller, *Württembergische Geschichte* (Stuttgart: Silberburg-Verlag, Werner Jäckh, 5th edn, 1963).
71 Karl Bosl, 'Repräsentierte und Repräsentierende. Vorformen und Traditionen des Parlamentarismus an der gesellschaftlichen Basis der deutschen Territorialstaaten vom 16. bis 18. Jahrhundert' in Bosl and Möckl (eds.), *Der Moderne Parlamentarismus*.

strength. For the nobility of the area opted out of the Duchy of Württemberg in favour of becoming independent imperial knights (*unmittelbare Reichsritter*) and the prelates joined the commoner representatives of the towns and land areas (*Städte und Ämter*) in a single-tiered Diet.[72] Ducal officials, the *Amtleute*, were finally excluded from the Diet in 1629; and at the same time the privy council (*Geheime Rat*) was made responsible to the Estates as well as the Duke. The Duke thus lacked a fully independent personal bureaucracy.[73] Although succeeding Dukes attempted to co-opt the prelates into ducal service, and at times succeeded in reducing their effective political autonomy, ducal attempts to provoke serious disunity within the Estates were never wholly successful. Regionally unified, and socially and culturally homogeneous, the Württemberg Estates were in a far better position to confront their ruler than were the scattered and disunited regional landed and urban Estates of Brandenburg-Prussia.

Socioeconomically, too, Württemberg was quite different from Prussia.[74] South-western Germany never developed the pattern of large landed estates, *Gutsherrschaft*, in which landlords had a variety of political, juridical and personal rights over their agricultural workers, as well as purely economic control. Rather, *Grundherrschaft* remained the basic pattern of south-west German development. Small property-ownership, in which peasants remained personally free and held their land on relatively favourable conditions, was the basic pattern in Württemberg. The lack of consistent rules of primogeniture led to the division of land into ever smaller units, and peasants frequently had to work at the same time at a trade; thus the distinction between artisans – who supplemented their income with produce from small plots of land – and peasants was blurred. Towns were interpenetrated with agricultural interests and activities; villages participated in trade and craft production.[75] While towns had certain political and juridical privileges – it was members of the urban elite who sat as deputies in the Diet – they were mostly small in size and in many cases hard to differentiate from the larger villages. As late as 1787, on the eve of the French Revolution, Württemberg had only three towns with more than 5,000 inhabitants: the capital, Stuttgart, with 22,000; Tübingen, the university town, with 6,059; and Ludwigsburg, the Versailles-style ducal residence town, with 5,318. The next five largest towns had only between 3,000 and 4,000 inhabitants each.[76] Since in 1790 Württemberg's population lived in 69 towns, 709 villages,

---

[72] See Lehmann, 'Württembergische Landstände'; Grube, *Stuttgarter Landtag*; Carsten, *Princes and Parliaments*.

[73] Carsten, *Princes and Parliaments*, p. 60.

[74] See Lütge, *Sozial- und Wirtschaftsgeschichte* and *Agrarverfassung*; Bechtel, *Wirtschafts- und Sozialgeschichte* and *Wirtschaftsgeschichte*, vol. 2; Helen P. Liebel, 'The Bourgeoisie in Southwestern Germany, 1500–1789: A Rising Class?', *International Review of Social History* 10 (2) (1965): 283–307.

[75] Schott, 'Wirtschaftliches Leben'; and Mantel, *Wildberg*.

[76] Schott, 'Wirtschaftliches Leben', p. 314.

379 hamlets and 827 farmsteads, it can be seen that the remaining 61 towns can have been barely distinguishable from the villages in all but status. The growth of population in the eighteenth century – population density rising from 48 per square mile in 1734 to 67 per square mile in 1790 – took place largely in the villages, towns remaining more constant in size. Culturally, too, since the introduction of universal primary education in 1649 (Württemberg was highly precocious in this respect), differences between town and country were lessened.[77]

Associated with the personal freedom of the peasantry was a certain political autonomy of the local community. In a three-field agricultural system with rotation of crops, community organisation was strongly developed. Lacking a patrimonial system with noble domination, villages had their own courts to deal with minor breaches of the law; and village communities elected their own local officials. Towns similarly enjoyed a high degree of independence in local government, and it was from their ranks that the representatives of town and land areas to the Diets were chosen. Between the late seventeenth and the mid-eighteenth centuries, villages developed an increasing influence on wider political affairs: the basis of election of deputies to the Diet, who were mandated delegates bound by the instructions of their electorate, widened to include large numbers of the peasant population in this period.[78] As we shall see, these local developments of increasing political participation and influence (somewhat parallel to processes in early seventeenth-century England, despite differences in scale) took place in a fashion somewhat at odds with ducal attempts at centralisation of power; although the Dukes attempted to harness village politics in their battles with the Estates. During the course of the eighteenth century, with economic change and population expansion, the socioeconomic differences within the peasantry began to increase, stratification becoming more marked; and

---

[77] Karl Weller, 'Geistiges Leben' in *Herzog Karl Eugen… und seine Zeit*, vol. 1; Eugen Schmid, 'Das Volksschulwesen' in ibid., vol. 2; Grube, *Stuttgarter Landtag*, p. 401; Carsten, *Princes and Parliaments*, pp. 3–4; but Lehmann, 'Württembergische Landstände', pp. 188–9 and n. 8, warns against over-minimising the differences between large towns and prelates on the one hand, and small towns and villages on the other. See also Liebel, 'Bourgeoisie', for discussion of Württemberg stratification, and differences between the *Honoratioren* or *Ehrbarkeit* and the lower levels of the population. Nevertheless, the relative social egalitarianism of Württemberg in comparison with Prussia is worth stressing; and as we shall see in Chapter 5, this was a society in which social mobility through the educational system was possible at least in principle and frequently also in practice. Walter Grube, 'Israel Hartmann. Lebensbild eines altwürttembergischen Pietisten', *Zeitschrift für Württembergische Landesgeschichte* 12 (1953): 250–70, charts the rise of a modestly born boy who rose through his profession of schoolmaster to become part of the highest circles in the land; this was by no means an unusual or isolated example. Apart from such mobility, however, the personal freedom and even minimal education of Württemberg's peasant population had important consequences for politics.

[78] Walter Grube, 'Dorfgemeinde und Amtsversammlung in Altwürttemberg', *Zeitschrift für Württembergische Landesgeschichte* 13 (1954): 194–219; Friedrich Wintterlin, 'Landeshoheit' in *Herzog Karl Eugen… und seine Zeit*, vol. 1.

(again, somewhat parallel to English developments) there were increasing attempts by elites to suppress aspects of popular culture, developing a comprehensive system of *Sittenpolizei* regulating behaviour and morality in secular and spiritual affairs. Nevertheless, in the late eighteenth century a traveller to Württemberg was still able to comment:

Sonderlich sind die württembergischen Bauern so klug und witzig, als in andern Ländern kaum die gemeinen Bürger; wozu meines Erachtens nicht wenig beiträgt, dass sie ihre kleinen Dorfgerichte selbst halten und auf diese Weise nicht ihrem Vogt oder Amtmann auch in den geringsten Dingen blinden Gehorsam zu leisten haben.[79]

All this stands in marked contrast to life in Prussia at the time.

Let us look now at the salient features of the political history of Württemberg, focussing on the ways in which Duke, Estates, and social groups interrelated and responded to changing circumstances. The Thirty Years War had had a devastating impact on Württemberg, which was overrun by armies and suffered immense destruction through the impact of plague and economic disruption as well as the direct consequences of warfare. Four years after the start of the war, in 1622, the population was 445,000; in 1634 it had been reduced by 30,000 to 415,000; but only five years later, in 1639, there were only 97,000 inhabitants remaining in the Duchy. More than three-quarters of the populace had been wiped out in the sufferings of the preceding years.[80] The situation improved only briefly after the Peace of Westphalia, before the wars of Louis XIV of France further ravaged the country. The opening decade of the eighteenth century witnessed the War of Spanish Succession; it was not until after the Treaty of Utrecht, when Württemberg was able to enjoy four decades of peace, that a measure of expansion and prosperity returned to the country.[81] It is against this background of warfare and devastation that the relationship between Duke and Estates must be viewed; and it is notable that the serious constitutional crisis of the 1760s, culminating in the *Erbvergleich* of 1770, was precipitated by the impact of the Seven Years War on Württemberg's policies and resources.

The mid-seventeenth century was a period in which, in general, Duke and Estates were able to work harmoniously together in the perceived interests of the country. The Thirty Years War and the rebuilding necessitated by its consequences in general strengthened the Estates. The introduction of an excise tax in 1638 had, unlike in Prussia, the effect of

---

[79] 'It is remarkable that in Württemberg the peasants are as clever as are barely the ordinary townspeople in other countries; for which it is not unimportant, in my opinion, that they hold their small village courts of justice themselves, and do not have to give blind obedience in even the smallest matters to their governor or administrator.' Quoted in Weller, 'Geistiges Leben', p. 397.

[80] Bechtel, *Wirtschaftsgeschichte*, p. 28. On the general consequences of the Thirty Years War, see Lütge, *Sozial- und Wirtschaftsgeschichte*, pp. 287–98.

[81] Schott, 'Wirtschaftliches Leben'.

augmenting the power of the Estates rather than the ruler, since it was the former, through the *Städte und Ämter*, who were responsible for collecting it, and since it was paid into the *Landschaftskasse* under the control of the Estates as well as the ruler.[82] The Estates could refuse to grant it, as they did in 1642–4. After the war was ended, the Diet of 1651–2 was followed by eleven more in the reign of Duke Eberhard up to 1674 – an average of one every two years. Despite certain frictions over foreign and military policy – frictions which could only be expected in a system of dual sovereignty – this was a period in which the old constitutional ideal of co-operation between ruler and Estates appeared to be realised in practice. The decades immediately following the Thirty Years War have indeed been termed the 'Blütezeit des Landtags'.[83]

The French Wars of the 1670s, '80s and '90s, subjecting the Duchy in the invasion of summer 1693 to its worst experience of destruction since the Thirty Years War, provoked increasing hostility between Duke and Estates. The ruler (from 1674 to 1677, Wilhelm Ludwig; in the period of minority of Eberhard Ludwig, the ducal regent Friedrich Karl, from 1677 to 1692; and from 1692 to 1733, Eberhard Ludwig) increasingly attempted to make independent policy decisions and sought to raise money from sources other than the grants of the Estates. In 1691 the regent transformed the defence militia into a permanent paid army; in 1692 he introduced forced conscription without consulting the Estates.[84] In September 1692 the regent was taken prisoner by the French; in 1693, Eberhard Ludwig, declared to have attained the age of majority, continued the regent's policies of independent rule. With the Treaty of Ryswick in 1697, Eberhard Ludwig wanted to keep on the army in peacetime; but the Estates, in the Diet of 1698–9, obstinately refused, and, on the sacking from ducal service of their major spokesman, Sturm, appealed to the Emperor in Vienna for support. The Duke attempted to circumvent the Diet by appealing directly to the local *Amtsversammlungen* – notably, Tübingen had the courage to oppose the Duke – and also forced the prelates to sign an agreement not to appeal to the Emperor again, thus striking a blow at the unity of the Estates. In 1699 the Diet was dissolved, and no further Diet was called for nearly forty years.

The early years of the eighteenth century were a low point for the cause of constitutional rule in Württemberg. In 1701 war started again; and the inevitable strains consequent on raising and financing troops were further complicated by the affair of the Duke's mistress, Wilhelmina von Grävenitz, who occasioned a long-running battle between ruler and Estates on moral as well as political issues. The Estates, who were not

---

[82] Grube, *Stuttgarter Landtag*, pp. 315–16.
[83] Ibid., p. 341; also Lehmann, 'Württembergische Landstände', p. 192.
[84] Grube, *Stuttgarter Landtag*, Book 2, ch. 9; Schneider, *Württembergische Geschichte*, ch. 12; Weller, *Württembergische Geschichte*, pp. 169–71; Carsten, *Princes and Parliaments*, sections 6 and 7.

summoned to a full Diet by the Duke, were represented by their two permanent committees, the *Engerer* and *Grosse Ausschüsse*, which had the power to convene themselves. Following the Treaty of Utrecht in 1713, and a partial resolution of the problem of 'die von Grävenitz', representatives of the Estates, led by the conciliatory Bishop Osiander, became more compliant; in 1724 the Duke achieved a limited gain for absolutism in obtaining at least short-term financial support for a small standing army. This was partly achieved by the method of the Duke again circumventing the Estates by appealing directly to the local *Amtsversammlungen* and pressurising them, through ducal officials, to instruct the Large Committee to agree to ducal proposals.[85] The subsequent 'Soldatenspielerei' of the Duke was effectively impotent in terms of the external defence of the country, but made some difference in the internal balance of forces, as was to become evident in succeeding decades. Still, since no permanent taxation had been agreed, there was no sense in which the limited powers of the Estates had been entirely dispensed with. Nor could the Large Committee be completely browbeaten by the Duke's tactics of appealing directly to the local assemblies: in 1728, even after pressures were put on the local deputies of each *Amt*, the Large Committee refused to make a grant for more than two years' financial support.[86]

In 1733 Karl Alexander became ruler. A Catholic since 1712, Karl Alexander had little sympathy for the Protestant, constitutional traditions of Württemberg. While in the *Religionsreversalien* Karl Alexander had to consent to the transference of the *summus episcopus* of the church to the *Geheime Rat*, thus losing control of the economic and political as well as spiritual jurisdiction of the church (and restoring the political independence of the bishops), he nevertheless pursued policies designed to attain equal status for his own Catholic religion, to destroy Protestantism as the established state religion, and to demolish the related powers of the Estates who stood as its guardian. With his army commander, the Catholic General von Remchingen, and his financial adviser and factotum, the Jew Süss Oppenheimer, Karl Alexander set about making himself independent of the Estates. Advised by his Catholic friend Bishop Friedrich Karl of Würzburg and Bamberg, Karl Alexander set in train the typical policies of absolutism: sale of offices, raising of unconstitutional taxes, increases in the size of the army; General von Remchingen even started developing a *Generalkriegskommissariat* for military organisation on the Prussian model. When the Large Committee was unwilling to concede to ducal demands for more money for troops, Remchingen used force to obtain money from the Estates' chest.[87] The situation was saved

---

[85] Carsten, *Princes and Parliaments*, pp. 120–2; Grube, *Stuttgarter Landtag*, pp. 384–5.

[86] Carsten, *Princes and Parliaments*, p. 122. Carsten suggests, p. 123 n. 1, that Grube (p. 388) goes too far in saying that at this time the Estates were becoming a tool of the absolutist state.

[87] Grube, *Stuttgarter Landtag*, pp. 391–3. On the Jew Süss, see Selma Stern, *The Court Jew*

for the Estates less by their persistent if passive opposition than by a historical accident: in 1737, on the eve of a trip to gain further support from the Bishop of Würzburg and Bamberg, Karl Alexander died. It was commonly supposed, either that this was assassination, or that the devil had come to take him away; neither supposition has received empirical confirmation, and modern historians tend to espouse the theory of an opportune heart attack.

Karl Alexander's successor, Karl Eugen, was only nine at the time of his father's death; a period of ducal minority therefore followed. There was an unsuccessful attempted coup by the army under General von Remchingen, ending in the escape of the General; order was re-established, the hated Jew Süss Oppenheimer arrested, put on trial, and executed; and a general Diet, the first in the eighteenth century, called in July 1737. It was at this Diet that the growing popular pressures from village communities for greater representation became apparent; but the elite of the Estates, in more conservative style, were concerned largely with attempts to maintain the ancient constitution.[88] Increasingly during the mid- and later eighteenth century the divergence between popular demands and the oligarchical concerns of the elite became evident. The Württemberg Estates, like the English Parliamentarians, were caught between opposing pressures: on the one hand, the ruler's attempts to attain absolute power and dispense with their participation in sovereignty; and on the other hand popular pressures for more radical programmes contrary to the perceived interests of a conservative elite. In Württemberg, as in England, this development was associated with rapid demographic expansion – the population of Württemberg increased by nearly fifty per cent during the sixty years' reign of Karl Eugen – and with increasing socioeconomic polarisation and cultural differentiation.[89]

After the passing of measures relatively favourable to the cause of the Estates during the period of ducal minority, Karl Eugen was declared old enough to rule at the age of sixteen in 1744. Within a few years, the frictions of two opposing conceptions of rulership arose again: Karl Eugen's open practice of Catholicism, his luxurious, spendthrift court life, his demands for vast revenues and his unconstitutional methods of raising income, his proclivity for entering into alliances abroad without consulting the Estates, were bound sooner or later to lead to confrontation.[90] The

---

(Philadelphia: The Jewish Publication Society of America, 1950). Refreshingly, Stern takes the side of Süss and the Duke against the Estates – an unusual position in the historiography.

[88] Grube, *Stuttgarter Landtag*, pp. 413–14.

[89] Carsten, *Princes and Parliaments*, p. 133. It is notable that Bishop Weissensee was protected by the Estates against mob violence despite his associations with Süss and the absolutist policies of Karl Alexander; an instance of elite social solidarity overriding ideological differences. (On the incident, see Grube, *Stuttgarter Landtag*, p. 411.)

[90] See generally, Albert Pfister, 'Hof und Hoffeste', and Pfister, 'Militärwesen', and Eugen Schneider, 'Regierung', and Alb. Eugen Adam, 'Herzog Karl Eugen und die Landschaft'

immediate cause of the confrontation that occurred was, as in the case of England, the necessity to raise troops for war. In 1756 the Seven Years War broke out; in January 1757 the Estates discovered that five years earlier the Duke had entered into a secret agreement with France, in which for annual payments he had agreed to raise 6,000 infantry troops for French service. The payments had in fact aided Karl Eugen in his luxurious lifestyle; it now transpired that most of the 6,000 troops, in addition to those owed by Württemberg to the Swabian *Kreis*, had yet to be found; as did the money with which to support the soldiers. Forced conscriptions followed, with mass desertions of soldiers who had no sympathy with an unpopular French fight against their Prussian Protestant brethren; unconstitutional measures were taken to raise money, including forced loans, debasement of the coinage, increased labour services, the introduction of salt and tobacco monopolies, and, in January 1759, the use of troops to force the Estates to hand over 30,000 guilders from the *Landschaftskasse*, a measure repeated six months later. Moser, seen as the leader of the opposition, was imprisoned; the *Geheime Rat* was functionally demoted and personal government with the aid of a few ministers, led by Graf Montmartin, took its place; and assaults were made on the autonomy of local government. In 1762 the village communities were reorganised into *Unterämter* under the direct control of ducal officials, the *Amtleute*. But with the ending of the Seven Years War in 1763, and with a more favourable international situation (no longer at war with one of the guarantors of the Protestant constitution, Prussia), the Estates petitioned the Emperor and the three powers guaranteeing the *Religionsreversalien*, Prussia, Denmark, and England–Hannover. A Diet was called, but with no effective resolution of differences; meanwhile, internal opposition to the Duke's regime was growing in strength. The weak and disunited Small Committee was now supplemented by the full Diet, subject to popular pressures from the localities; and in 1764, when the Duke attempted to introduce a poll-tax by appealing directly to the local *Amtsversammlungen* he met such resistance that it proved impossible to implement, despite the imprisonment of the Tübingen *Oberamtmann* Huber and the use of troops in Tübingen, the centre of resistance. The Estates finally made a formal complaint to the *Reichshofrat* in Vienna; in the meantime, international pressure forced the Duke to release Moser from his incarceration.

The case in Vienna dragged on, with twists and turns in the fortunes of each side, until 1770. In January of this year, a compromise was reached between Duke and Estates in the *Erbvergleich*, which confirmed the rights of the Estates, in return for financial support for the Duke, in the six areas of purported constitutional violation: politics, the Church, the

(an extremely detailed account), in *Herzog Karl Eugen... und seine Zeit*, vol. 1, in addition to Carsten, Grube, Schneider and Weller.

army, financial affairs, forests and wild life, and local government. A number of measures introduced by the Duke in previous years were formally rescinded, thus restoring the rights of the Small and Large Committees to convene themselves, and re-establishing the independence of local government and the rights of Estates and Church to control their own finances. This agreement was ratified in December 1770, apparently sealing the fate of absolutism in Württemberg. In practice, tensions continued in the next two decades; and the form of constitutional rule was one of a narrow, nepotistic oligarchy rather than a democratic parliamentarism. Nevertheless, the absolutist project in Württemberg was defeated, thanks both to the internal alignment of forces and to the external support of foreign powers guaranteeing the constitution and aiding the Estates in the Imperial Court.

Three patterns of attempted absolutism

Such were the three patterns of sociopolitical development in the periods of attempted absolutism. As we have seen, in each case there were incipient tendencies in a similar direction: rulers were attempting to build up financial and organisational independence, such that in one way or another they could dispense with the co-rulership of Estates or Houses of Parliament. In these attempts, three factors were of crucial importance: taxation, bureaucracy, and military organisation. There are debates among scholars as to just how important any one of these elements might be in explaining the success or failure of attempts at absolutism; nevertheless, taken together, if a ruler could achieve independent sources of revenue, an independent bureaucratic apparatus for extracting revenue and controlling local government, and a standing army which could be used for internal repression as well as external defence and agression, he was likely to reduce the Estates to ineffectiveness even if he did not dispense with them entirely. In Prussia, this is precisely what was able to occur: the eighteenth century saw the development of a highly efficient militarised bureaucratic absolutism. In Württemberg, considerable steps were taken in such a direction; but in the end the ruler faced too strong an opposition, both internally and externally, to be able to carry it through. In England, the balance of forces internally, and the political situation internationally, was such that it took a Civil War to resolve – or to transform – the tensions inherent in the early Stuart regime. In order to understand more fully the parts played by the Pietist and Puritan movements in these patterns of development, we must now turn to analysis of the location of the established church in each regime. For it is through the relationships among church, state, and social/ political groups that the political responses of Puritans and Pietists were refracted and developed.

4

The established church and toleration

The structural location of the established church, and the degrees and sources of toleration accorded to the precisionist movements for religious reform, are crucial factors mediating the relationships between precisionism and the state. In this chapter we shall examine first the economic, political, and sociocultural location of the established church (or orthodoxy) in each case; and then we shall turn to the question of the degree to which the church could tolerate or incorporate its reformist wing, or, on the other hand, seek to suppress it and denounce it as heretical. This discussion, in conjunction with the analysis of the attempts at absolutism in the previous chapter, will complete the picture of the elements together conditioning the different political trajectories of Puritans and Pietists. The following chapters will then treat each case separately, showing in detail how the different patterns of development can be explained in terms of the different structural relationships among church, state and society in each case.

The structural location of the established church

Traditional to the characterisation of Lutheran state churches is the comment about the inevitable subservience of the church to the state as a consequence of the post-Reformation principle of 'cuius regio, eius religio'. However useful as an overall generalisation about the territorial pattern of European politico-religious settlements, this generalisation like others admits of exceptions; and it happens that neither Württemberg nor Prussia conform to the rule. In the course of development of both these states, it in fact became the Estates who were most closely tied to the outlook and interests of the established church, often in some tension with the policies and even the professed faith of the ruler. Conversely, however, the generalisation would be most suited to characterising the post-Reformation Church of England: a church intimately linked, in a variety of ways, with the interests, fortunes, and policies of the ruler. But in each case, there were ambiguities inherent in the role and status of the church, which cannot be adequately described in terms of a single dimension. The following sketches highlight aspects of the economic,

76

political, and sociocultural locations of the three Protestant state churches.

Undoubtedly the church enjoying the most favourable economic situation was that of Württemberg. The Reformation in Württemberg, after something of a faltering start, had been consolidated under Duke Christoph (1550–65), when the church was able to collect together and receive constitutional guarantees for its wealth.[1] The *Grosse Kirchenordnung* of 1559, which remained the basic law of the duchy in religious and educational matters until 1806, stipulated that the wealth and income of the church was to be used for the good of the church, the schools, and the poor, and was to be administered by the central church authority, the *Kirchenrat*, in Stuttgart. Although the *Kirchenrat* became subordinated to the Privy Council (*Geheimer Rat*) in 1629, the latter was, as we have seen, not purely an organ of the ruler but rather was at this time made responsible to the Estates as well as the Duke.[2] Use of the church income was expressly stipulated in the constitution and guaranteed by the Estates. Needless to say, such guarantees did not deter successive rulers from attempting to benefit from church wealth: unconstitutional uses of church income included the maintenance of foreign dignitaries, court music and theatre, the building of the palace at Ludwigsburg and other town and castle-building projects, and maintenance of the 'Kriegsspielereien' and generally luxurious baroque lifestyle of late seventeenth- and eighteenth-century rulers.[3] The church was the loser in debates over the claims that, since mediaeval abbeys had supplied hounds for hunts, the church should foot the bill for the extensive *Parforcejägerei* enjoyed by eighteenth-century Dukes; and that, since the singer in the Stuttgart *Stiftskirche* was paid by the church, the latter was financially responsible also for such musical endeavours as the immensely expensive Italian opera at Karl Eugen's court. Such grievances formed part of the complaints eventually leading to the *Erbvergleich*. Nevertheless, despite such encroachments on the intended uses of its wealth, the church in Württemberg enjoyed considerable financial independence in the eighteenth century. Possessing 24 *Klöster* and their lands, 450 or so villages, hamlets, and estates, and numerous miscellaneous properties, sources of revenue and jurisdictions scattered over the country, comprehending altogether about one third of the Duchy of Württemberg, the church constituted a veritable 'state within a state', as

[1] See particularly F.L. Carsten, *Princes and Parliaments in Germany* (Oxford: Clarendon Press, 1959), chapter 1.
[2] See Chapter 3, above.
[3] Martin Leube, 'Die fremden Ausgaben des altwürttembergischen Kirchenguts', *Blätter für Württembergische Kirchengeschichte* 29 (1925): 168–99, partic. pp. 179–80, 186, 195–6; also Walter Grube, 'Altwürttembergische Kloster vor und nach der Reformation', *Blätter für Deutsche Landesgeschichte* 109 (1973): 139–50, p. 147.

Hasselhorn has put it.[4] Such wealth ensured at least financial autonomy for the church.

The uniquely favourable economic situation of the Württemberg church was reflected at the parochial level.[5] In contrast to other Lutheran churches – and in accordance with the reformed ideal unsuccessfully argued for by certain English Puritans – pastorates were not local benefices. Rather, pastors received fixed salaries in money, wood, wine, and produce from the central income of the church. Tithes existed, but went directly to the *Kirchenrat*: a part, mainly the so-called Great Tithes and income from major privileges, was paid straight to the central administration; the 'small tithes', only nominally paid into central funds, were administered locally for the church by incumbents. Pastors were thus protected both economically and socially: they were not constrained directly into conflicts with their parishioners over income; their fixed salaries protected them to some degree against poor harvests and bad years; and they did not have to worry unduly about such matters as raising money for the upkeep of the fabric of church buildings, since these were linked to the Great Tithes. This is not to suggest that there were no deficiencies in practice: there were variations in the amounts of land and types of rights and income attached to different pastorates; inflation meant a decline in value of the money part of the salary; and most pastors needed at least a vegetable garden, a couple of cows, and some vines for wine, to supplement their salaries. Nevertheless, while not affluent, pastors in Württemberg enjoyed a certain respectability in standard of living, with an independence from local pressures, and a style of life a cut above that of the local farmers, butchers, bakers, and artisans. It may have been true, as the saying went, that pastors bequeathed 'only books and children'; but they were able to send their sons to college and, with much saving, to ensure respectable dowries for their daughters.

Economic independence was mirrored by considerable political independence for the Württemberg church. In 1565 the Estates obtained from Duke Christoph (who was compelled by acute financial need) a guarantee of their rights of preservation of the Lutheran church settlement. In conjunction with the *Kirchenordnung* of 1559,

Christoph thus not only had to renounce many of the financial benefits accruing to other princes from the secularization of church property, but even the *Jus Reformandi*, which the German princes possessed since the peace of Augsburg of 1555; concessions of great importance for the future history of the country.[6]

There was little increase in the power of the Württemberg Dukes through the Reformation; and in the eighteenth century, when from 1733 to 1797

[4] Martin Hasselhorn, *Der Altwürttembergische Pfarrstand im 18. Jahrhundert* (Stuttgart: W. Kohlhammer Verlag, 1958), pp. 1–2.
[5] This paragraph is largely based on Hasselhorn.
[6] Carsten, *Princes and Parliaments*, pp. 28–9.

the Dukes were personally openly professing Catholics, the summ-episcopacy of the church went to the *Geheimer Rat*.[7] The closest consti-tutional and practical political links of the Württemberg church were with the Estates. As mentioned in Chapter 3, above, prelates sat with deputies from town and country areas in a single-tiered Diet; and influen-tial prelates always sat on the *Engerer Ausschuss*, the Small Committee preserving the parliamentary tradition in periods when no full Diet was called. Estates and church were united in working to protect 'das Alte Recht', their inherited constitutional rights and privileges, against encroachments by the ruler. Dukes made periodic attempts, ultimately unsuccessful, to gain the prelates as ducal servants; the most they achieved was the muzzling of the prelates' articulation of discontent in complaining to Vienna, between 1699 and 1733.[8] Interestingly, also, prelates were subject to fewer pressures from below than were the secular deputies in the Diet, and could thus less easily be co-opted for the Duke's policies in this way: for prelates represented only themselves and the interests of the church in the Diet, and were not mandated delegates from the geographical areas under their control.[9]

Enjoying such economic and political advantages, it is scarcely surpris-ing that the personnel of the Württemberg church had a high social and cultural status. In a society lacking an indigenous aristocracy, there were three main social groups: at the bottom, the peasantry; then the *Klein-bürgertum*; and at the top, the notables of society – the *Honoratioren* or *Ehrbarkeit*. In principle, status was achieved rather than ascribed: the ladders of education and career would determine one's adult position. In practice, of course, the usual networks of intermarriage and nepotism ensured the perpetuation of oligarchical privilege from generation to generation, and sons tended to inherit the positions of their fathers. In this commoner society, culturally united in its dislike of absolutist court culture and the ways of the foreign nobility, the clergy formed part of the *Ehrbarkeit* or *Honoratioren*.[10] Links with leading political figures in the Estates were not merely a matter of strategic alliance: the same families, tied by relationship as well as common social interest, played important roles in both the spiritual and the secular affairs of Württemberg.[11] The church had a central part in the educational, cultural, and political life of

---

[7] Hasselhorn, *Altwürttembergische Pfarrstand*, pp. 66–7.
[8] Cf. Chapter 3, above.
[9] Grube, 'Altwürttembergische Kloster', pp. 147ff. The converse of this was, of course, that those subjects living on lands owned by the church had no effective method of ensuring that their grievances and interests would be represented at Diets.
[10] Cf. Hasselhorn, *Altwürttembergische Pfarrstand*; also Helen P. Liebel, 'The Bourgeoisie in Southwestern Germany, 1500–1789: A Rising Class?', *International Review of Social History* 10 (1965): 283–307.
[11] F. Fritz, 'Die evangelische Kirche Württembergs im Zeitalter des Pietismus', *Blätter für Württembergische Kirchengeschichte* 55 (1955): 68–116 and 56 (1956): 99–167, pp. 102–3.

Württemberg, and tremendous popular interest focussed on the yearly
Landexamen, when boys from all over the country would come to
Stuttgart to compete for places in the *Klosterschulen* which prepared the
way for university studies in Tübingen. There was no less general interest
in the subsequent *Lokationen*, ranking the pupils in the *Klosterschulen*
supposedly in order of achievement and having great influence on their
future career prospects.[12] Members of the *Kleinbürgertum* and even
peasantry were continually trying to push their sons forward through the
educational process; in the eighteenth century, periodic attempts were
made to restrict eligibility for university entrance. At the university, twice
as many students studied theology as all the other disciplines together;
and about one third of all theology students had finally to take up careers
outside the church, there being too few vacancies for the numbers trained
and qualified for the clerical profession.[13] Once in the job, the pastor in
Württemberg found that his main obligation was fulfilment of his duties
as understood by the central church authorities. Unlike the position in
other German states, the Württemberg pastor was not pre-eminently
active in the role of state servant: while pronouncements about morality
were frequently made from the pulpit, and new church regulations were
read out to the congregations, it was very rare for any political decrees to
be communicated via the church.[14] Nor were the laity given much of an
active role in church affairs: they had veto rights over the choice of
pastor, and could of course make their feelings known over particular
issues, but it was ultimately the central church authorities who decided
where pastors should be placed and who determined church policies.[15]
Thus in the late seventeenth and early eighteenth centuries, the church
had an assured status in Württemberg life.

The situation of the post-Reformation English church was more complicated than that of Württemberg. Economically, politically, and culturally
its position under Elizabeth and the early Stuarts was ambiguous and

---

[12] There is a nice indication in the novel by Seybold, *Hartmann: Eine Württembergische
Klostergeschichte* (Leipzig: In der Weygandschen Buchhandlung, 1778), that social
status and nepotism still had their place beside intellectual achievement in determining
scholastic rank: the novel's young hero, Hartmann, has to take third place after a
Stuttgart boy 'von vornehmer Familie' ('from a distinguished family') and 'einem Vetter
des Prälaten' ('a cousin (relative) of the bishop') (p. 118).

[13] See Martin Leube, *Die Geschichte des Tübinger Stifts* (Stuttgart: Verlag Chr. Scheufele,
vol. 2, 1930), pp. 318–25; also the critical comments of Friedrich Nicolai, in
*Beschreibung einer Reise durch Deutschland und die Schweiz im Jahre 1781. Nebst
Bemerkungen über Gelehrsamkeit, Industrie, Religion und Sitten* (Berlin und Stettin,
1795), vol. 11, Book 3, section 12, 'Aufenthalt in Tübingen'.

[14] Hasselhorn, *Altwürttembergische Pfarrstand*, pp. 61–2.

[15] This centralisation of control in the Württemberg church had a history developing from
the sixteenth century. Cf. for example, Martin Brecht, *Kirchenordnung und Kirchenzucht in Württemberg vom 16. bis zum 18. Jahrhundert* (Stuttgart: Calwer Verlag,
1967).

subject to a number of tensions. While in many ways the post-Reformation Church of England was most closely linked with and dependent on the Crown, in a variety of respects the laity had a considerable interest in and degree of control over church affairs. Because of the peculiar economic basis and political location of the English church in the eight decades preceding the outbreak of Civil War, it constituted an essentially contested territory.

Christopher Hill begins his classic work on *Economic Problems of the Church* with the sentence: 'The Henrician Reformation impoverished the church and weakened it politically.'[16] Recent research has refined and deepened our detailed knowledge of church finances and personnel, but has done little to alter the general picture evoked by Hill.[17] Over the course of the mid- and later sixteenth century the church was, at times gradually and at other times more rapidly and rapaciously, relieved of a considerable proportion of its wealth and assets. Under Somerset, there was a decimation of church property; halted, but not reversed, under Mary, the pillage of the church was taken up again in Elizabeth's reign. This pillage had important consequences for the status and role of members of the church hierarchy, for their capacity to carry out traditional and new tasks, and for the perceptions, expectations, and interventions of the laity in relation to the church.

Starting at the top, bishops were 'transformed from feudal potentates, powerful in their own right as landowners, to hangers-on of the court, making what they could of their office whilst they held it'.[18] The loss of manors in return for rectories, tithes, and other spiritualities meant that bishops no longer had the automatic status and power accruing to large landowners in sixteenth-century England, however adeptly some of them might have managed to maintain the general level of their income.[19] Furthermore, Elizabethan bishops were of lower social origins than their pre-Reformation predecessors. While the Reformation initially appeared to have little impact on the social origins of the episcopate, by Elizabethan times 'the majority [came] from backgrounds with no pretensions to influence or were of unknown [and hence probably humble] parentage'.[20] Nor did the post-Reformation bishops manage to compen-

[16] Christopher Hill, *Economic Problems of the Church* (Oxford: Clarendon Press, 1956), p. 3.

[17] See for example: Felicity Heal and Rosemary O'Day (eds.), *Church and Society in England: Henry VIII to James I* (London: Macmillan, 1977); Rosemary O'Day and Felicity Heal (eds.), *Continuity and Change: Personnel and Administration of the Church in England 1500–1642* (Leicester: Leicester University Press, 1976); Rosemary O'Day, *The English Clergy: The Emergence and Consolidation of a Profession, 1558–1642* (Leicester: Leicester University Press, 1979); Felicity Heal, *Of Prelates and Princes: A Study of the Economic and Social Position of the Tudor Episcopate* (Cambridge: Cambridge University Press, 1980).

[18] Hill, *Economic Problems of the Church*, p. 28.

[19] See partic. Heal, *Prelates and Princes*.

[20] Ibid., p. 245.

sate by marrying high-status wives; and they compounded their economic and social problems in their attempts to make suitable financial arrangements for members of their families, a new problem for clerics who did not always make clear distinctions between public and private assets and income. Yet the post-Reformation bishops of the Church of England had not been transformed into the pastoral superintendents of the Reformed ideal. They were still expected, in addition to their pastoral functions, to maintain the pomp, ceremony, and worldly dignity appropriate to high secular office, and to indulge in generous hospitality as part of their social and political functions, as well as supporting the more spiritual causes of education and the poor. It was difficult for distraught and insecure bishops, concerned with problems of finance and administration in straitened circumstances, always to fulfil all the varied and partly conflicting demands of their station.

Similar tensions were evident in the position of the lower ranks of the clergy. There has been some debate over the changing levels of clerical incomes: but it is certainly clear that while many rectors may have prospered as a result of rising prices in a century of inflation, a great number of vicars and curates remained or became impoverished, with an increasing inequality in the values of livings.[21] A combination of factors, including the decreasing real value of fixed tithes with commutation of dues, the reluctance of many lay impropriators to give more than 'leavings, not livings', and the inequitable distribution of clerical taxation, led to undesirable consequences at the parochial level. If the living was insufficient to attract a 'learned minister', the parish might have to make do either with a relatively incompetent person simultaneously engaged in other income-raising activities, or with a non-resident pluralist dividing his attentions among a number of parishes. Yet at the same time the qualifications required of a minister in post-Reformation England were rather different from those of the mediaeval parish priest, whose main duties had been of a ritual nature. With the Protestant rejection of quasi-magical conceptions of the sacrament, combined with a heightened emphasis on preaching the Word of the Lord, literacy and education were increasingly important qualifications for the ministry. There was in fact a massive rise in the educational qualifications of the clergy between the accession of Elizabeth and the mid-seventeenth century, such that in the reign of Charles I almost all ordinands were at least graduates and some had higher degrees; there may even have been an overproduction, in the first half of the seventeenth century, of qualified candidates for the ministry.[22] But it seems that this development was related to the general

---

[21] O'Day, *English Clergy*, ch. 13.
[22] See Mark Curtis, 'The Alienated Intellectuals of Early Stuart England', *Past and Present* 23 (November 1962): 25–43; but cf. Ian Green, 'Career Prospects and Clerical Conformity in the Early Stuart Church', *Past and Present* 90 (1981): 71–115.

massive expansion of education and literacy, and to the rising status of the clergy as a profession, rather than to any marked improvement in clerical income or prospects; and it did little to resolve continuing problems of pluralism and non-residence.

Stripped of considerable wealth, the Church of England was much dependent on the patronage of others. The Crown was initially the major beneficiary of the plunder of the church; but by the end of the sixteenth century, through the direct mechanism of re-sale of church properties to laymen and through the indirect but no less powerful mechanism of influence and patronage at court, the laity had a very large say in the affairs of the church.[23] Through the possession of advowsons and impropriations, laymen had rights of nomination to livings; through augmentations of insufficient livings, wealthy individuals and congregations could also influence the type of preaching and pastoral care they were to receive; those with the right connections could even succeed in influencing nominations to livings nominally under Crown patronage. Outside the regular parochial structure, lectureships could be endowed to ensure an alternative source of preaching sympathetic to the ears of a particular congregation.[24]

The relationship of the Church of England to the Crown was not purely one of economic dependence: it offered, in return, vital political and administrative services. The parish was the basis of administration of such matters as poor relief; church courts functioned alongside secular courts for the administration of justice and the maintenance of social order; and, of great importance in an age of compulsory church attendance and lacking the modern mass media of communication, the pulpit served the Crown as a direct organ for political propaganda. The wishes and dictates of the sovereign could be communicated rapidly and effectively to a large proportion of the populace through the parish network. As Heylyn said, for example, when Queen Elizabeth 'had any business to bring about amongst the people, she used to *tune the pulpits*, as her saying was; that is to say, to have some preachers in and about London, and other great auditories in the kingdom, ready at her command to cry up her design'.[25] King James' Book of Sports was ordered to be read in all churches, causing problems for Puritan ministers who viewed its recommendations as sacrilegious.[26] Ironically, the church which had been plundered for revenue by the Crown was gradually perceived to be an important bureaucratic apparatus aiding monarchical administration

---

[23] Cf. Hill, *Economic Problems of the Church*; and the references in n. 17, above.

[24] See particularly Paul Seaver, *The Puritan Lectureships: The Politics of Religious Dissent, 1560–1662* (Stanford: Stanford University Press, 1970).

[25] Quoted in ibid., p. 58.

[26] See the reprint, as reissued by Charles I, in H. Gee and W.J. Hardy, *Documents Illustrative of English Church History* (London: Macmillan and Co., 1896), pp. 528–32, for its deliberately offensive attitude towards 'Puritans and Precisians' (p. 530).

and the maintenance of the social order. Contemporaries tended to agree with the assertion of Sir John Eliot that 'Religion it is that keeps the subject in obedience', however much they might disagree over the right form of religion.[27] Under James I, the contradictory and self-defeating long-term consequences of further reducing the wealth and status of the church for immediate economic gain were recognised, and a more positive policy of economic support began, starting with the legislation of 1604 forbidding bishops to alienate further lands to the Crown. By the time of Charles I's reign, the intimate relationship between Crown and church was consolidated, as high churchmen came again to occupy important political posts and to have an influential voice in secular affairs of state.[28]

The ambiguous position of the church in matters relating to finance and patronage was mirrored by theoretical ambiguities and tensions. As Claire Cross remarks, 'Elizabeth almost immediately after her accession came under attack on two fronts, from clerics of very different beliefs concerned for the autonomy of the church, and from laymen eager for a voice in deciding upon church policy.'[29] The fact of the lay supremacy of the church posed a number of questions which, arising in relation to quite practical issues of policy and control, were the subject of continual and unresolved debate in late Tudor and early Stuart England. If a lay person was head – or supreme governor – of a church, the doctrine and ritual of which had been established by Act of Parliament, then why should not laymen in general participate more fully in affairs of church government? But, on the other hand, the church's realm was that of things spiritual, and the first allegiance of churchmen must be to God; God's commands could only be adequately understood by the trained interpreters of the Scriptures; hence should not the affairs of the church be determined by those belonging to a separate, spiritual order? Varieties of erastian and clericalist position proliferated in the decades following the Reformation, and, in their political implications at both national and local levels, were to be of consequence for the fortunes of Puritanism in England.

The Lutheran state church in Prussia found itself in an even more ambiguous position than the post-Reformation Church of England. Failing to conserve its wealth in the manner of the church in Württemberg, the church in Prussia was, like the English church, economically weak and dependent; but its political position was considerably more compli-

[27] Quoted in H.R. Trevor-Roper, *Archbishop Laud, 1573–1645* (London: Macmillan, 2nd edn, 1962), p. 5.
[28] This development can in fact be traced back to late Elizabethan times; it was not entirely new.
[29] Claire Cross, *The Royal Supremacy in the Elizabethan Church* (London: George Allen and Unwin, 1969), p. 18.

cated than that of either of the other two state churches. For a start, the Hohenzollern rulers had been, since 1613, of the Reformed religion; they retained the summepiscopacy of the church, but relinquished the *Jus Reformandi* to the Estates, allowing the established state church to remain Lutheran. In the composite state that formed late seventeenth- and eighteenth-century Brandenburg-Prussia, there were considerable pockets of other religious minorities, including relatively large Catholic populations as well as a number of immigrant sects. The rulers of Brandenburg-Prussia favoured, for a variety of personal, political, and economic reasons, a policy of religious toleration, and there were at times active plans for achieving a union of the Reformed and Lutheran faiths. The political status of the Lutheran church was insecure in another way too: linked with the regional Estates, it became part of the terrain on which the struggle between centralising state and local *Stände* was waged, as rulers sought to reduce the independence of the church and transform it into a functional arm of the central state apparatus. Tensions were inscribed in the very nature of the economic and political situation of the church in Prussia; and these tensions were reflected in the sociocultural role and status of its personnel. Altogether, the Lutheran state church of late seventeenth- and eighteenth-century Brandenburg-Prussia was in a very much weaker position than its contemporary counterpart in Württemberg.

The economic resources of the Prussian Lutheran church were much reduced with the secularisation of church properties, and the church found itself dependent on income from parishioners, from noble and municipal patrons, and from royal patronage.[30] Patronage, as in England, was a piece of private property assuming a variety of guises and associated with a variety of other rights, privileges, property, and income. Patronage was in no way tied to the religious faith of the patron: a Catholic could be patron of a Lutheran church and vice versa; the King, a Calvinist, had by virtue of his landed estates rights of patronage in a large number of Lutheran churches.[31] Sometimes patronage might be mixed, as when ruler and a town were co-patrons; sometimes the same pastor served different churches, under several different patrons. In practice, most pastors were dependent on local nobles: in the *Landtagsrecess* of 1653, the rights of the Prussian Junkers of church patronage had been explicitly confirmed as part of a package deal in recompense for financial contributions towards a standing army.[32] The income of pastors being in

---

[30] On the Prussian church, see particularly Georges Pariset, *L'État et les Églises en Prusse sous Frédéric-Guillaume 1er (1713–1740)* (Paris: Armand Colin et Cie, 1897); Otto Hintze, 'Die Epochen des evangelischen Kirchenregiments in Preussen', *Historische Zeitschrift* 97 (1906): 67–118.

[31] Pariset, *L'État et les Églises*, Book 3, ch. 5, section 2.

[32] Klaus Deppermann, 'Pietismus und moderne Staat' in K. Aland (ed.), *Pietismus und Moderne Welt* (Witten: Luther-Verlag, 1974), p. 77.

general inadequate, pastors might develop into a form of factotum for their patron and engage in a variety of unspiritual but remunerative pursuits in the locality. This was hardly conducive to good relations with the parishioners: as Pariset comments,

si le pasteur avait su se faire bien venir du patron, dont il devenait souvent l'homme à tout faire, les fidèles n'avaient aucun recours contre ses exactions. Il devenait pour sa paroisse un insupportable petit despote.[33]

Patrons also gained services of a more symbolic, but no less important, nature. They might obtain a place of honour in the church, an impressive tomb after their death, the family coat of arms on the church door, and, not least in significance, patrons might be mentioned in the public prayers in church. In such a context, the Lutheran doctrine of obedience to authority meant obedience to the local lord rather than to some far-distant and abstract notion of a nation-state.[34]

The economic dependence of the clergy was compounded by the low social status of the clerical profession. Pariset, in his study of church and state under Friedrich Wilhelm I, found that ninety-eight per cent of the Lutheran pastors he studied were of humble social origin. Only two per cent could boast the noble 'von', and even these were not from the 'feudal' landed nobility, having no landed estates or wealth in their possession. There were clerical dynasties, nearly a third of pastors being sons of pastors; one fifth were sons of very minor functionaries, teachers, or traders; and nearly a half were of unknown parentage, hence probably the sons of peasants or artisans never deemed worthy of mention in the sources which have survived.[35] Not a single pastor was the son of an army officer. The nobility in general disdained the clerical profession; and a career in the church was not even to be considered for the offspring of the socially aspiring.[36] All this is in stark contrast to the situation in Württemberg.

The church is an institution playing an important role in the political and social order, however, and the energetic Hohenzollern state-builders of the mid-seventeenth to mid-eighteenth centuries naturally set about

[33] 'If the pastor had been able to get in well with his patron, for whom he frequently became a factotum, the parishioners had no recourse against his extortions. For his parish he became an insupportable petty despot.' Pariset, *L'État et les Églises*, p. 303.
[34] As Bofinger and Carsten point out, Hintze and others have overestimated the role of the Reformation in strengthening the powers of princes; frequently it was the Estates who became the protectors and supporters of the state churches in the subsequent two centuries. See Carsten, *Princes and Parliaments*, p. 437; and Wilhelm Bofinger, 'Zur Rolle des Luthertums in der Geschichte des deutschen Ständeparlamentarismus', in H. Liebing and K. Scholder (eds.), *Geist und Geschichte der Reformation: Festgabe Hanns Rückert* (Berlin: Walter de Gruyter, 1966), pp. 398ff. See also Carl Hinrichs, *Preussentum und Pietismus* (Göttingen: Vandenhoek und Ruprecht, 1971), p. 179, p. 242.
[35] Pariset, *L'État et les Églises*, table on p. 258, and pp. 255ff. generally.
[36] Ibid., p. 260; Klaus Deppermann, *Der Hallesche Pietismus und der Preussische Staat unter Friedrich III. (I.)* (Göttingen: Vandenhoek und Ruprecht, 1961), pp. 9–10; Hinrichs, *Preussentum und Pietismus*, p. 179.

attempting to reform and harness it to their own advantage.[37] In 1648, the Great Elector introduced parity among the Lutheran, Reformed, and Catholic churches, and tolerance for dissenting sects. The consistories having administrative authority over the different churches in different territories of Brandenburg-Prussia were able to retain considerable independence in the seventeenth century (with variations: Lutherans, for example, supervised the Reformed churches of East Prussia). But from the 1690s onwards, there was a gradual centralisation and rationalisation of administration, with a corresponding subordination of church to state. From 1695, there was a *de facto* administering of spiritual affairs from the Privy Council in Berlin, initially by Paul von Fuchs. From the accession of Friedrich Wilhelm I in 1713, the Berlin Lutheran consistory started to interfere with the separate territorial consistories and to centralise administration, a development finally formalised legally by Friedrich II in 1750 when all consistories were officially subordinated to the Brandenburg Lutheran consistory. At the same time, since the 1690s the consistories had been becoming bureaucratic, executive organs of the Privy Council, having less independent importance. In 1730 the Spiritual Department, combined with the Judicial Department, was founded, and in 1738 it received independent status with the formation of the state's Ministry for Spiritual Affairs. At the local level, encroachments were simultaneously being made on the powers and privileges of private patrons. In 1701, when Friedrich crowned himself first King in Prussia, he introduced a measure requiring even pastors under noble patronage to be ratified by the consistorium under his control.[38] The Crown thus gained a political advantage at the expense of the nobility, which was to be of some importance for the subsequent history of Pietism in the area. Friedrich Wilhelm I made a series of further attempts to restrict and redefine the powers of patrons, reducing their rights largely to duties. In practice, many of his proposed reforms could be effected only in churches under royal patronage, since state inspectors could do little to enforce the execution of edicts in areas where noble patrons had great local power. One reform which did achieve some success was that concerning public prayers for authorities: a uniform prayer was introduced, naming only official state functionaries, and it was forbidden to mention by name any particular local persons in the public prayers.[39] By the time of the Russian occupation of East Prussia in 1758–62, pastors were sending 'dringende Fragen... für welchen Landesherrn nun in den Kirchen gebetet werden

---

[37] See R.A. Dorwart, *The Administrative Reforms of Frederick William I of Prussia* (Cambridge, Mass.: Harvard University Press, 1953); Dorwart, 'Church Organization in Brandenburg-Prussia from the Reformation to 1740', *Harvard Theological Review* 31 (4) (1938): 275–90; Hintze, 'Epochen'.

[38] Walter Hubatsch, *Geschichte der evangelischen Kirche Ostpreussens* (Göttingen: Vandenhoek und Ruprecht, 1968), vol. 1, p. 174.

[39] Pariset, *L'État et les Églises*, p. 428; see also pp. 407–10.

sollte, für den preussischen oder für den russischen...'.[40] Rulers also
weakened the church institutionally, as in the case of removing effective
powers of excommunication from the Lutheran church in Brandenburg by
forbidding insistence on private confession before receipt of the sacraments.[41] The Hohenzollerns did not scruple to take ample advantage of
their argument that *Kirchenhoheit* was an attribute of *Staatshoheit* and
that the political rulers had supreme powers of intervention in the interests
of the good of the state.

Briefly, we may summarise the positions of the three Protestant state
churches in the table below. It is evident that the structural locations of the
established state churches in England and Prussia rendered them essentially politically contested territory, with different strains and tensions in
each case; whereas the church in Württemberg enjoyed a far more
autonomous position, having only its own interests to consider and being
less of a battleground for different groups with differing conceptions of the
social order.

Church	England	Württemberg	Prussia
Economic basis	Weak Divided patronage: crown, laity, church	Strong Independent wealth and income	Weak Divided patronage: crown, laity, church
Status of clergy	Rising status, frequently economically dependent	High status, economically independent	Low status, economically dependent
Political links	Constitutional and political links with Crown; but lay interventions and ambiguities	Constitutionally and socially allied with Estates as independent partner	Theoretically linked with ruler; in practice allied to regional Estates and local nobles

The church and toleration

Their different structural locations affected the different ways in which
the state churches of England, Württemberg and Prussia responded to
their respective movements for religious reform; and their different
responses in turn conditioned the different patterns of politicisation of
the Puritan and Pietist movements. The church in Württemberg had the

---

[40] 'Urgent questions ... concerning which ruler should now be prayed for in the churches,
the Prussian or the Russian...' Quoted in Albert Nietzki, *D. Johann Jakob Quandt.
Generalsuperintendent von Preussen und Oberhofprediger in Königsberg 1686–1772*
(Königsberg: Kommissionsverlag Ferd. Beyers Buchhandlung, 1905; Schriften der Synodalkommission für Ostpreussische Kirchengeschichte, Heft 3), p. 104.

[41] See Helmut Obst, *Der Berliner Beichtstuhlstreit* (Witten: Luther-Verlag, 1972).

greatest freedom of movement in terms of determining its response to the challenges from within; whereas the churches in England and Prussia were rather more constrained by external pressures, since in both these cases the state and the laity had a high degree of participation in the affairs of the church. Let us look at the more complicated cases first.

The relation of Puritanism to the wider state church in England was ambivalent and changing. Since Puritanism arose out of the attempt to achieve completion of what was seen initially as only a temporary religious settlement, Puritanism was in many ways constitutive of the very nature of the Church of England at its formation, and it is necessary to be sensitive to this fact when discussing the responses of 'orthodoxy' or 'the established church' to its Puritan wing.[42] Nevertheless, Puritan attempts at reform were never entirely successful, and while at certain times, under certain conditions, Puritan non-conformity within the church was tolerated, at other times active attempts were made to stamp out Puritan attitudes and activities and to impose a more rigid uniformity.

Given the dependent situation of the Church of England as an institution, the hierarchy was much constrained by the wishes and policies of the ruler. Thus while many individuals of Puritan sympathies may at various times have attained high office in the church, they were limited in their freedom of action to effect policies in line with their personal inclinations. These limits on freedom of action were at times quite crudely explicit: Grindal, Archbishop of Canterbury, was suspended for his refusal to obey the Queen's order for suppression of prophesyings; Curteys, Bishop of Chichester, was suspended and eventually deprived for his overzealous activities in Sussex.[43] In other cases the limits were subtler: with their humble social origins and need for economic support, many bishops were only too willing to toe whatever official line was in favour in the hope of preferment. Agents of the Crown, and dependent on the Crown, they were willing to act in the interests of the Crown in the localities in a way which feudal barons had not.[44] And perhaps most importantly in the long run, the very composition of the higher ranks of the church hierarchy was not an arbitrary affair. The monarch of course listened to the advances of patrons, but ultimately the choice was the Crown's; and it was noticeable, for example, that as Elizabeth's reign proceeded, the first generation of reforming bishops was replaced by more conservative men in line with the inclinations of the Queen. Similarly, under Charles I, the Laudians were able rapidly to take over the

---

[42] Cf. the discussion of the concept of 'Puritanism', above, Chapter 2. The same problem also exists of course for the two Pietist cases.

[43] See, for example, Patrick Collinson, *The Elizabethan Puritan Movement* (London: Jonathan Cape, 1967), pp. 159–207 on Grindal and prophesyings; and R.B. Manning, *Religion and Society in Elizabethan Sussex* (Leicester: Leicester University Press, 1969), on the fate of Curteys.

[44] Cf. Trevor-Roper, *Laud*, pp. 150–1.

higher echelons of the church apparatus by virtue of central government favour.

What then were the interests of the state church in relation to Puritanism? Because of the direct links between church and state, any demands for religious reform were considered in terms of their social and political implications. Thus the Queen, at the close of the Parliamentary session of 1585, declared that she would not 'tolerate new-fangledness' or its proponents: 'And of the latter, I must pronounce them dangerous to a kingly rule: to have every man, according to his own censure, to make a doom of the validity and privity of his prince's government, with a common veil and cover of God's word, whose followers must not be judged but by a private man's exposition.'[45] The Archbishop of York, Matthew Hutton, a tolerant man sympathetic to the ethical and pastoral concerns of Puritans, made a similar point in a letter of October 1603 to the Archbishop of Canterbury concerning the more radical Presbyterians: 'They that so much magnify the government of the presbyteries, like better of a popular state than of a monarchy... Therefore the King's majesty, as he is a passing wise King, and the best learned prince in Europe, had need to take heed, how he receiveth into his kingdom such a popular government ecclesiastical as is that of the presbyterie.'[46] This concern with the political implications of specific religious practices and policies was evident at every stage in the development of English Puritanism in its relations with the church hierarchy and official policies.

It became clear at a very early point, in the debate of the 1560s over vestments. Ostensibly a relatively trivial question of 'adiaphora', or things indifferent to salvation, the refusal to wear a surplice – a garment redolent of the Catholic faith – became seen as a political gesture of disobedience to the commands of the secular ruler.[47] As such, it could not – at least where enforcement was feasible – be tolerated. Similarly, the hierarchy's responses to the Puritan concern with preaching depended to a large extent on the political implications of such preaching in any particular set of circumstances. In 1584, just after the death of Grindal, who had been suspended for his refusal to suppress prophesyings in the south, a completely different official policy was being adopted in north-west England. There, where Catholicism was the major political-religious problem faced by the London regime, exercises and prophesyings were officially approved, in which Puritan ministers could act as moderators with disciplinary powers. Exercises, stamped out in the

---

[45] Quoted in Collinson, *Elizabethan Puritan Movement*, p. 286.
[46] Quoted in S.B. Babbage, *Puritanism and Richard Bancroft* (London: S.P.C.K., 1962), p. 58.
[47] Cf. Collinson, *Elizabethan Puritan Movement*, Part 2; M.M. Knappen, *Tudor Puritanism* (Chicago and London: University of Chicago Press, 1939), ch. 10; H.C. Porter, *Reformation and Reaction in Tudor Cambridge* (Cambridge: Cambridge University Press, 1958), ch. 6.

south in the 1590s, were not seriously attacked in the north until the 1630s and survived in some places until the outbreak of the Civil War.[48] It suited the government to ensure that the energies of Puritan preachers were expended in evangelising the 'dark corners of the land', and where Catholicism posed the greater political problem, Puritanism could be harnessed and indeed encouraged. Conversely, however, when Puritan activities appeared the greater threat to political stability, a stronger line was required. In the 1560s and '70s, with the initial need of the Elizabethan regime to establish itself, some ambiguity was possible; but from the 1570s onwards, and particularly in the 1580s and '90s, it was Puritanism which at least in the south-east of the country appeared potentially more subversive of government. This was especially the case when the threat from international Catholicism appeared somewhat reduced after the defeat of the Spanish Armada.[49] A movement capable of developing a separate presbyterian form of organisation, irrespective of the policies of Parliament or Convocation, and capable of maintaining secret printing presses for propaganda warfare, culminating most notoriously in the Marprelate tracts – such a movement was evidently a danger and subversive of both state and church; such a movement must evidently be suppressed. Suppression of Puritanism became the task of Whitgift and Bancroft, with the aid of the High Commission, in the 1580s and '90s.

But the ambiguities in the relations between the established church and its Puritan wing remained. In the localities, Puritan ministers continued to receive the protection of powerful lay patrons, as well as to enjoy the toleration of certain well-disposed, or lazy, individual bishops: the church was by no means consistently or effectively anti-Puritan, even when circumstances favoured delimited anti-Puritan campaigns of the sort led by Whitgift. And at the centre of government, too, the policies of the church were determined in no simple manner: at least until the 1590s, Puritans had powerful sponsors at court and in the Privy Council. It was the latter that pressurised Whitgift into compromising over subscription to his Articles of 1584, for example; and men such as Essex, Walsingham, even Cecil, were able to influence the Queen favourably towards Puritans in certain respects or particular cases. There was also a continuing problem of detection and enforcement of any anti-Puritan policy. Churchwardens – particularly if the opinions of the congregation were in line with those of the minister – were unwilling to present for nonconformity, and thus many Puritan ministers succeeded in evading detection

---

[48] Christopher Haigh, *Reformation and Resistance in Tudor Lancashire* (Cambridge: Cambridge University Press, 1975), pp. 301ff.; R.C. Richardson, *Puritanism in North-West England* (Manchester: University of Manchester Press, 1972), ch. 1, and pp. 65–7.

[49] Cf. Patrick McGrath, *Papists and Puritans under Elizabeth I* (London: Blandford Press, 1967).

for such matters as not wearing a surplice; indeed, many Puritan ministers may never have appeared in the visitation records at all.[50] And in
the late 1600s and 1610s, after the initial crisis of the introduction of
new church canons in 1604, there was little serious attempt to impose
effective uniformity at all, until the rise of the Laudians. There was also
a continuing ambiguity in the relations between clergy and laity, such
that while the clericalist implications of presbyterianism might ultimately have run contrary to the interests of the lay governing classes,
the latter were far more aware of, and opposed to, the social and
political pretensions of bishops. This first became a real problem in the
1590s, and flared up again with force in the 1630s.

These developments will be examined in greater detail in the following chapter. But it is worth briefly making one more point here, concerning toleration in the English church. The late 1620s and '30s, when
the so-called Arminians took over key positions in the church, are a
crucial period in the formation of opposition to the regime of Charles I.
Arminianism has recently been interpreted as the 'really revolutionary'
movement in early Stuart England, while Puritanism is cast in the role
of conservative reaction and counter-revolution.[51] Be this as it may, the
possible differences of theological opinion are far less important in the
present context than the political implications of the Laudian takeover.
In a country where church and state were so closely linked, and in a
period when the King was attempting to develop the apparatus of prerogative rule and the centralisation of power, then the use of the church
in an attempt to impose a new uniformity, the use of bishops as agents
of central government, and the attempts to restore to the church its
pre-Reformation wealth and power, together represented integral
aspects of a developing absolutism. The theoretical and religious elevation of the bishops, and the re-introduction of Catholic forms of ritual
and ceremonial, were not merely aspects of a theological position but
rather were elements of a total political programme of change. And it
was their political and social implications that determined much of the
response.

For the moment, it is enough if the point has been made that, in
England, it was impossible to separate the implications of policies in the
church from those of the state, and that actions in relation to the one

---

[50] Cf. e.g.: R.A. Marchant, *The Puritans and the Church Courts in the Diocese of York,
1560–1642* (London: Longmans, Green and Co., 1960), p. 182; Ogbu Kalu, 'Bishops
and Puritans in Early Jacobean England: A Perspective on Methodology', *Church
History* 45 (4) (1976): 469–89; Kalu, 'Continuity in Change: Bishops of London and
Religious Dissent in Early Stuart England', *Journal of British Studies* 18 (1) (1978): 28–
45; M. Spufford, *Contrasting Communities: English Villagers in the Sixteenth and
Seventeenth Centuries* (Cambridge: Cambridge University Press, 1974), pp. 265–70.
[51] N. Tyacke, 'Puritanism, Arminianism, and Counter-Revolution' in Conrad Russell (ed.),
The Origins of the English Civil War (London: Macmillan, 1973).

inevitably affected the other. The ways in which the ambivalent tolerance and opposition of the church towards Puritanism affected the political development of the latter will form the subject of Chapter 5.

The orthodox church in Brandenburg-Prussia was in general less ambivalent towards its reformist wing: it was actively hostile. It could be said that there were three main sets of sociological (as opposed to theological) reasons why this was the case, all fundamentally arising out of the weak, dependent position of the church. One set of reasons had to do with social fears: fears of lower-class movements with chiliastic beliefs and levelling tendencies. Another set was related to this, but was professionally more specific: fears concerning the status and institutional power of the clergy and the trained teachers of orthodox Lutheranism. The third set of reasons arose out of the dependence of the established church on local noble patrons: where the interests of the latter conflicted with the activities of Pietists, orthodox pastors were limited in their freedom of action and were unlikely to contradict the wishes of their patrons.

The social fears, concerning the development of lower-class radical sects with egalitarian conceptions of the priesthood of all believers, were similar to the social fears of the governing classes in England and Württemberg about popular disorders and chiliastic sects. Again, there were ironies in the situation: while orthodoxy in Prussia was concerned about political and social disruptions arising from the spread of Pietism among the lower ranks of society, the Pietist leaders themselves were centrally concerned with the immoralities of the people and the failure of the established church to control the lifestyles and morals of the people through an effective Christian discipline. The Pietists, like Puritans, wanted better observance of the Sabbath, stricter measures against conduct such as swearing, drunkenness, sexual offences; and they felt that the established church was in practice condoning popular immorality by the lifeless church services, the incomprehensible and ornate sermons, the emphasis on receipt of salvation through outward rites and ceremonies mechanically performed in the physical context of the institutional church. A central part of the impetus lying behind Pietism was the desire to make living Christianity a real force for the transformation of the way of life of the masses. Yet, of course, there were differences in the way the message was received and interpreted by the followers of Pietism: refracted through the experiences of lower-class life, an egalitarianism and an increased sense of self-confidence and freedom to act in unrestrained and anti-authoritarian ways might be an unintended consequence among the chiliastic groups inspired by the Pietist message. It was these consequences which aroused the fears and distaste of the established church.

The initially hostile reaction to Francke on his arrival in Brandenburg-Prussia was not without foundation. Francke had been forced to leave Leipzig, in the electorate of Saxony, and then Erfurt, under the governance of Mainz, because of the social implications of his activities. The Dresden inquisition into Francke's activities in Leipzig, for example, had been concerned that he was having discussions with common people, preaching in fields, and that he was reputed to have called a linen weaver a 'brother in Christ'; what effects would such notions of spiritual brotherhood with the lower ranks have on the maintenance of the social hierarchy![52] In Erfurt, the main opponent of the Pietists among the town ministry complained that 'sich unter-schiedene Leute ... von Leipzig und andern Orten eingefunden, die unter den Schein der Gottseligkeit falsche Lehren verbreiten und allerlei Zusammenkünfte bei Tag und nächtlicher Zeit veranstalten'.[53] One suspects that the gatherings by night of the assorted people caused as much concern as the supposed falsity of the teachings. Even gatherings of the common citizens of Leipzig on a Sunday afternoon for edificatory discussions in their own houses aroused the concern of the Elector of Saxony, who felt that the very existence of conventicles was a threat to social order and the peace of the church.[54] It is hardly surprising that Francke should receive a cool reception on his arrival at Halle, geographically so close to Leipzig and the scenes of previous troubles.[55]

Such social fears were not based merely on the evidence of past experience and trouble elsewhere, however. The development of Pietism in Königsberg, for example, far over into eastern Europe well away from Saxony, soon revealed a similar pattern of problems, including the radicalisation of the followers of Pietism. The activities of the latter, dissociated from the teachings of the leaders, were soon sufficient to provoke the concern of the secular authorities as well as the orthodox pastors. By 1707, the *Magistrat* of Königsberg was backing up the complaints of the consistory and clergy about the activities of the Pietist Lysius, who encouraged his audiences, 'die doch nur aus lauter einfältigen schlechten Bürgers- und Handwerksleuten bestänen', to open up and explicate texts of the Bible 'gleich den heutigen Quäckern, Mennoniten, Enthusiasten und andern phantastischen Irrgeistern'.[56] The split between the teach-

---

[52] See Erich Beyreuther, *August Hermann Francke 1663–1727: Zeuge des Lebendigen Gottes* (Marburg an der Lahn: Verlag der Francke-Buchhandlung, 1956), pp. 68–71.

[53] 'Various people... from Leipzig and other places had come together, who under the appearance of godliness spread false doctrines and arrange all sorts of gatherings by day or at night-time.' Gustav Kramer, *August Hermann Francke: Ein Lebensbild* (Halle: Verlag der Buchhandlung des Waisenhauses, Part 1, 1880), p. 75.

[54] Ibid., p. 52.

[55] Cf. also E. Selbmann, 'Die Gesellschaftlichen Erscheinungsformen des Pietismus Hallischer Prägung' in *450 Jahre Martin-Luther-Universität Halle-Wittenberg*, vol. 2 (Halle-Wittenberg: Selbstverlag der Martin-Luther-Universität Halle-Wittenberg, 1952).

[56] 'Who after all only consisted of nothing but simple poor townspeople and artisans'; 'like

ings of the leaders and their reception and translation into practice by followers continued to be evident twenty to thirty years later: while neither Rogall nor Schultz, now the leaders of 'official' Pietism, propounded chiliastic teachings, belief in ecstatic revelations, perfectionism, or the belief that a sinless state could be achieved here and now, nevertheless the Pietist movement in Königsberg indulged in its own form of 'Schwärmerei'.[57]

These fears of the levelling tendencies of a movement which, in however unintended a fashion, helped to emancipate individuals from hierarchical bonds by emphasising the individuality of spiritual experience, the direct relationship of man to God, the priesthood of all believers, were heightened in Brandenburg-Prussia by being overlaid with professional fears on the part of the clergy. As we have seen, the Lutheran church in Prussia was in a weak position socially and politically, and had to defend itself against any threat to its institutional power and professional status. Pietism constituted in several ways such a threat. Most immediately, Pietism implied not only that the institutional church was not the only source of grace or salvation, but even that salvation might not be obtainable at all from the services of the institutional church. Pietists in Königsberg appeared to be accusing orthodoxy of keeping the people in sin, because it was impossible to be converted by outward ceremonies alone, lacking an internal understanding and a genuine experience of conversion to a new life.[58] The clergy in Königsberg complained that Lysius, an early Pietist leader, was accusing orthodoxy

als richteten sie ihre Predigt so ein dass das Volk in dem Wahn behalten werde, es könne kein Mensch from werden, es könne keiner von seiner bösen wegen abstehen, sondern jeder müsse bleiben wie er sey und fortfahren in der Sünde wie vorhin ... Sie führten die Leute nur auf äusserlichen Ceremonien und an den Gottesdienst ... Sie verkauften Taufe, Abendmahl, Absolution, trieben Wucher und Schacherey mit den Geheimnissen Gottes ... Die Beichte das Kirchengehen das Abendmahl führt er als Einrichtungen an, die wohl geschehen und gebraucht werden könnten denn man aber auch entbehren könnte, so dass keine grosse Gefahr dabey zu besorgen. Er ruft dabey die prediger als Babilonier und als gottloser Leute aus, umb derer willen der Zorn Gottes über das Land gekommen...[59]

the contemporary Quakers, Mennonites, Enthusiasts and other fanciful mistaken souls'. Walther Borrmann, *Das Eindringen des Pietismus in die ostpreussische Landeskirche* (Königsberg i. Pr.: Kommissionsverlag Ferd. Beyers Buchhandlung Thomas und Oppermann, 1913; Schriften der Synodalkommission für Ostpreussische Kirchengeschichte, Heft 15), p. 69.

[57] See Nietzki, *Quandt*, pp. 77–8.
[58] Ibid., p. 29; Borrmann, *Eindringen des Pietismus*, p. 75.
[59] 'As though they ordered their preaching such that people would be kept in error, that no-one could become pious, no-one could give up his bad ways, but rather everyone must stay as he was and continue in sin as before... They were said to direct people only to external ceremonies and to the public service.... They were said to sell baptism, communion, absolution, to be profiteering and haggling with the secrets of God,... Confession, going to church, communion, he alleges to be arrangements that could be

In Halle, Francke was certainly quite explicit in his 1698 sermon about 'false prophets', 'wolves in sheep's clothing', in identifying as false prophets 'vornehmlich die *vorgewandte Orthodoxie*, oder reine Lehre', professing only the letter, not the spirit, of the law.[60] The false prophets of orthodoxy, according to Francke, by their stress only on purity of doctrine and not on a total conversion of life, allow the people to take the broad path to damnation. Salvation could only be obtained by a genuine spiritual experience, not available from the sermons and ceremonies of orthodox pastors who were themselves unconverted. Francke's preaching may have had little initial impact on the disorderly lower classes of Glaucha, who preferred the less demanding religion of the orthodox churches in neighbouring Halle, but in Königsberg at any rate the effect was to empty the established churches of much of their previous audience. Widely advertised through the anti-Pietist polemics of orthodox sermons, the Pietist alternative services soon gained huge attendances, as people flocked to hear the Pietist message either out of curiosity or from a genuine concern about the best means of attaining salvation.

Fears about retaining their audiences were compounded by orthodoxy's fears for the professional and institutional status of the church. The Berlin controversy of the 1690s, concerning the question of whether there should be a choice between private or general confession before communion, provoked such public disorder that a special investigative commission with a final decision by the ruler was necessitated. By the latter's finding in favour of the Pietist position proposing freedom of choice, the institutional monopoly of orthodoxy was weakened; and this consideration was a major factor in the motivation of orthodoxy's position, impelled by the 'Furcht ... vor einem Machtverlust bei Aufhebung der Privatbeichte'.[61] In Königsberg, the clergy feared a loss of professional status as the rise of 'unberuffenen Winckelprediger' decreased status differences between clergy and laity. Gehr, who started the Pietist school and church in the late 1690s, was trained neither as pastor nor as teacher; yet by his activities he was depriving 'real' teachers of their rightful income. Pastors who were prepared to be taken in by untrained upstarts were prostituting their status and rank, as Hofprediger Wegner complained:

Ordinierte Prediger prostituiren ihr Ampt, wenn sie sich oft und vorsetzlich in die Versammlung derer unberuffenen Winckelprediger einfinden. Bekand ist es, dass

---

well done and well used, but that could also be dispensed with, without any great danger. At the same time he proclaims the preachers to be Babylonians and godless people, for whose sake God's wrath has come over the land...' Nietzki, *Quandt*, p. 29.

[60] Sermon reprinted in Erhard Peschke (ed.), *August Hermann Francke: Werke in Auswahl* (Evangelische Verlagsanstalt Berlin: Luther-Verlag, 1969), pp. 305–35; quotation is from p. 310.

[61] 'Fear... of a loss of power with the giving up of private confession.' Obst, *Beichtstuhl-streit*, p. 77.

die Winckelprediger weil sie mit dem geistlichen Priestertum grob schwanger gehen, den Unterschied der Lehrer und Hörer, wo nicht genzlich auffheben, doch zum wenigstens auf gut quäckerisch einschränken wollen. Wenn nun ordinierte Prediger zu den Winckelpredigern sich begeben, sie loben und admiriren, begeben sie sich tatsächlich ihres Cantzels und Altars, werden aus Lehrern Zuhörer, verkauffen ihre Reverend und kleiden in dieselbe Leinweber und Schuster ein, worüber die Winckelprediger sehr mögen ins Fäustche lachen ...[62]

And even so sympathetic a proponent of orthodoxy as Löscher, more than prepared to try to reach agreement with Pietists and achieve some form of reconciliation within the church, was concerned that the Pietist emphasis on experience would dissolve the theological unity of the church and further weaken its position against the external threats of enlightenment and other ideologies.[63]

Not least in importance in determining orthodoxy's response to Pietism in Brandenburg-Prussia were the constraints imposed by dependence on local patrons. The latter were frequently inclined to oppose the Pietist programme for economic and political reasons. For example, with the major school- and church-building programme supported by Friedrich Wilhelm I, as part of his cultural colonisation of East Prussia, landowners found they had to make heavy financial contributions to particular local projects. Less directly, they found that Pietist educational endeavours even without the benefit of adequate material surroundings were detrimental to their interests: for, if landowners released their agricultural labourers for catechism and Bible lessons, they lost valuable working time; and, perhaps more serious, once labourers had been confirmed and received Holy Communion, they were socially counted as 'adults' and had to be paid adult wage rates accordingly. As one pastor, responding to directives for improvement of religious education, reported in 1736:

Es sind viele Erwachsene von 20 bis 24 Jahre alt, die noch nicht zum Abendmahl gewesen, welche selten oder garnicht zur Präparation kommen. Die Herrschaften schicken sie nicht zum Pfarrer, denn das Geheimnis dahinter steckt, dass kein Knecht eher Knechtslohn erhält, ehe er zum hl. Abendmahl kommt. Deswegen lassen sie die Jugend erst etliche 20 Jahr aufwachsen und dann mag der Prediger sehen, was er ihnen beibringt.[64]

---

[62] 'Ordained preachers prostitute their office, if they often and purposefully turn up at the gatherings of these unqualified back-street preachers. It is known that the back-street preachers, because they are grossly full of notions of spiritual priesthood, even if they do not quite dissolve the distinction between teacher and audience, nevertheless in good Quaker fashion they at least want to limit it. Now if ordained preachers go to the back-street preachers, praise and admire them, then in fact they renounce their pulpit and altar, turn into listeners rather than teachers, sell their reverence and appear just like the linen weavers and cobblers, about which the back-street preachers must have a good laugh behind their backs...' Borrmann, *Eindringen des Pietismus*, p. 28.

[63] Martin Greschat, *Zwischen Tradition und neuem Anfang. Valentin Ernst Löscher und der Ausgang der Lutherischen Orthodoxie* (Witten: Luther-Verlag, 1971).

[64] 'There are many adults of 20 to 24 years old, not yet having been to Communion, who seldom or never come to the preparation. Their masters do not send them to the pastor,

One can well imagine that a poor pastor, himself ill-educated and eking out his miserable income by acting as factotum for his patron, would make little effort to overcome such powerful obstacles to Pietist activity. Politically, too, local nobles were threatened by Pietism, particularly after the state had started to take a strong hand in its development. The pillars of local government objected to outside commissions with extraordinary powers stepping in to transform the nature of local arrangements.[65] Patrons objected to the limiting of their patronage rights after the introduction in 1730 of the requirement for Pietist testimonials even to obtain positions under private patronage.[66] Nor were they pleased by the measures to centralise political authority, through the use of the church, initiated by the state but largely effected through the medium of Pietist pastors, and expressed in such measures as changing the 'authorities' to whom obedience was due and who were to be mentioned in public prayers.

As in England, there were of course ambiguities, tensions, and exceptions in the responses of orthodoxy to precisionism. And, as over time the Pietist movement entered into a closer relationship with the state and in many respects gained support from the state, it became itself gradually institutionalised as the new orthodoxy. Such developments make it difficult to distil and compress the complex movements of history into a few clear and simple positions, a few well-defined characterisations. Nevertheless, an overall comparison would suggest that the social pressures and constraints in the Prussian situation were such as to render the established church in general hostile towards the Pietist movement and, where conditioned by interests of groups outside the institutional framework of the church itself, to pressure the church into supporting the local patrons on which it was economically and politically dependent against the innovations implied by Pietism.

Social and political considerations operated very differently in Württemberg. Here, where the church enjoyed considerable independence and high social status, it was less seriously threatened by any movements for reform. Furthermore, many of those arguing for reform, and criticising existing church practices, were of high social standing. Where the Pietists were themselves clergy, the members of the church hierarchy dealing with errant pastors were not, as in England, constrained by the wishes of the ruler and perceived needs of the state; nor were they under obliga-

and the secret behind this is, that no servant or farm-hand receives a servant's wages until he has been to Holy Communion. For this reason they let the young people grow up for some twenty years, and then the preacher may see what he can impart to them.' Quoted in Nietzki, *Quandt*, p. 55; see also Erich Riedesel, *Pietismus und Orthodoxie in Ostpreussen* (Königsberg und Berlin: Ost-Europa-Verlag, 1937), pp. 132–3.

[65] Cf. Pariset, *L'État et les Églises*, Book 4, ch. 3, section 4.
[66] Cf. Riedesel, *Pietismus und Orthodoxie*, p. 57.

tions to powerful local lay patrons, as in Prussia. This meant that the debate over Pietism in Württemberg was very much less fraught and overlaid with political pressures and external considerations than were similar controversies in England and Prussia. Social considerations and questions of moral codes and political authority of course entered into and affected the response of the church to Pietism in Württemberg; but because of the more independent position of the established church, the pressures put on the Pietists were of a more subdued, indirect nature, which was to have important consequences for the different pattern of political development.

Spener had visited Württemberg in 1662, when he had made friends and contacts among Württemberg theologians, who followed with interest the later developments of his ideas and the organisation of conventicles. The leaders of the Württemberg church themselves then took a new interest in the indigenous reforming tradition of Johann Valentin Andreae, and in the 1680s and '90s a number of measures of reform along Spener's lines were introduced in the Württemberg church. In 1681, catechetical teaching was established; there were measures to improve church discipline, the quality of preaching, the education of pastors, particularly on the practical side, and much emphasis was laid on 'studium pietatis'.[67] Some measures took longer to be accepted. Confirmation, for example, proposed by Hochstetter in 1692, by Hedinger in 1701, by Pfaff in 1719, was only finally agreed by the Duke in 1721 and put into practice in 1723.[68]

The reception of Pietism in Württemberg was not without some ambivalence on the part of authorities, however; particularly since, as elsewhere, there were more radical implications to the ways in which the Pietist message might be refracted through the experiences of lower-class groups. The controversies ensuing from later publication of Tübinger Kanzler Müller's 1692 attack on Pietism gave rise to the 1694 edict requiring theologians to refrain from polemics; the growth of lay separatist groups and of separatist tendencies among theological students and pastors in the 1690s and 1700s demanded further measures. Inter-

---

[67] See: Martin Brecht, 'Philipp Jakob Spener und die Württembergische Kirche' in Liebing and Scholder (eds.), *Geist und Geschichte*; Heinrich Fausel, 'Von Altlutherischer Orthodoxie zum Frühpietismus in Württemberg', *Zeitschrift für Württembergische Landesgeschichte* 24 (1965): 309–28; Heinrich Hermelink, *Geschichte der Evangelischen Kirche in Württemberg von der Reformation bis zur Gegenwart* (Stuttgart und Tübingen: Rainer Wunderlich Verlag Hermann Leins, 1949); Christoph Kolb, 'Die Anfänge des Pietismus und Separatismus in Württemberg', *Württembergische Vierteljahresheft für Landesgeschichte* 9 (1900): 33–93, 368–412; 10 (1901): 201–51, 364–88; 11 (1902): 43–78; Martin Leube, *Tübinger Stift*; Hartmut Lehmann, *Pietismus und Weltliche Ordnung in Württemberg vom 17. bis zum 20. Jahrhundert* (Stuttgart: W. Kohlhammer Verlag, 1969).

[68] F. Fritz, 'Die evangelische Kirche Württembergs im Zeitalter des Pietismus', Part 2, *Blätter für Württembergische Kirchengeschichte* 56 (1956): 99–167; Hermelink, *Geschichte der Evangelischen Kirche*, p. 181; Kolb, 'Anfänge des Pietismus'.

estingly, while the social implications of separatist groups in Württemberg might in principle be similar to those in Prussia, the reactions of the church authorities were far more conciliatory and tolerant in the former state. This tolerance already had roots in Württemberg traditions: in 1657, for example, Anna Bechthold, wife of a *Weingärtner*, on having ecstatic revelations was simply treated as medically ill and requiring the help of a doctor.[69] When in 1702 and 1703 the *Weingärtner* of Tübingen became interested in having further instruction and religious education from *Repetenten* of the *Tübinger Stift*, the investigators decided that while private gatherings in the fields or in citizens' houses were unwise, such spontaneous interest and desire for reform on the part of the lower orders was in general a good thing which should be carefully nurtured under the supervision of the church.[70] The wild behaviour of a separatist group in Stuttgart led to imprisonment of some members in 1710, and certain pastors elsewhere were at various times deprived of their positions. Nevertheless, the measures concerning Pietism and separatism of 1704, 1706, 1707, 1711 and 1715 were on the whole tolerant in tone, even if limited in scope. Orthodox Lutherans such as Jäger – who still had a high opinion of Spener – were particularly concerned to set limits to what could be allowed, in the interests of preserving the purity of doctrine of the Lutheran church.[71] But supporters of Pietism such as the Hochstetters were far more interested in combating what they saw as '*Im*pietisten', and not with undue restraint of those genuinely seeking after religious edification and a deeper Christian awareness, however much this search might lead to mistaken opinions along the way. The ambivalence, tending towards toleration, evidenced in the reaction of church authorities to the growth of Pietist groups in Württemberg was even more marked when the social status of a separatist group was high, and the religious conventicle did not imply at the same time a sociopolitical threat. This was the case, most importantly, in relation to the separatist Pietist group at Calw, which was investigated in 1713.[72] Calw was a major manufacturing and trading centre in Württemberg, and it turned out that the leading Pietists were powerful and wealthy members of the *Calwer Compagnie* itself, who had been influenced by Pietist literature brought back from trading expeditions in north Germany. These upper-middle-class entrepreneurs were upset by the poor state of

---

[69] F. Fritz, 'Konsistorium und Synodus in Württemberg am Vorabend der pietistischen Zeit', *Blätter für Württembergische Kirchengeschichte* 39 (1935): 100–31, pp. 129–30.
[70] Leube, *Tübinger Stift*, pp. 266–8.
[71] Cf. Kolb, 'Anfänge des Pietismus'; F. Fritz, 'Konventikel in Württemberg von der Reformationszeit bis zum Edikt von 1743', *Blätter für Württembergische Kirchengeschichte* 49 (1949): 99–154; 50 (1950): 65–121; 51 (1951): 78–137; 52 (1952): 28–65; 53 (1953): 82–130; 54 (1954): 75–119; Lehmann, *Pietismus und Weltliche Ordnung*.
[72] Cf. Hermelink, *Geschichte der Evangelischen Kirche*; Lehmann, *Pietismus und Weltliche Ordnung*, and Lehmann, 'Pietismus und Wirtschaft in Calw am Anfang des 18. Jahrhunderts', *Zeitschrift für Württembergische Landesgeschichte* 31 (1972): 249–77.

affairs in the local church, and drew attention to the inadequacy of the services of the institutional church by their withdrawal from it. The official investigators sympathised with the Pietists' attitudes and concerns, and were hence prepared to see separatism in this case as a 'nützliches Übel', helping the church in diagnosis and reform of its deficiencies. The intervention of Jäger with the Duke blocked the positive measures of toleration envisaged in the Pietist edict of 1715. Nevertheless, Pietism was in this general climate able to gain in practice a niche within the established church, both through the respectability and security of influential members of the church hierarchy itself and through the *de facto* acceptance of Pietist conventicles under the supervision of pastors and within certain limits. Despite some setbacks, particularly under the brief rule of Duke Karl Alexander, the gradual toleration of innerchurchly Pietism was finally formalised in the *Pietistenreskript* of 1743. By 1776, one of the main arguments against a Pietist gathering that lasted well into the night was that having so many people in a confined space constituted a fire risk.[73] This was far removed from English and Prussian assumptions about the potential dangers inherent in conventicles.

It can only be suggested that this unique degree of tolerance in Württemberg – the only German state to pass a measure explicitly permitting the special gatherings of Pietists – was possible because of the particular sociopolitical configuration and specifically the structural location of the established state church. In a strong political position, the church did not perceive reformist pressures as a threat to its institutional status, as in Prussia; nor were differences of opinion over *adiaphora*, 'things indifferent', to be construed as political gestures of rebellion, as they were in England. Uniquely independent, the church in Württemberg could afford to expand the limits of the differences which could be tolerated within the broad confines of a latitudinarian church. By the mid-eighteenth century, after the joint activities of representatives of the Enlightenment (Bilfinger) and Pietism (Moser) had achieved institutional toleration of Pietist activities, it became an accepted strand or orientation within the broad, official, church.

Such were the different modes of reception and toleration or otherwise experienced by earnest, pietistic or puritanical members of the state churches in England, Württemberg, and Prussia, at the times when the rulers of these states were incipiently attempting to develop the apparatus of absolutist rule. We are now in a position to look in more detail at the different patterns of development of the three religious movements, as the political attitudes, alliances and activities of the Puritans and Pietists were shaped and formed in the contexts of their times.

[73] Christoph Kolb, 'Strenge Handhabung des Edikts von 1743', *Blätter für Württembergische Kirchengeschichte* 6 (1902): 90–2. (There were also fears of the social disturbances that might be occasioned by the gathering.)

5

From reform to revolution: Puritanism in England

English Puritanism was not an inherently revolutionary movement. At no time prior to 1640 did Puritans develop any coherent doctrine of revolution. And Puritanism was not simply a 'class' ideology, carried by some 'rising class' seeking to attain more power for itself. Puritans were those ardent Protestant members of the Church of England who wished, in a variety of ways, to further the process of reformation and purge the church of Catholic survivals. At certain periods, some Puritans were politically active and organised; at other times, many Puritans represented a more passive piety, earnestly going about their local business seeking to live according to the Word of the Lord as revealed in the scriptures. But by the 1630s, Puritanism had become politically salient; and by the early 1640s it played a key role in the opposition to attempted Stuart absolutism. This chapter will seek to reinterpret the development of Puritanism, from a movement for religious reform to one of revolution, in terms of the peculiar configuration of state, church, and society in late Tudor and early Stuart England.

Puritanism and the Elizabethan Reformation

The Elizabethan religious settlement of 1559 was less the reflection of a positive set of religious policies than the ambiguous result of political compromise.[1] For committed Protestants, returning from the heady days of religious experiment while exiled on the continent, such a settlement could hardly be considered as final. In Collinson's summary:

A reformed doctrinal confession had been grafted on to a Church which had renounced the Roman obedience (but preserved, within the limits imposed by the act of supremacy, a Catholic ministry and order), and which was bound by the act of uniformity to the use of a liturgy which was essentially Catholic, although accommodated in some places to Protestant doctrines.[2]

Many thought that this was merely an interim arrangement, pending

---

[1] J.E. Neale, *Elizabeth I and her Parliaments*, vol. 1 (London: Jonathan Cape, 1953), Part 1, chs. 2 and 3; Neale, 'The Elizabethan Acts of Supremacy and Uniformity', *English Historical Review* 65 (1950): 304–32. Elton, in his 1978 Neale Lecture, comments that recent research has suggested no forcing of the pace in 1559 by the Commons.

[2] Patrick Collinson, 'John Field and Elizabethan Puritanism' in S. Bindoff et al. (eds.), *Elizabethan Government and Society: Essays presented to Sir John Neale* (London: Athlone Press, 1961), pp. 127–8. See also G.R. Elton, *The Tudor Constitution* (Cambridge: Cambridge University Press, 1960), documents 184 and 195.

further alteration. Those who became known as Puritans believed that the Elizabethan church, as established in 1559, possessed the essentials of a true Protestant church, but was open to considerable improvement.

The belief that Elizabeth would be amenable to further reform was soon dissipated. The first major controversy – and that which gave rise to the widespread use of the epithet 'Puritan' – was over vestments. The Act of Uniformity provided that 'such ornaments of the church and of the ministers thereof shall be retained and be in use as was in the Church of England by authority of Parliament in the second year of the reign of King Edward the Sixth until other order shall be therein taken by the authority of the Queen's Majesty...'.[3] Ministers who found what they considered to be the 'Pope's attire' repugnant generally thought that this provision was temporary and would not be insisted on in practice. It was generally agreed, however, that vestments were *adiaphora*, matters indifferent to salvation, and therefore within the province of the secular ruler to decide. Elizabeth's first bench of bishops were generally committed to reform, and sympathetic to Puritan scruples about wearing the surplice; but, as officials of Elizabeth's state church, they held it best to obey the prince over a matter indifferent. Some of the more radical clergy, however, could not stomach such a position, and attempted instead to make fine distinctions between things truly indifferent, and things not quite so indifferent. Robert Crowley, discussing the 'Outwarde Apparell and Ministring Garmentes of the Popishe Church', argued that:

Wee graunt, that of themselves, they be things indifferent, and may be used or not used, as occasion shall serve: but when the use of them will destroy, or not edifie, then ceasse they to be so indifferent ... If the using of the outwarde and ministring garmets of the popes church, cannot now edifie the church of Christ, then doe they ceasse to be so indifferent that we may use them.

Crowley summarised the position of many when he concluded that now was not the time to obey the secular ruler on these matters:

Lest we shoulde therfore encourage the obstinate and blinde Papistes to sticke still in their popishe puddle: lest we should beat back those that are by oure cryinge unto them begynning to craule out of that puddle: lest we should shake off and hurle headlong into that puddle, those that are by our meanes plucked out thereof, and yet not so freed from the filth thereof, but that they have neede to be made cleane by our helpe, and stayed from slyding in againe: yea and lest we shoulde make sorowfull and pyerce the heartes of them, that be quite escaped, when they should see us by whose meanes they have escaped, bewadled in the same filth our selves: and so bring al that we have taught into doubt, and all that we shall teache into suspicion, we have thought it meete for us, utterly to refuse all those thinges that now are urged.[4]

---

[3] Elton, *Tudor Constitution*, p. 403.

[4] Robert Crowley, *A Briefe Discourse against the Outwarde Apparell and Ministring Garmentes of the Popishe Church* (n.p.: 1566), no pagination. See also Antony Gilby, *A Pleasaunt Dialogue... betweene a Souldier of Barwick, and an English Chaplain...*

For the ruler, however, there were other considerations. At a time when Elizabeth was attempting to establish her authority among both Catholic and Protestant subjects at home, and to avoid antagonising any major powers abroad, it was important to retain a certain conservative ambiguity in church affairs. Furthermore, there were questions of constitutional significance involved: should the clergy, the laity, Parliament, or the secular head of state have ultimate power to determine ecclesiastical affairs? Elizabeth was certain that the ruler should retain control of the state church, and she blocked attempts to introduce measures of religious reform in the Parliament of 1566. But at the same time, she did not wish to lay open her own person to criticism by ardent Protestants; thus Archbishop Parker had to publish his 'Advertisements' concerning vestments on his own authority alone. Elizabeth was an astute politician, and it was important also that fundamental constitutional questions concerning authority in ecclesiastical policy were disguised behind an apparently trivial debate over the wearing of vestments. For the less committed of Elizabeth's subjects, scruples over the surplice must have seemed a quite irrelevant and superficial affair.[5]

The 'vestiarian controversy' aroused considerable debate, particularly in London and the universities, but there was no clear resolution, either theoretical or practical. The continental reformers whom Puritans had consulted advised conformity as a matter of expediency at this time, but many found that their consciences would not allow this. Conformity was in any case not easily achieved in many areas. In London, where bishops had a reasonable degree of control, many ministers were forced to conform despite strong pressures from their congregations to make a stand on this point. In Cambridge, troubles provoked by refusals to wear a surplice rumbled on for a couple of years or more after the initial protests of Longworth and Fulke at St John's in 1565. In north-western areas of England, nonconformity over vestments was generally overlooked by ecclesiastical authorities, in the interest of promoting Puritan energies against the worse problem of Catholicism. And in Kent, shortage of clergy effectively undermined attempts at achieving conformity.[6]

(1581). Patrick Collinson, *The Elizabethan Puritan Movement* (London: Jonathan Cape, 1967), pp. 92–7, stresses the importance of lay pressures on ministers not to conform, in contrast to Walzer's clericalist interpretation.

[5] Neale, *Elizabeth I and her Parliaments*, vol. 1, Part 3, ch. 3; Collinson, *Elizabethan Puritan Movement*, Part 2; M.M. Knappen, *Tudor Puritanism* (Chicago: University of Chicago Press, 1939), ch. 10; Claire Cross, *The Royal Supremacy in the Elizabethan Church* (London: George Allen and Unwin, 1969), p. 74.

[6] Collinson, *Elizabethan Puritan Movement*; H.C. Porter, *Reformation and Reaction in Tudor Cambridge* (Cambridge: Cambridge University Press, 1958), Part 2, ch. 6; Christopher Haigh, *Reformation and Resistance in Tudor Lancashire* (Cambridge: Cambridge University Press, 1975), p. 300; R.C. Richardson, *Puritanism in North-West England* (Manchester: University of Manchester Press, 1972); Peter Clark, *English Provincial Society from the Reformation to the Revolution: Religion, Politics and Society in Kent, 1500–1640* (Sussex: Harvester Press, 1977), p. 163.

Over succeeding decades, this problem continued unresolved. In the late seventeenth century, Baxter commented about his scruples over vestments as a young man in the 1630s: 'The surplice I more doubted of; but more inclined to think it lawful; and though I purposed, while I doubted, to forbear it till necessity lay upon me, yet could I not have justified the forsaking of my ministry for it (though I never wore it to this day).'[7] Conformity in the state church was evidently not attained; but it also became clear, in the course of the initial controversy, that further reform of the church was not going to be so easily achieved as had at first been assumed. The Puritan solution at this early stage was to combine passive resistance with a determination to change the nature of the religious settlement.

By the 1570s, a new note was entering Puritanism. It began to become clear to some ardent Protestants that what was required was a fundamental reconstruction of the English church. Reform of ceremonial should take second place to reform of church polity. In 1570 the Lady Margaret Professor of Divinity at Cambridge University, Thomas Cartwright, delivered a series of lectures on the Acts of the Apostles. In these lectures, Cartwright expounded what he considered to be the scriptural justification for a presbyterian form of church government. Cartwright's ideas were not in themselves new; what was new was that they were given the authority of a university teacher at a time favourable to their reception. Cartwright himself had to leave for Geneva; but following the Queen's obstruction of parliamentary measures for religious reform in 1571, Field and Wilcox produced the *Admonition to Parliament* in the course of the Parliament of 1572, putting the case for a presbyterian organisation of the church. This occasioned a lengthy public dispute between Whitgift and Cartwright over state and church government. In the following years, the presbyterian movement gained strength, as a more radical Puritanism began to be dissociated from the earlier, milder reforming tradition. At the same time, the earlier united front with reform-minded bishops was dissolving, as bishops increasingly became conservative agents of the Crown. Out of the inconclusive and inchoate Elizabethan settlement, distinct and firmly held positions were beginning to emerge.[8]

The presbyterian movement might never have gained momentum had it not been for the ruler's blocking of more moderate measures for reform.

---

[7] Richard Baxter, *Autobiography*, ed. J.M.L. Thomas (London: J.M. Dent and Sons Ltd, 1931, abridged from the 1696 *Reliquiae Baxterianae*), p. 17.

[8] Collinson, *Elizabethan Puritan Movement*; A.F. Scott Pearson, *Church and State: Political Aspects of Sixteenth-Century Puritanism* (Cambridge: Cambridge University Press, 1928); Pearson, *Thomas Cartwright and Elizabethan Puritanism 1535–1603* (Cambridge: Cambridge University Press, 1925); Porter, *Reformation and Reaction*, chs. 7 and 8; W.H. Frere and C.E. Douglas, *Puritan Manifestoes* (London: S.P.C.K., 1954); J.E. Neale, 'Parliament and the Articles of Religion, 1571', *English Historical Review* 67 (1952): 510–21.

Underlying all Puritan activities was the concern to achieve an adequate, preaching ministry, capable of bringing the means of salvation, the Word of the Lord, to all who heard. This concern was shared by many high up in the ecclesiastical hierarchy; most notably, Elizabeth's reforming Archbishop, Edmund Grindal. Elizabeth might be insistent on her right to dictate church policy and to forbid Parliament to meddle in religious affairs; but many moderate Protestants saw a variety of non-parliamentary paths to improving the nature of the ministry. One such means was the practice of 'exercises', or 'prophesyings', in which ministers would meet together to preach, expound the scriptures, indulge in mutual criticism and exhortation. Archbishop Grindal, and many bishops, viewed this practice as a useful form of further education which should be encouraged. Even Grindal's more conservative predecessor, Parker, had at one time been in favour of prophesyings, and it is possible that he had initiated such activities in East Kent to help combat Catholicism. Bishop Curteys encouraged exercises in Sussex, and Bishop Parkhurst in Norwich similarly saw Puritans and the promotion of a preaching ministry as important in the fight against popery. Nevertheless, the Queen commanded Grindal to suppress the prophesyings. Grindal refused, arguing that exercises constituted 'the best means to increase knowledge in the simple and to continue it in the learned'. The Queen was not convinced by Grindal's suggestion that 'By preaching also due obedience to Christian princes and magistrates is planted in the hearts of subjects: for obedience proceedeth of conscience; conscience is grounded upon the word of God; the word of God worketh his effect by preaching. So as generally, where preaching wanteth, obedience faileth ... ' Grindal was suspended from duty, and the Queen made it clear that she did not favour Grindal's 'moderate courses' in her state church. It has been suggested by one expert historian that had Grindal's programme been carried out, there would have been 'little ground' for the continued existence of a Puritan party in England. As it was, Elizabeth appointed the virulently anti-Puritan Archbishop Whitgift as Grindal's successor.[9]

The delicate development of ardent Protestants into Puritans with doubts about the episcopal structure of the state church, through frustration at the obstacles put in the way of reform, is illustrated by the attitude of Edward Dering. Dering was representative of the Puritan tradition of Christ's College, Cambridge; and he had more of a practical concern with the abuses of ecclesiastical office than an explicit theoretical critique

[9] Knappen, *Tudor Puritanism*, pp. 251ff; Grindal quotations from reprinted documents in Elton, *Tudor Constitution*, p. 442, and Joel Hurstfield and Alan Smith, *Elizabethan People: State and Society* (London: Edward Arnold, 1972), p. 126; Collinson, *Elizabethan Puritan Movement*, Part 4; Clark, *English Provincial Society*, pp. 163–4; R.B. Manning, *Religion and Society in Elizabethan Sussex* (Leicester: Leicester University Press, 1969), chs. 4 and 10; Ralph Houlbrooke, *Church Courts and the People during the English Reformation 1520–1570* (Oxford: Oxford University Press, 1979), p. 255.

of the ecclesiastical polity *per se*. As Clark puts it, Dering's 'real significance was that he exemplified the increasing suspicion felt by more progressive, though not necessarily extreme, Protestants that the hierarchy was no longer on their side, that it was more interested in preserving its own status than in defeating Popery, ignorance and ecclesiastical abuse'.[10] The most frequently reprinted Elizabethan sermon was the one preached by Dering to the Queen on 25 February 1570. In this, he complained in outspoken terms of the state of Elizabeth's church:

I would first leade you to your Benefices, and behold some are defiled with impropriations, some with sequestrations, some loaden with pensions, some robbed of their commodities. And yet behold more abhominations than these. Looke after this upon your Patrons, and loe, some are selling their Benefices, some farming them, some keepe them for their children, some give them to Boyes, some to Servingmen, a very few seeke after learned Pastors. And yet you shall see more abhominations than these. Looke upon your Ministery, and there are some of one occupation, some of another: some shake Bucklers, some Ruffians, some Hawkers and Hunters, some Dicers and Corders, some blind guides, and can not see, some dumb dogs and will not barke. And yet a thousand more iniquities have now covered the Priesthood. And yet you in the meane while that all these whordoms are committed, you at whose hands God will require it, you sit still and are carelesse, let men doe as they list...[11]

The Queen was not amused, and Dering was eventually forbidden to preach, having to find other outlets for his religious energies. But his sense of outrage at the slowness of reform was shared by many, and in the course of the 1570s and '80s more practical steps were taken to try to transform the state church while circumventing the head of state.

Field, Wilcox, Cartwright, Travers and others set about establishing a presbyterian network of organisation within the episcopal state church. Parliamentary campaigns continued in the 1570s and '80s, to attempt to introduce reform by parliamentary means; but at the same time, reforms were being unofficially introduced, so far as possible within the bounds of law, at the local level. Ministers organised *classes* and conferences, meeting in small groups in their local area and coming together occasionally on a wider, regional basis. One early *classis* was the group who started meeting at Dedham, near Colchester, in October 1582. The minutes of meetings of this group from 1582 to 1589 reveal the concerns of the participants. Themes range from general religious education (reading of the scriptures, prayer, fasting), through discussion of particular questions (such as Sabbatarianism), to specific practical problems (what

---

[10] Clark, *English Provincial Society*, p. 165; see also Patrick Collinson, *Mirror of Elizabethan Puritanism: The Life and Letters of 'Godly Master Dering'* (London: Dr Williams's Trust, 1964); and Cross, *Royal Supremacy*, pp. 58–9.

[11] E. Dering, 'A Sermon preached before the Queenes Maiestie the 25. day of February...' in Dering, *WORKES More at large than ever hath heere-to-fore been printed in any one Volume* (London, 1597), p. 27.

to do if suspended for nonconformity, how to deal with difficult cases among parishioners). An interesting feature which emerges from this fascinating record is the continuing legalism of the Puritans' approach. On 5 October 1584, for example, when Mr Negus, who had been suspended by the Bishop from preaching, 'alleged the B[ishop] had proceeded with him against law, and therefore he thought he might preach agayne, it was said unto him, that he might aske advise of some wise and discreet lawyers tutching that point and if it be not against law then to proceed'. In 1586 the brethren debated

what might be done with the excommunications that were sent out: some said they might answere by a proctor ... Others thought bicause we were subiecte to their governmente in other thinges, they saw noe cause why they shuld not yeld in this except they shuld renounce the whole. Some thought it not safe to answer by a proctor, to let that be done by another which he wold not doe himself, so yt in thend it was concluded, that the advise of some Lawyer shuld be asked how farre law did bind us to it.[12]

Collinson, in his magisterial survey of Elizabethan Puritanism, suggests that the Dedham *classis* was, at least in 1582, 'precocious and unusual'. But by 1583 the Lewes exercise in Sussex, for example, had been re-organised as a presbyterian *classis*, and in the 1580s and '90s other *classes* developed elsewhere. Even if there was not the vast conspiracy postulated by the anti-Puritan Bishop Bancroft, henchman and later successor of Whitgift, there was a very real network of Puritan organisa-tion developing. This organisation was partly forged in the adversity of the years following the elevation of Whitgift to the position of Archbishop of Canterbury in September 1583.[13]

Whitgift began his primacy with an attempt to achieve in practice the uniformity and conformity in religion so desired by the Queen. In Octo-ber 1583 he issued his 'Three Articles' for subscription by ministers. The second article demanded total endorsement of the Prayer Book: 'That the Book of Common Prayer, and of ordering bishops, priests, and deacons, containeth nothing in it contrary to the Word of God. And that the same may be lawfully used; and that he himself will use the form of the said book prescribed, in public prayer and administration of the sacraments, and none other.'[14] It was not merely extremists and presbyterians who would be troubled by this demand: a majority of moderate Puritan clergymen would find it difficult to subscribe to Whitgift's formula. Prominent lay people were also opposed to Whitgift's move. Even the

[12] R.G. Usher (ed.), *The Presbyterian Movement in the Reign of Queen Elizabeth as illustrated by the Minute Book of the Dedham Classis 1582–1589* (London: Offices of the Royal Historical Society, 1905), p. 39, p. 65.
[13] Collinson, *Elizabethan Puritan Movement*, p. 232 and Part 4 generally; Manning, *Elizabethan Sussex*, ch. 10.
[14] Elton, *Tudor Constitution*, pp. 444–5.

Council opposed the Archbishop's lack of moderation and tolerance, and Whitgift was eventually forced to back down somewhat, requiring subscription only of those about to be ordained or admitted to livings. Some Puritans appear to have been restored unconditionally to their positions, particularly if protected by powerful patrons. As Richard Rogers later reported:

[The Archbishop] protested none of us should Preach without conformity and Subscription. I thanke God I have seen him eate his Words as Great and as Peremptory as he was. For after Thirty Weeks I was Restored by Dr. Aylmer, Bishop of London, to whome Sir Robert Wroth Writ in favour of me, and bad me Preach and he would beare me out, and so I have continued about 20 yeares to the end of Archbishop Whitgifts Life who deceased the first of March 1604.[15]

Nevertheless, although Whitgift retreated somewhat from his initial position, accepting only partial success on this point, he continued his campaign of harrying Puritans. (The presbyterian Field was upset at Whitgift's new moderation, since this tended to split the Puritans, isolating those who were more radical.) Whitgift's new weapon was the use of the twenty-four articles, or interrogatories, to be answered on *ex officio mero* oath, which effectively meant that the person interrogated was required to incriminate himself.[16]

The alliances of the Puritans were now broadening. Lay patrons in the localities continued to protect Puritan ministers; and at court and in Parliament there was considerable opposition to Whitgift's approach. Even Burghley wrote to the Archbishop complaining of the use of the *ex officio* oath: 'I think the Inquisitors of Spain use not so many questions to comprehend and to trap their preyes... According to my simple judgement, this kind of proceeding is too much savouring of the Romish Inquisition; and is rather a device to seek for offenders, than to reform any.'[17] At the same time, parliamentary campaigns continued to be mounted to try to change the nature of the laws. On 4 January 1585, the Minutes of the Dedham *classis* record that 'Mr. Dow moved this, whether it were not needfull that ther shuld (be) praier and fastinge agayne because of the assembly of parliament: yt was thought necessary and that the brethren of London shuld be written unto, to know when they appoint to have theirs, that we might ioigne with them, and that some shuld contynue to solicite the cause of the Churche there.'[18] According to Collinson, the Parliament of 1584–5 saw a 'political campaign without precedent in parliamentary history', as the Puritan press

---

[15] Richard Rogers in M.M. Knappen (ed.), *Two Tudor Puritan Diaries* (Chicago: American Society of Church History, 1933), p. 29.

[16] Collinson, 'John Field', pp. 150–1; Collinson, *Elizabethan Puritan Movement*, Part 5.

[17] Quoted in S.B. Babbage, *Puritanism and Richard Bancroft* (London: S.P.C.K., 1962), p. 19.

[18] Usher (ed.), *Presbyterian Movement*, p. 41.

poured out propaganda, numbers of lay Puritans were returned to Westminster, M.P.s were systematically lobbied by Puritans, and surveys were conducted to expose the sad condition of the ministry in the country. These surveys, finally completed for the Parliament of 1586, revealed the extent of incompetence and 'scandalous life' among the clergy, as named individuals were variously accused of such offences as being 'a very ridiculous preacher', 'a dicer, a carder, a pot companion, a company keeper of riotous persons, living very offensively to all men', 'by reason of ... age not able to preach nor distinctly to read, yet ... provideth none... to do good', and so on.[19] The complaints, now attached to specific persons and backed by supposedly hard evidence, echoed those of Dering's sermon to the Queen; and the refrain was to be reiterated again and again by Puritans in subsequent decades. In the 1584–5 Parliament, while pressure was applied in the form of petitions, Peter Turner's attempt to introduce a 'bill and book' (proposing establishment of the Genevan Prayer Book and a presbyterian polity) was diverted. The majority were in favour of moderate reforms of the church, which might be achieved by appeal to the ruler, rather than outright and immediate presbyterianism. But the Queen once again made it quite clear that she would not countenance the 'meddling' of Parliament in matters of religion, and that she intended the 1559 settlement, viewed by Puritans as temporary, to be permanent.[20]

The parliamentary campaign, led by the Puritan M.P.s Peter Wentworth and Anthony Cope, was continued in the Parliament of 1586. Cope's 'bill and book' was radical, to say the least: 'the bill containing a petition that it might be enacted that all laws now in force touching ecclesiastical government should be void'.[21] The Queen – one would have thought predictably, by now – firmly suppressed this initiative, and Wentworth and others were committed by the House to the Tower. It was not merely the contents of the proposals which offended the ruler; it was also the wider constitutional significance of the manner of parliamentary attempts to reform the state church. As Collinson comments:

Peter Wentworth took the floor ... in a celebrated defence of the imagined liberties of the House of Commons. In the rhetoric of his ringing, prophetic questions, Parliament was entrenched in the fundamental constitution of the country with prerogatives of its own, a deadly threat to the Tudor conception of kingship. On this showing, Elizabeth was more than justified in regarding puritanism as a more insidious enemy than popery.[22]

---

[19] Collinson, *Elizabethan Puritan Movement*, p. 273; Elton, *Tudor Constitution*, pp. 328–9.
[20] Neale, *Elizabeth I and her Parliaments*, vol. 2 (London: Jonathan Cape, 1957), Part 1, ch. 4.
[21] Elton, *Tudor Constitution*, p. 312.
[22] Collinson, *Elizabethan Puritan Movement*, p. 311; see also J.E. Neale, 'Peter Wentworth', *English Historical Review* 39 (1924): 36–54 and 175–205.

Committed Puritans could not be swayed from pursuit of their goals by the failure of the parliamentary path to the Holy Commonwealth. Field, Travers and others determined that a presbyterian organisation must be effected in practice, whatever the formal state of settlement of religion. Accordingly, a Book of Discipline, written by Travers with some assistance from Field and others, was sent out to the provinces to aid in the *de facto* reformation of the church. Puritan preaching and Puritan propaganda from the secret printing presses continued to pour forth, culminating, most notoriously, in the scurrilous Martin Marprelate tracts of 1588.[23]

It was the concerted opposition of the Queen and the Archbishop of Canterbury, aided by certain members of an increasingly conservative bench of bishops, which served to transform Puritanism in the 1580s into an organised, disciplined movement, with distinctive forms of political activity and a network of contacts united in service of a cause rather than a personal faction. It was also because of the tactics of the anti-Puritan campaign that Puritans now developed a new alliance, with lawyers, as well as gaining sympathy from more members of the lay governing classes. One aspect of the conservative ascendancy on the bench of bishops was the emergence – tentative at first – of a *iure divino* claim for episcopacy. This was intimated by Richard Bancroft in his St Paul's Cross sermon of 5 February 1589, and presaged the developments of the 1620s and '30s. (The 1590s also saw the rise of early Arminian opinions, equally foreshadowing developments under Charles I.) Simultaneously, there were increasing clashes over spheres of jurisdiction between the lay governors and the bishops in the localities. These developments served to blind the eyes of prominent members of the laity to the clericalism inherent in presbyterianism, and to render them sympathetic to the Puritans' critique of episcopacy. Puritanism began to become closely interrelated with local political struggles, as in the competition for places on the Commission of the Peace in Norfolk. Politically, Puritanism began to be associated with local opposition to prerogative rule. This was connected, too, with the developing alliance of Puritans with common lawyers. The use by Whitgift and Bancroft of the prerogative court of High Commission, with its use of the self-incriminating *ex officio* oath, helped to forge this alliance. Although these patterns of development should not be exaggerated, clear lines of affiliation were beginning to emerge. The way was in principle still open for different developments; but Puritanism was becoming firmly embedded as the religious orientation of sectors of English society in a wider manner than the early campaigns for reform of ceremonial had implied.[24]

---

[23] Collinson, *Elizabethan Puritan Movement*, and 'John Field'.
[24] Knappen, *Tudor Puritanism*, ch. 13; Cross, *Royal Supremacy*; Porter, *Reformation and Reaction*, chapters 11, 15, 17, 18; A. Hassell Smith, *County and Court: Government*

Reaction and retreat: Puritanism from the 1590s to the 1620s

In the late 1580s and '90s, through the efforts of Whitgift and Bancroft, the Puritan movement in the narrower sense was effectively extinguished. The search for the originators and printers of the Marprelate tracts led, not to the discovery of 'Martin', but at least to the discovery of the Book of Discipline and the covert presbyterian organisation. In the winter of 1589–90, scores of preachers were interrogated by the High Commission, and a number of individuals who refused the *ex officio* oath were sent for trial in Star Chamber. The proceedings were ultimately inconclusive, and the Puritans were eventually released without any martyrs having been made. But the Puritan movement, in the strong sense, had already been weakening and crumbling from within, as well as losing some of its most important support at court. A generation of great Puritan patrons and parliamentarians were coming to an end – Leicester died in 1588, his brother Warwick in 1590, Mildmay in 1589, Walsingham in 1590, the Earl of Bedford in 1585 – and Burghley found himself powerless to prevent the rise of the reactionary party of Hatton, Bancroft, Cosin, Sutcliffe and others at court. Puritans in the 1589 Parliament were on the defensive, and the presbyterian movement in the localities was weakening. Field had died in 1588, and the last presbyterian conference took place at St John's College, Cambridge, in September 1589. In the Parliament of 1593, Whitgift was able to turn a bill against recusants into one against Protestant sectaries.[25]

At the same time as the first generation of Puritans was passing – those who had direct experience of the 'best reformed churches' of the continent – changes were taking place in the character of the Church of England as established. New men who had no experience or little personal memory of the early days of the Elizabethan settlement did not perceive it as a temporary, impermanent and unstable compromise. In the decades following the Spanish Armada, the Church of England became closely identified with English nationalism, and began to be perceived as a positive arrangement with its own validity. At the accession of James I, according to Usher,

The Church, which the fathers had tolerated from political necessity, the sons supported because they approved of it as a religious institution and found comfort in its ministrations: the same force of tradition and habit which had prejudiced their sires against the Church biassed them in its favour, while round it

    and Politics in Norfolk, 1558–1603 (Oxford: Clarendon Press, 1974), ch. 10 and pp. 338ff; R.G. Usher, *The Rise and Fall of the High Commission* (Oxford: Clarendon Press, 1913), ch. 6; Babbage, *Richard Bancroft*, pp. 27–9; Ronald Marchant, *The Church under the Law* (Cambridge: Cambridge University Press, 1969), pp. 4–5.
[25] Collinson, *Elizabethan Puritan Movement*, Part 8; Porter, *Reformation and Reaction*, ch. 9; Usher, *High Commission*, ch. 6; Babbage, *Richard Bancroft*, ch. 1; Elton, *Tudor Constitution*, pp. 447–50.

came to circle that halo of splendour with which the awakening nationality and solidarity of the English people was beginning to invest Elizabeth's reign. To the Englishman of 1603 Catholicism reeked of the Spanish Inquisition: Calvinism was made in the image of Amsterdam, Geneva, or Charenton: Anglicanism alone was English, and the pent-up force of national pride, loosened by the victory of the Armada, began to contemplate its own church with satisfaction and even with complaisance.[26]

Whatever doubts we may have about identifying with any certainty the feelings of 'the Englishman of 1603', it is true that there were changes in the justifications of the English church at this time. No longer were official justifications couched in defensive terms referring to political authority and necessary compromise in imperfect conditions; rather, the Elizabethan settlement of the Church of England was given an explicit, positive evaluation. The first volumes of Hooker's *Laws of Ecclesiastical Polity* gave coherent expression to a self-confident conception of a definitively English form of church. In Cragg's opinion, Hooker provided the Church of England 'with a position strong enough to meet its rivals on equal terms ... Hitherto the Church of England had borne only too clearly the marks of a political expedient; at last it could appeal to a massive statement of fundamental religious principles.'[27]

Nevertheless, Puritanism in the wider sense was too firmly entrenched in civil society to be engulfed by a more self-confident establishment or to succumb to concerted attacks from the centre. In numerous areas, *classes* survived because of the failure of church courts to invoke effective sanctions. As Manning points out, the ecclesiastical machinery was 'too feeble to compel universal adherence to the established church'. Because of the decentralised nature of English local government, the Crown was heavily reliant on the co-operation of lay local governors. But, as Manning found in his study of religion and society in Elizabethan Sussex, 'in the case of Puritanism the government could not turn to the temporal magistrates to carry out the suppression of a movement which so many of the local governors actively patronized or at least sympathised with'. The dissolution of *classes* in the diocese of Peterborough in 1588–90 changed only the nature, but not the existence, of Puritan activity, which continued to grow in the area. In the diocese of York, particularly after the lenient Matthew Hutton took over from John Piers, 'men with moderate or radical Puritan views could usually escape with little more than a reprimand for their nonconformity, which was thought to be more than outweighed by their zeal in performing their pastoral duties'. All

[26] R.G. Usher, *The Reconstruction of the English Church* (New York: D. Appleton & Co., 1910), vol. 1, p. 287.
[27] G.R. Cragg, *Freedom and Authority* (Philadelphia: The Westminster Press, 1975), p. 97. See also H.R. McAdoo, *The Spirit of Anglicanism* (London: Adam and Charles Black, 1965), ch. 1; and H.J. Hillerbrand (ed.), *The Protestant Reformation* (London: Macmillan, 1968), pp. 267–90.

114 Piety and politics

over England, there continued to be earnest, pious individuals and groups, still concerned to achieve higher standards of morality and discipline, and a more adequate preaching ministry. Clerical nonconformity was frequently not reported by sympathetic churchwardens, or was protected by lay patrons, or overlooked by tolerant or incompetent authorities; while at the same time lectureships, private chaplaincies, and donative cures provided institutional means for evading certain regulations. This broader Puritanism, based as it was in the peculiarities of the economic and political location of the English state church, could not so easily be disturbed.[28]

Nor had hopes for a legislated reform of the state church been entirely given up, and when the Scottish Calvinist James succeeded Elizabeth as ruler there was renewed political activity among Puritans. A great campaign was mounted to petition the new King for reform, a campaign revealing considerable tactical skill on the part of Puritans: 'There must be sundrie petitions of Ministers of sundrie parts, and yet but a fewe in a petition to *avoyde the suspition of conspiracie*, and the petitions to varie in woords, but agree in the *desire* of reformation to be according to the woord, and all reformed Churches about us...'[29] The so-called Millenary Petition was presented on behalf of 'the ministers of the gospel in this land, neither as factious men affecting a popular parity in the Church, nor as schismatics aiming at the dissolution of the state ecclesiastical; but as the faithful servants of Christ, and loyal subjects...' The petition assured King James that the ministers desired 'not a disorderly innovation, but a due and godly reformation'.[30] The Puritan programme of 1603 was indeed relatively moderate in its proposals. The King agreed to a conference between representatives of the Puritans and certain bishops, which took place at Hampton Court in early 1604. There is some disagreement among recent historians concerning evaluations of this conference. According to Curtis, the King was by no means as opposed to the moderate Puritan proposals as had sometimes been supposed, and indeed was quite surprised at the mildness of the Puritan position. But it was left to the bishops to implement those reforms which had been agreed upon, and, not surprisingly, they failed to implement reforms to which they were opposed. According to Shriver, King James had an

[28] Manning, *Elizabethan Sussex*, p. 216, p. 217; William Sheils, 'Some Problems of Government in a New Diocese: the Bishop and the Puritans in the Diocese of Peterborough' in R. O'Day and F. Heal (eds.), *Continuity and Change: Personnel and Administration of the Church in England, 1500–1642* (Leicester: Leicester University Press, 1976), pp. 180–1; R.A. Marchant, *The Puritans and the Church Courts in the Diocese of York, 1560–1642* (London: Longmans, Green and Co., 1960), p. 24; and for insights into lay Puritanism, D.M. Meads (ed.), *Diary of Lady Margaret Hoby, 1599–1605* (London: George Routledge and Sons, 1930).

[29] Quoted in Babbage, *Richard Bancroft*, p. 49.

[30] J.P. Kenyon, *The Stuart Constitution, 1603–1688* (Cambridge: Cambridge University Press, 1966), p. 132, p. 134.

independent policy from the start, while determined to support episcopal institutions: 'On the puritan side, the best that can be said for the king is that he tried to treat them graciously while intending all the while to force them to submit.' Whatever the relative merits of these interpretations, the outcome is not in doubt. When Bancroft succeeded Whitgift as Archbishop of Canterbury, he instituted a new campaign to achieve uniformity, requiring subscription to the three articles of canon 36 of the 1604 church canons. The House of Commons viewed these canons with disapproval, and drew up a bill declaring key canons, including the one requiring subscription, invalid and void. A similar bill in the House of Lords received two readings before being stopped. James I, despite his relative lenience towards moderate Puritans, continued his predecessor's tradition of monarchical opposition to parliamentary meddling with affairs of religion, and insisted on conformity to the canons.[31]

Bancroft's campaign to achieve conformity probably resulted in not more than about ninety deprivations of nonconforming ministers, about one fifth of whom later conformed. Many bishops continued to be tolerant of those who had scruples of conscience. Hutton and his successor Matthew in York were both lenient towards Puritans, and Puritan preachers were able to consolidate their hold over the hearts and minds of large numbers of the laity. In Nottinghamshire, the ejected clergy of 1605 and 1606 appear to have enjoyed considerable freedom to continue preaching. Smyth and Robinson were even able to travel around advocating separatism, and in 1608 incumbents and churchwardens were still allowing separatists the use of the pulpit to expound their opinions. In Lancashire, when Bishop Vaughan attempted to impose the canons of 1604, the intervention of twelve Puritan Justices of the Peace ensured that in the end no clergy were deprived. In the diocese of Peterborough, leading Puritan gentry insisted that deprived ministers were not nonconformists; rather, the new canons were attempting to outlaw practices accepted for forty years. Lay patrons continued to support deprived ministers, refusing to fill supposedly vacant livings, or replacing deprived Puritans with a new batch of Puritans. The Bishop soon discovered that there were awkward social consequences if he was forced into a conflict with the leading gentry families of the area, and Puritan activities continued. Similarly in Kent, the Jacobean regime turned out to be not as oppressive in practice as had been feared in 1604.[32]

31 Mark Curtis, 'Hampton Court Conference and its Aftermath', *History* 46 (156) (1961): 1–16; Frederick Shriver, 'Hampton Court Re-visited: James I and the Puritans', *Journal of Ecclesiastical History* 33 (1982): 48–71, p. 70; see also Usher, *Reconstruction*, vol. 1, Book 2, ch. 2; Collinson, *Elizabethan Puritan Movement*, Part 8, ch. 5; Babbage, *Richard Bancroft*, ch. 3; Kenyon, *Stuart Constitution*, pp. 137–42 and pp. 134–7.
32 Ogbu Kalu, 'Bishops and Puritans in Early Jacobean England: A Perspective on Methodology', *Church History* 45 (4) (1976): 469–89; Babbage, *Richard Bancroft*, p. 217; Marchant, *Church under the Law*, pp. 132–3; Marchant, *Puritans and Church Courts,*

Despite the initial disappointment following the Hampton Court Conference and the 1604 canons, the early years of the seventeenth century were in fact a relatively fruitful period for English Puritanism. Many Puritans at this time found it preferable to continue preaching by conforming; others, as indicated, found it possible to evade being silenced despite nonconformity. The first two decades of the seventeenth century were the great period of Puritan preaching and theological elaboration, firmly implanting Puritan ethical, religious, and social concerns in the hearts and minds of wide sections of the laity. The 'spiritual brotherhood' of the 'physicians of the soul', whose strivings and passions William Haller has evoked, spoke to the condition of many men and women deeply concerned about the state of their souls. The Puritan experience of 'spiritual warfare' corresponded to the Puritan view of theology, as systematised by William Perkins, as 'the science of living blessedly for ever'. The Puritanism of this period was largely an inward-turning struggle, concerned with conscience and spirit rather than politics and structure. Richard Greenham, who had little success with his own recalcitrant parishioners at Dry Drayton, near Cambridge, emphasised the supreme importance of the battle for the soul: '... if then a good conscience helpeth all evils, and all other benefites in this life, in themselves cannot helpe a troubled conscience; we see it true in proofe, which here is in proverbe, *the spirit of a man will sustaine his infirmity: but a wounded spirit who can bear it?*'. Temporal penalties could be escaped; but the consequences of sinning against God were inescapable. The main focus of interest of Puritans, when they were free from harassment, was in the watchful leading of the godly life. The early Jacobean church put few serious practical obstacles in the way of these endeavours.[33]

This is not to suggest that attempts at further formal reformation had been entirely given up. While there was not the strong Puritan organisation of the 1570s and '80s, in diverse ways Puritans continued to press for changes, in alliance with other groups. Puritanism was one element in the common lawyers' attack on the powers and legality of the High Commission in the early years of James' reign. The flood of writs of prohibition issued by common lawyers, and the explicit attacks on the

pp. 145–7; C. Haigh, *Reformation and Resistance in Tudor Lancashire*, p. 304; Sheils, 'Problems of Government', pp. 171–2; Clark, *English Provincial Society*, pp. 304–6.

[33] William Haller, *The Rise of Puritanism* (Philadelphia: University of Pennsylvania Press, 1972 (orig. 1938)); Owen C. Watkins, *The Puritan Experience* (London: Routledge and Kegan Paul, 1972), ch. 1; M. Spufford, *Contrasting Communities: English Villagers in the Sixteenth and Seventeenth Centuries* (Cambridge: Cambridge University Press, 1974), pp. 327–8; Richard Greenham, 'The First Treatise for an afflicted Conscience...' in Greenham, *The Workes of the Reverend and Faithfull Servant of Iesus Christ...* (London: Printed for William Welby, 1612), p. 97; cf. also William Perkins, *A Golden Chaine: Or, the Description of Theologie, containing the Order of the Causes of Saluation and Damnation, according to God's Word* (Printed by John Legat, Printer to the Universitie of Cambridge, 1600).

High Commission led by Sir Edward Coke, involved a wide range of issues; but Puritans were participants in this attempt to delimit the activities of the prerogative court. Religion continued to be an issue in parliamentary grievances: in 1610, Parliament was prorogued without a resolution of James' pressing financial problems, partly because of disagreements over religion. The *Petition of Grievances* included complaints about the High Commission. The *Petition concerning Religion* complained that 'the laws are not executed against the priests, who are the corrupters of the people in religion and loyalty', while 'divers painful and learned pastors that have long travailed in the work of the ministry with good fruit and blessing of their labours' were prevented from performing their duties merely 'for not conforming in points of ceremonies, and refusing the subscription directed by the late canons'. Thus 'the whole people that want instruction are by this means punished, and through ignorance lie open to the seducements of Popish and ill-affected persons'. The petition complained also of the perennial ills of pluralism, nonresidence, and the misuses of excommunication, but to little practical effect.[34]

Archbishop Bancroft, who has been credited with the 'reconstruction of the English Church' in the first decade of the seventeenth century, died in late 1610. His successor was the moderate Abbot, whose sympathetic attitude towards the less radical Puritans helped to reduce tension in religious affairs. In general, Abbot continued his predecessor's policies in a rather passive manner, doing little either to innovate or to enforce uniformity in an energetic fashion. But while the moderation of the Archbishop defused any strong opposition, the interests of the ruler in a particular form of state church remained at odds with the conceptions of Puritans. Conflict was latent, rather than resolved. While James remained personally a committed Calvinist, supporting opposition to the Arminians at the Synod of Dort, there were many issues other than purely theological ones which separated the interests of the ruler from those of the Puritans. Considerations of the political contribution made by a state church to the running of secular affairs influenced James' 'Declaration of Sports' of 1618, which opposed the Puritans' conception of the Sabbath and argued that the prohibition of 'honest mirth or recreation ... barreth the common and meaner sort of people from using such exercises as may make their bodies more able for war, when we or our successors shall have occasion to use them, and in place thereof sets up filthy tippling and drunkenness, and breeds a number of idle and discontented speeches in their ale-houses'. And despite his own enjoyment of debate and dispute, James shared Elizabeth's concern with the possible consequences of

---

[34] Usher, *Presbyterian Movement* and *Reconstruction*; J.R. Tanner (ed.), *Constitutional Documents of the Reign of James I, 1603–1625* (Cambridge: Cambridge University Press, 1930), pp. 148–56, pp. 78–9.

preaching. His 'Directions to Preachers' of 1622 included admonitions to desist from delving into the 'deep points of predestination', or using the pulpit 'to declare, limit, or bound out, by way of positive doctrine, in any lecture or sermon the power, prerogative, and jurisdiction, authority, or duty of sovereign princes, or otherwise meddle with these matters of state and the differences betwixt princes and the people...'.[35] The point at issue has less to do with the personal beliefs or theological attitudes of any particular incumbent of the English throne than with the more general considerations concerning the political implications of a particular form of state church in England at this time.

The early Jacobean church escaped the turmoils and conflicts of the Elizabethan period largely because no very effective measures were taken to make use of the state church in a uniform fashion, and in practice a diversity of opinions and approaches found a relatively tolerant environment in which expression was possible. A certain latitudinarianism in reality meant that, although the ruler was hardly in complete control of the state church (and Puritanism was able to take firm root across the country), he yet did not have to contend with any strong, organised and aroused opposition. But this period of relative peace and diversity was not to last. From the later years of James' reign onwards, religious conflict began to increase, in a context of economic slump and depression combined with political problems. In the 1620s, the pressures of war transformed the nature of English politics, and with the rise of the so-called Arminian faction religious differences once again attained political salience. The complex developments of the 1620s and '30s were to eventuate – however far this may have been from any participants' intentions – in what has become known as the 'Puritan Revolution'.

Religion and absolutism: the politicisation of Puritanism

A strong refrain of the revisionist history of recent years has been to view the pre-revolutionary decades 'in perspective'. The conflicts and clearly opposed parties of the 1640s should not be read back into earlier years. Nevertheless, the 1620s and '30s saw the breakdown of parliamentary government in England, replaced by a period of personal rule. And associated with this political change was a change in the nature of the religious orthodoxy of the state church. It was the concurrence of these changes which helped to politicise Puritanism. The transformation of the state church, under the Arminians or Laudian faction, was not purely theological: it had considerable social, economic, and political implications. And these implications coincided very closely with other, secular,

---

[35] Tanner, *Constitutional Documents*, p. 55; Kenyon, *Stuart Constitution*, p. 146; cf. also Conrad Russell, *The Crisis of Parliaments: English History 1509–1660* (London: Oxford University Press, 1971), Part 5, ch. 3.

aspects of Charles' personal rule. The coincidence of Laud's concerted attempt to impose a certain sort of religious uniformity with simultaneous changes in other spheres of government ensured that, when the crisis erupted in 1640–2, Puritanism would fall on the Parliamentarian side. A much broadened Puritanism played a major role in parliamentary opposition to absolutist rule.

In picking out the key elements in the development of this configuration, it must not be assumed that there was a steadily rising crescendo of conflict. But whatever the ups and downs, twists and turns of the story, in relation to particular incidents and issues under particular circumstances, the overall profile is clear. In the course of the 1620s, the fact of England's financial and administrative weakness in the matter of pursuing an active foreign policy placed increasing strains on the relations between Crown and Parliament. This was already becoming clear towards the end of James' reign, but became particularly acute with the accession of the new King, Charles I, in 1625. Refusal to grant Charles tonnage and poundage for more than one year led to the ruler's having to raise this without the authority of Parliament. The Forced Loans and the Five Knights' Case increased the mistrust which was developing between Charles and some important members of his Commons. Mistrust may have been based in structural weaknesses, as those representing the localities and responsible for raising supply refused to meet the needs of the state for waging war, or indeed financing domestic activities; but this mistrust was exacerbated by problems of communication with the Crown, since Charles, unlike his loquacious father, was taciturn and reticent about giving reasons for his actions. Moreover, the ascendance of Buckingham and the emergence of only one dominant party at court reduced the accessibility of the Crown, such that opposition increasingly found that the only location in which it could make itself heard was Parliament. It may well be true that in the course of the 1620s there were no coherent, well-organised, clearly identifiable parties of 'government' and 'opposition'. But there were certainly continued clashes over issues of principle. Individuals may have shifted or modified their positions, but strains were emerging which, even if not clearly conceptualised by many, were threatening the tradition of co-operation between Crown and Parliament. In the Parliament of 1628, these strains began to have an impact on consciousness: the *Petition of Right* both created and reflected the increased concern of some M.P.s with the policies of the Crown. When Parliament was dissolved in 1629, many must have echoed Sir Benjamin Rudyerd's sentiment of 1628: 'This is the crisis of Parliaments: we shall know by this if Parliaments live or die . . .'[36]

---

[36] Quoted in Russell, *Crisis of Parliaments*, p. 299. See in more detail, Conrad Russell, *Parliaments and English Politics, 1621–1629* (Oxford: Clarendon Press, 1979); and K. Sharpe (ed.), *Faction and Parliament* (Oxford: Clarendon Press, 1978); Kenyon, *Stuart Constitution*, pp. 82–5.

At the same time as affairs of government were changing in nature, the nature of orthodoxy in the English Church was being transformed. In the early 1620s, the Puritan John Preston had been supported by Buckingham and had been chaplain to Prince Charles. But Preston was dropped in 1626; and from the early 1620s also the moderate Archbishop Abbot was beginning to be eclipsed at Court. From the mid-twenties, new religious orientations were given preferential treatment by the Crown. The new party were known as Arminians, after the Dutch Arminius. The basic theological tenet was a rejection of the Calvinist doctrine of predestination, although this was not sufficient to define those who actually became known as Arminians in the late 1620s and '30s. Nor was this theological idea as such new in England: similar ideas had been aired already in the Cambridge debates over Barrett, Baro, and others in the 1590s. More to the point, perhaps, was another aspect of the Arminian advance at this time – an aspect encapsulated in the much-quoted contemporary joke concerning the question of what the Arminians held. (The reply was, they held the best bishoprics and deaneries in England.) For there were many aspects of the rise of Arminians in the English Church which had crucial practical implications.[37]

Many strong Protestants in the 1620s and '30s were actually incensed by Arminian beliefs as such, and saw in them a Catholicising threat to Protestant orthodoxy in England. The House of Commons sub-committee for religion of February 1629 spoke of the 'subtle and pernicious spreading of the Arminian faction; whereby they have kindled such a fire of division in the very bowels of the State ... by casting doubt upon the religion professed and established, which ... will be rendered suspicious to unstable minds ... and incline them to Popery, to which those tenets, in their own nature, do prepare the way...'.[38] The fears that Arminianism opened the way to popery were reinforced in a number of ways. One straightforward fact which gave cause for thought was Charles' marriage to the Catholic Henrietta Maria, who particularly after the death of Buckingham had great influence over her husband. Catholicism was openly practised at Court, and papal agents were received in 1634 and 1636. The major ways in which the Arminian church appeared to be reverting to popery were however evident in parish churches all across the country. Arminians de-emphasised the role of preaching, and re-elevated the role of ceremonial and the sacraments. The campaign to achieve uniformity included numerous directives concerning the material

---

[37] Irvonwy Morgan, *Prince Charles's Puritan Chaplain* (London: George Allen and Unwin, 1957); N. Tyacke, 'Puritanism, Arminianism, and Counter-Revolution' in Conrad Russell (ed.), *The Origins of the English Civil War* (London: Macmillan, 1973); Porter, *Reformation and Reaction*, Part 3; H.R. Trevor-Roper, *Archbishop Laud, 1573–1645* (London: Macmillan, 1940).

[38] Kenyon, *Stuart Constitution*, p. 157.

context of worship, of which the most notable was the one concerning the communion table. This was to be removed from its position in the centre of the church, and railed in, altar-wise, at the eastern end. This in itself was redolent of popery; and it had further symbolic implications. It elevated the role of the clergy, from that of a pastor in the Protestant tradition to that of a priest acting as sole mediator between man and God. The clergy were to be elevated in other ways too: it was an integral part of the programme of the Laudian church to restore to its personnel the wealth and power of pre-Reformation times. Laud's religious concerns may in many ways have been quite puritanical in tone; but his practical policies for the church savoured of attempts to nullify the practical consequences of the Reformation.[39]

Conrad Russell has suggested that it was a mere 'coincidence' that Charles I chose to challenge prevailing religious opinion by favouring Arminians at the same time as he came into conflict with his Parliaments over policy and finances.[40] It is arguable whether or not it was 'coincidence' that Arminian ideas were available, and so eagerly picked up by members of the church, at this particular time. Having postulated that Puritanism cannot simply be reduced to specific class interests, it would be inconsistent to be less generous to the Arminians. Nevertheless, the ecclesiastical policies of the Arminians had quite specific consequences for the nature of personal rule as Charles' reign proceeded. Without wishing to make the functionalist suggestion that these beneficial consequences can explain the initial adoption of Arminianism, it would be foolish to overlook the practical implications of the Laudian church for Charles' attempt at prerogative rule.

In the first place, bishops were agents of the Crown, and many were of lowly social origins. Unlike the lay governing classes in the localities, they did not have high individual status in terms of family background, and they were not caught between the possibly conflicting pressures of 'country' and 'court'. For decades before the 1620s, members of the lay governing classes had found a certain harmonious tension in mediating between 'country' and 'court'; but after 1629 this mediation was endangered under the personal rule. For a great part of the 1630s local governors may have attempted to carry out Crown policies in the provinces; but they were subject also to local pressures and personal interests which conflicted in many ways with the policies of the Crown. Bishops, on the other hand, were in a rather different situation. They depended for power, wealth, and advancement, on the goodwill of the Crown. In a state which lacked a specialised state bureaucracy, the bishops were structurally best placed to act as royal officials. When royal policies also

---

[39] Trevor-Roper, *Laud*; Christopher Hill, *Economic Problems of the Church* (Oxford: Clarendon Press, 1956), ch. 14, partic. p. 337.
[40] Russell, *Origins*, p. 31.

included the elevation of clerical status, and in particular that of the episcopacy, members of the episcopal hierarchy had an added incentive to support, wholeheartedly, the programme of the Crown. The 1630s saw the return to high secular office of a number of ecclesiastical officials.

In the second place, the Laudian programme implied the eradication, or control, of potentially dangerous tendencies in religion as viewed from the perspective of the state. One of these tendencies was preaching; and, what was perhaps worse, uncontrolled democratic organisation within the church – bypassing the official authorities – for the promotion of a preaching ministry. In 1625 the Feoffees for Impropriations had been formed – an association of merchants, ministers, and lawyers – to buy up impropriations and advowsons and ensure that adequate preaching ministers filled vacant livings. Although only on a small scale, and not necessarily strictly 'Puritan' in aims, this operation was manifestly threatening to royal and episcopal control of the church. The Decree against the Feoffees, of February 1633, may have indulged in some exaggeration, but very real fears were voiced in the assertion that 'the proceedinge of the said Defendants was against the lawes and customes of the Realme and that they tended to the drawinge to themselues in tyme a principall dependencye of the whole Clergie of this Realme that should receive reward from them in such measure, and on such condiccions as they should fancye thereby introduceinge many novelties of dangerous consequence both to the Church and Common Weale, and were vsurpacions vppon his Majestys Regalitie ... '.[41] The Laudian church also made other attacks on 'Puritan' activities. In 1633 Charles reissued his father's 'Declaration of Sports', in direct conflict with the sabbatarian conceptions of Puritans. The activities of church courts, and the machinery for detection of offenders and nonconformists, were tightened up.[42] For the first time in decades, Puritans were under serious threat. Charles' drive for increased efficiency in local government was echoed in his state church. 'Thorough' may have been a vague term in an era when government policies were less than definite; but it conveyed the essential flavour of the personal rule in church and state. The 'coincidence' certainly seems to have produced a rather harmonious partnership in practice; and it is unlikely that Arminians would have been favoured for so long if it had been otherwise.

There were however considerable obstacles to the implementation of these policies. Just as the decentralised nature of English local government posed problems for Charles' attempt at ruling without the co-oper-

---

[41] I.M. Calder (ed.), *Activities of the Puritan Faction of the Church of England, 1625–1633* (London: S.P.C.K., 1957), p. 139.

[42] S.R. Gardiner (ed.), *The Constitutional Documents of the Puritan Revolution, 1625–1660* (Oxford: Clarendon Press, 3rd edn, pbk, 1979), pp. 99–103; and cf. Ogbu Kalu, 'Continuity in Change: Bishops of London and Religious Dissent in Early Stuart England', *Journal of British Studies* 18 (1) (1978): 28–45.

ation of local governors, so the peculiar structure of the English church aided resistance to attempts at the imposition of a stringent and unpopular uniformity in religion. The 1630s saw the radicalisation and broadening of Puritanism in England. This was true both of those who might strictly be called Puritans on religious grounds, and of those many moderate men and women who had previously considered themselves to be in the mainstream of English orthodoxy. The very term 'Puritan' now expanded its meaning; as Henry Parker later commented, 'they which are the Devils chief Artificers in abusing this word when they please, can so stretch and extend the same, that scarce any civill honest Protestant which is hearty and true to his religion can avoid the aspersion of it ...'.[43] The Laudian bishops' attempts to increase their control over religious affairs, in which the laity had played such an autonomous role for so long, and to impose a new form of conformity which was at odds with both the ideas and the interests of prominent members of the laity, could only produce opposition. The expansion and politicisation of Puritanism, in response to the pressures of the Arminian church, is repeatedly illustrated in local studies of the period. Arminian dominance destroyed the relative peace of the tolerant early Jacobean church.

In Durham, the Arminian Neile was Bishop from 1617 to 1627, and he and his followers, including John Cosin, were of humble social origins with large pretensions concerning the status of the clergy. Neile, in his dual capacity as prelate and as Lord Lieutenant of Durham, managed to antagonise 'powerful elements in the ruling class' by his temporal magistracy. Both dissident clergy and lay anti-clericals disliked the accumulation of offices and benefices of the Arminian clergy who were preferred. When Peter Smart attacked Cosin, his parliamentary allies in 1628 made it into a national case; but after the dissolution of Parliament, Smart was deprived by the York High Commission Court, fined, and imprisoned until the Long Parliament in 1640. Bishop Morton, who succeeded in retaining his bishopric from 1632 until the abolition of episcopy, tried to moderate the disputes; but as Lord Lieutenant and an agent of the Crown, Morton could only preside over increasing controversies between Arminians, Puritans, and anti-clerical lay magnates. By 1639–40, Puritans were pushed into political radicalism by the strength of Arminian opposition: Puritans 'were forced, as a result of their firm rejection by the dominant Church and political order, to make the

[43] Henry Parker, *A Discourse Concerning Puritans* (London, 1641), p. 11. Cf. also the much earlier comments of Joseph Mead, in a letter of spring 1623, on the different types of Puritan: 'First, a Puritan in politicks, or the Politicall Puritan, in matters of State, liberties of people, prerogatives of sovereigns etc. Secondly An Ecclesiasticall Puritan, for the Church Hierarchie and ceremonies, who was at first the only Puritan. Thirdly A Puritan in Ethicks or Moral Puritan sayd to consist in singularity of living, and hypocrisie both civil and religious which may be called the Vulgar Puritan, and was the second in birth and hath made too many ashamed to be honest.' Quoted in Kenneth Shipps, 'The "Political Puritan"', *Church History* 45 (2) (1976): 196–205, p. 196.

progression from a religious to a political radicalism as soon as circumstances provided the opportunity'.[44] A similar story of radicalisation is told on a smaller scale for the Puritans of Newcastle: before the 1630s, Puritanism was generally characterised by 'unconnected activity ... a number of individuals preaching the word and then disappearing...', but in face of Arminianism a more definite Puritan organisation and leadership emerged. Newcastle Puritans appear to have been united by little except their religious concerns – a unity provoked by adversity.[45]

Neile became Archbishop of York in 1632, and instituted a firm campaign against Puritans. But in Yorkshire, because of the support of the laity – the gentry of the East Riding and the Plain of York, the merchants of Hull and Beverley – Puritan clergy were able to continue preaching. According to Marchant, although Neile had some success in obtaining outward conformity, he 'never convinced the Protestant laity that his ideas were not more Roman than Reformed, and he had to support a government that governed the north, not through the local squirearchy but through a bureaucracy directed from London [the Council of the North]'.[46] Again, the religious programme of the Arminian church was so closely connected with political issues that grounds for opposition can only artificially be disentangled. In Nottinghamshire, in the Laudian period, detailed administration was brought directly under the control of York, and procedures were tightened up under Neile's Official Mottershed. By the end of the 1630s, the hierarchy's campaign had produced only outward conformity, combined with increased hostility and resistance: churchwardens refused to co-operate, there was widespread antagonism to the church courts, and the Laudian regime had lost the confidence of the local governors.[47]

The story is repeated again and again in the different counties of England, with minor local variations being played on the same national theme. In Cheshire, Puritans were increasingly harassed from 1633 onwards, and the 'effect of this persecution was to polarize attitudes, creating a radical anti-episcopal movement where none had existed before'. Many moderates in Cheshire seem to have been turned against the government simply because the Crown's policies were provoking radical discontent.[48] In Somerset, Barnes tells us that Laudianism 'prob-

[44] Mervyn James, *Family, Lineage, and Civil Society. A Study of Society, Politics and Mentality in the Durham Region, 1500–1640* (Oxford: Clarendon Press, 1974), p. 175; see generally chs. 5 and 6.
[45] Roger Howell, *Newcastle-upon-Tyne and the Puritan Revolution* (Oxford: Clarendon Press, 1967), pp. 85ff.
[46] Marchant, *Puritans and Church Courts*, p. 130. Cf. also J.T. Cliffe, *The Yorkshire Gentry from the Reformation to the Civil War* (London: Athlone Press, 1969), ch. 12.
[47] Marchant, *Church under the Law*, pp. 195–203; Marchant, *Puritans and Church Courts*, ch. 10.
[48] J.S. Morrill, *Cheshire 1630–1660: County Government and Society during the English Revolution* (London: Oxford University Press, 1974), p. 20, p. 30.

ably did manage through oppressive measures ... to raise the level of uniformity and decency a very slight degree. But it left an immense residue of resentment ...'.[49] In Cambridgeshire, Protestant beliefs in the importance of preaching and the scriptures were strongly held among the laity, even among villagers of the lowest social levels, and there was considerable opposition to what were regarded as the popish innovations of Laudianism. During the 1630s Puritans deliberately filled a high proportion of lay parochial offices, and systematically biassed the presentations drawn up for episcopal visitations, effectively undermining Laudian control.[50] Religious polarisation started in Kent already at the beginning of the 1620s, with the eclipse of the moderate Abbot at court. Religious and civic, urban, radicalism began to overlap, in common opposition to Crown policies. During the 1630s, private conventicles grew as many were driven into some form of separatism from the Laudian church, which no longer permitted the forms of religious gathering and worship they desired. By 1640, Puritans were part of a virtually united front against Crown policies, which appeared to pose a major threat to provincial social and political order.[51] And in Sussex, according to Fletcher, even though 'there was no sustained Arminian campaign against Puritan nonconformity ... the Puritan gentry were shocked ... into a total rethinking of their attitude towards episcopacy. A radical party emerged on the Bench and among the gentry in the late 1630s determined to counter the Arminian innovations in the church.'[52]

These local developments took place in the context of wider, national issues and incidents. Events such as the spectacular trials and punishments of Prynne, Burton, and Bastwick served to give widespread publicity to the increasing opposition to the Laudian regime. The activities of the Laudian bishops served to create anti-episcopal feelings that Field and the sixteenth-century presbyterians never succeeded in producing to such an extent. A Laudian bishopric, 'whereby the man is preferred from the Church to the Court, from the Altar to some Tribunall, from Gods Spirituall to the Kings Temporall affaires', antagonised those who believed themselves to be the natural rulers of England, and led them to ally with more radical spirits with whom they would normally have had little sympathy. And the lack of toleration activated the antagonism. One is inclined to agree with Henry Parker:

Nay, it is thought that if our Bishops had been more gentle-handed all this while towards such as dis-relish't Ceremonies for Poperies sake, and had rather pitied

---

[49] T.G. Barnes, *Somerset 1625–1640* (London: Oxford University Press, 1961), p. 15.

[50] Spufford, *Contrasting Communities*, p. 237, pp. 269–70.

[51] Clark, *English Provincial Society*, chs. 11 and 12; see also Peter Clark, 'Thomas Scott and the Growth of Urban Opposition to the Early Stuart Regime', *The Historical Journal* 21 (1) (1978): 1–26.

[52] A. Fletcher, *A County Community in Peace and War: Sussex 1600–1660* (London: Longman, 1975), pp. 92–3.

them as men of tender consciences, then persecuted and defamed them, as seditious *Puritans*, these differences had not lasted so long: for when the Reformation was not yet fully perfected, the *Puritans* of those dayes were more fiery than now; but not being so odious in the Church, lesse combustion followed thereupon: whereas now they are so unmercifully treated, that no moderate complyance can serve the turne.[53]

The rising tide of anti-episcopal feeling was further incensed by Laud's canons of 1640, with the infamous 'etcetera oath', never to 'consent to alter the government of this Church by archbishops, bishops, deans and archdeacons, etc.'. On 11 December 1640, a 'humble petition of many of his Majesty's subjects in and about the City of London, and several counties of the kingdom' requested that 'whereas the government of archbishops and lord bishops, deans and archdeacons, etc., with their courts and ministrations in them, have proved prejudicial and very dangerous both to the Church and Commonwealth', then 'the said government, with all its dependencies, roots and branches, may be abolished, and all laws in their behalf made void, and the government according to God's Word may be rightly placed amongst us'. The final paragraphs in this petition succeeded beautifully in relating the Arminian ascendancy, and divine right episcopacy, to the rise of popery, the decay of manufacture, the decline in trade, the decreased value of wool, the increased unemployment and poverty, and the dangers to the kingdom of the Scottish Wars.[54]

By 1640, the interrelations between political and religious unease at the personal rule of Charles I were so intimate that the term 'Puritan' broadened to embrace all strands of opposition. Lucy Hutchinson captures the complex processes by which political, social, religious, moral and ethical aspects of the constitutional crisis were entangled:

The payment of civill obedience to the King and the lawes of the land satisfied not; if any durst dispute his impositions in the worship of God, he was presently reckon'd among the seditious and disturbers of the publick peace, and accordingly persecuted. If any were griev'd at the dishonor of the kingdome, or the griping of the poore, or the unjust oppressions of the subject ... he was a Puritane ... If any shew'd favour to any godly person, kept them company, reliev'd them in want, or protected them against violent or unjust oppression, he was a Puritane. If any gentleman in his country maintain'd the good lawes of the land, or stood up for any publick interest of his country, for good order of government, he was a Puritane; and in short, all that crost the interest of the needie Courtiers, the proud encroaching priests, the theevish projectors, the lewd nobillity and gentrie, whoever was zealous for God's glory or worship, could not endure blasphemous oathes, ribald conversation, prophane scoffes, sabbath breach, derision of the word of God, and the like; whoever could endure a sermon, modest habitt or conversation, or aniething that was good, all these were Puri-

[53] Parker, *Discourse*, p. 37, p. 39.
[54] Kenyon, *Stuart Constitution*, p. 169, pp. 171–2, p. 175.

tanes; and if Puritanes, then enemies to the king and his government, seditious factious hipocrites, ambitious disturbers of the publick peace, and finally the pest of [the] Kingdome, enemies of God and good men, according to the Court account... Thus the two factions ... grew up to greate heigths and enmities, one against the other ...[55]

It may well be true that no-one in this period intended to make a revolution; but the situation was inherently combustible. When the Scots refused to accept the Laudian religious impositions in Scotland, and took up arms against England instead, Charles was forced to terminate his attempt at an increasingly difficult rule without Parliament, and to try to obtain revenues with the consent of the people. This consent was not forthcoming. With the radicalisation and polarisation of the years 1640–2, the forceful emergence of popular pressures into national politics helped to provoke a conservative reaction by some, and the formation of a party supporting the King. In 1642, the troubles in Ireland which had erupted at the end of the previous year finally brought to a head the growing conflict and mistrust between opposing sides, unwilling as they might have been to enter into open and physical strife.

This is not the place to examine subsequent developments. In the course of the 1640s, as the turmoils progressed, sides emerged and were transformed, alliances were made and broken, coalitions shifted and changed, as the early unity of opposition was split apart over how to resolve the crisis.[56] But it is notable that of all the factors which historians have attempted to correlate with civil war allegiance, religion is the one that consistently produces the strongest patterns. Puritans were overwhelmingly Parliamentarian; Arminians and Catholics supported the King.[57] And at the centre of affairs, the Puritan network of contacts, the Puritan experience of propaganda and printing, and the Puritan passion and expertise at preaching, all aided in the organisation and the ideological arousal of the opposition to the ungodly rule of the would-be absolutist King.

That Puritanism fell apart as the troubles continued only highlights the fragility of the unity forged by Charles' personal rule in church and

---

[55] Lucy Hutchinson, *Memoirs of the Life of Colonel Hutchinson*, ed. James Sutherland (London: Oxford University Press, 1973), pp. 43–4.

[56] See for example, Christopher Hill, *The World Turned Upside Down* (Harmondsworth: Penguin, 1975); A.L. Morton, *The World of the Ranters* (London: Lawrence and Wishart, 1970); and for some general accounts, Ivan Roots, *The Great Rebellion, 1642–1660* (London: Batsford Academic, 1966); B. Coward, *The Stuart Age* (London: Longman, 1980), Part 3; R. Ashton, *The English Civil War* (London: Weidenfeld and Nicolson, 1978); Russell, *Crisis of Parliaments*, Part 7.

[57] For example: Morrill, *Cheshire*, p. 71; Cliffe, *Yorkshire Gentry*, p. 339, p. 344, p. 346; B.G. Blackwood, *The Lancashire Gentry and the Great Rebellion, 1640–1660* (Manchester: Chetham Society, 1978), p. 47 and pp. 63ff. See also J.S. Morrill, 'The Northern Gentry and the Great Rebellion', *Northern History* 15 (1979): 66–87.

state. Puritanism was formed into a revolutionary political movement, held together in opposition to prerogative rule, because of the peculiar relationship of church and state in England, and the particular structural location of the church in English society. Puritanism was not an inherently revolutionary movement, by virtue of its ideas or ethos, or because of the material positions of those who espoused Puritan ideas. For much of the time between the accession of Elizabeth and the reign of Charles, Puritans were in the main moderate men and women simply committed to the achievement of religious reforms. But because of the links of the church with the state, this commitment inevitably had political implications, however much Puritans might disavow any desire for alteration of secular affairs. They had a sufficient foothold in the church to be able to survive and spread, even through periods of persecution. But when the state wanted to use the church in particular ways, then Puritans were provoked into active political opposition. This is what happened in the particular set of historical circumstances eventuating in the Civil War of the 1640s. It was because of certain structural features of the socio-political landscape in which English Puritans sought to establish the Holy Commonwealth that they became embroiled eventually in the Puritan Revolution.

This chapter has appeared to recount a narrative of high politics. But it must be read in the light of the analyses of interrelationships among state, society, and church presented in the preceding two chapters. It was these interrelationships which conditioned the different responses to the Puritan movement for religious reform; it was these interrelationships which determined the spaces in which Puritanism could develop, and the alliances which it was likely to form. Puritanism had a relatively strong societal base against a relatively weak absolutism. Therefore, if it was to challenge absolutist rule, it would be more likely to appear to play an important historical role than if the relations of strength and weakness had been reversed. But Puritans would not have challenged absolutist rule had it not been for the ambiguous, politically contested location of the state church. It was the combination of the specific state/society and state/church relationships in England which rendered English Puritanism an historically important force against absolutist rule.

Yet history is made by people, not by structures. Structural relationships among church, state, and society circumscribed a given field of constraints and possibilities. Structural relationships are both sustained and transformed by particular actors, with different skills, ambitions, aspirations, and luck. History could have been different if different actors had been playing the game. (How far there could have been different actors to some extent depends on social role: archbishops can be appointed and removed, according to attitude and capacity, and therefore particular incumbents of the position are not entirely arbitrary; whereas monarchs tend more to be selected by accidents of pedigree.) Nevertheless, history could not have been very different: there were certain limits conditioning what was or was not possible in given circumstances, what eventuations were or were not likely. The narrative of agency presented in this chapter complements the analysis of structure presented in the preceding two to show how, in the English case, the particular set of relationships among state, church, and crucial social groups constrained and conditioned certain religiously motivated people into developing certain alliances and not others, forming certain political attitudes and not others, seizing certain opportunities for action in pursuit of their goals, and, eventually, appearing to make a historically crucial contribution to the defeat of attempts at absolutist rule in England. The following two chapters will recount how, under different sets of state/society/ church relationships in Württemberg and Prussia, different patterns of alliance and action developed, as Pietists responded with different strategies to the obstacles and opportunities they faced.

6

From reform to retreat: Pietism in Württemberg

In the early decades of Pietism in Württemberg – from the 1680s to 1715 or so – Pietism was a politically active force at both the inner-churchly and the separatist levels. Leading churchmen argued for reforms in church and state, and defended the interests of the Estates, with which the church was so closely linked, against the perceived political, social, and cultural dangers of absolutism. More humble pastors and groups of the laity met together and worked out criticisms of church and society, seeking to develop new ways of leading a godly life, and setting themselves apart from a sinful world in which the wrath of God was only too evident. Networks of organisation developed, as people joined together in conventicles, heard the message of travelling preachers or themselves went from place to place to hear the Word of the Lord. Social processes of mockery, labelling, splits in local communities, pushed many such groups into separation from the church, heightening their awareness of their own special status as true Christians, the godly, the reborn. At the local level, members of the laity were as active as were the more sober leaders of Spenerian Pietism in national affairs.

From perhaps 1715 onwards, such reformist and radical ferment subsided. The main Pietist reforms of the church were accomplished by the 1720s, which finally saw the introduction, after repeated earlier attempts, of catechism teaching, and which ended with the Pietist-influenced *Schulordnung* of 1729. After 1715, there was a marked wane of separatist activity, as conventicles in practice became tolerated as an aspect of church life. Briefly, under the reign of the Catholic Duke Karl Alexander, from 1733 to 1737, Pietism and the Lutheran church more generally found their positions threatened. But with the death of Karl Alexander, and the restored rule of the Estates under the new Duke-Administrator during a period of ducal minority, the danger was removed. The passing of the 1743 *Generalreskript* finally accorded Pietists in Württemberg a formal freedom of association and activity, under certain specified conditions. The Pietism of the mid-eighteenth century, incorporated into the state church, was politically defused, a passive form of gathering under the moral oversight of the pastor, without the radical charge of earlier decades. In the constitutional struggles of the 1750s and '60s, against the absolutism of Duke Karl Eugen, religion was not directly an issue. Pietists were generally disunited, failing to agree on any particular approach, and were in the main passive and withdrawn from politics. A few Pietists who were politically active failed to obtain any widespread support.

This chapter will seek to show in more detail how the retreat of Pietism from political radicalism in Württemberg was related to the delicate process of its incorporation and toleration within the state church, as affected by the latter's position in Württemberg state and society.

The early years: separatist rebellion and Pietist reform

Spener had visited Württemberg early in his career, and made lasting friendships with leading churchmen in Württemberg, many of whom shared his concerns and ideals. In the 1680s and '90s, as we have seen in Chapter 4, Pietist reforms of the church were discussed in the Synod and a number of measures were passed, particularly those concerned with the improvement of the religious education and moral discipline of the laity, and the theological and practical training of the clergy. These measures of reform were not attained without considerable discussion and some opposition; and certain proposed reforms, such as the introduction of presbyters, and religious discipline through house-visits, were eventually dropped. (The latter fell because of perceived embarrassments in attempting to visit and discipline persons of high social standing.) Nevertheless, Württemberg churchmen continued the tradition of reform exemplified earlier in the seventeenth century by the activities of Johann Valentin Andreae, who had introduced Genevan elements into the Lutheran state church in the form of the *Kirchenkonvente*. Spener's concern with fostering active religiosity in everyday life, to complement orthodox purity of doctrine or formally correct theology, found a favourable reception with influential prelates and theologians in the Württemberg church. Because of the relatively independent position of the state church, many of these measures could be adopted with little difficulty.[1]

Conditions were ripe for Pietist activity in a number of other ways. The Thirty Years War, and the continuing warfare and natural disasters of the later seventeenth century, evoked a variety of responses. Some members of

[1] See, generally: Martin Brecht, 'Philipp Jakob Spener und die Württembergische Kirche' in H. Liebing and K. Scholder (eds.), *Geist und Geschichte der Reformation. Festgabe Hanns Rückert* (Berlin: Walter de Gruyter, 1966); Martin Brecht, *Kirchenordnung und Kirchenzucht in Württemberg vom 16. bis zum 18. Jahrhundert* (Stuttgart: Calwer Verlag, 1967); Heinrich Fausel, 'Von Altlutherischer Orthodoxie zum Frühpietismus in Württemberg', *Zeitschrift für Württembergische Landesgeschichte* 24 (1965): 309–28; F. Fritz, 'Konsistorium und Synodus in Württemberg am Vorabend der pietistischen Zeit', *Blätter für Württembergische Kirchengeschichte* 39 (1935): 100–31 and 40 (1936): 33–106; Heinrich Hermelink, *Geschichte der Evangelischen Kirche in Württemberg von der Reformation bis zur Gegenwart* (Stuttgart and Tübingen: Rainer Wunderlich Verlag Hermann Leins, 1949), ch. 21; and cf. Chapters 2 and 4, above.

the church hierarchy might, as indicated, be receptive to reforms in the Spenerian mould; others reacted differently. At less elevated social levels, chiliastic groups flourished, receptive to the enthusiastic messages of travelling prophets and prophetesses. People wished to separate themselves off from an ungodly world, in which the reign of Anti-Christ was at hand, and to prepare for the Second Coming. Another type of response to the sociopolitical conditions of the time tended almost in the opposite direction: a spirit of hedonism flourished, evidenced in the secularity of large numbers of the populace, and, with greater resources, in the new baroque culture and sumptuous luxuries of the court. Inner-churchly Pietists found themselves fighting on a number of fronts: not merely did they have to achieve the formal passage of reformist measures in the Synod; they also had to deal, in different ways, with chiliastic, radical, and separatist groups; with immorality and irreligion among other members of the laity; and with a new style of culture and political ambition at court.[2]

At the level of court culture and national politics, early Pietists were notably outspoken and courageous. Johann Heinrich Sturm played a leading role in the Estates in the late seventeenth century, battling against the attempts of the Duke to introduce a standing army and reduce the consultative powers of the Estates. Even after three years imprisoned as a hostage following the French invasion of 1693, Sturm maintained his strength and conviction in opposing the absolutist policies of the ruler. In 1699, after the Estates had again refused money for troops, Sturm as the leading spokesman was sacked from his position as *Oberrat* – a position which, with its dual responsibilities to Duke and Estates, was becoming structurally untenable and subject to incompatible demands under absolutism. Other Pietists too were active in opposing the new absolutism at court. Hedinger, court preacher until 1705, delivered strong political invective in his sermons. Numbers of Pietist pastors refused to admit the Duke's mistress, von Grävenitz, to communion, and made a stand against the immoralities of the court. Pietist sermons in general appealed for the reform of the court as well as the people, to avert God's punishments on an ungodly land.[3]

More directly, Pietists in the Württemberg church were faced with

---

[2] Hartmut Lehmann, *Pietismus und Weltliche Ordnung in Württemberg vom 17. bis zum 20. Jahrhundert* (Stuttgart: W. Kohlhammer Verlag, 1969); Bassler, 'Die ersten Jahre nach dem dreissigjährigen Krieg im Bezirk Maulbronn', *Blätter für Württembergische Kirchengeschichte* 2 (1898): 119–28, 166–73; Werner Fleischhauer, *Barock im Herzogtum Württemberg* (Stuttgart: W. Kohlhammer Verlag, 1958); Eugen Schneider, *Württembergische Geschichte* (Stuttgart: J.B. Metzlerscher Verlag, 1896), chs. 12 and 13.

[3] Walter Grube, *Der Stuttgarter Landtag 1457–1957* (Stuttgart: Ernst Klett Verlag, 1957), Book 2, ch. 9; F. Fritz, 'Hedinger und der Württembergische Hof', *Blätter für Württembergische Kirchengeschichte* 40 (1936): 244–53; F. Fritz, *Altwürttembergische Pietisten* (Stuttgart: Im Quell-Verlag der Evangelischen Gesellschaft, 1950), ch. 2; Lehmann, *Pietismus und Weltliche Ordnung.*

internal problems of dissension, sectarianism, and schism. It was in dealing with clerical radicalism and lay separatism that the ambiguous nature of inner-churchly Pietism was revealed. For on the one hand, leading Pietists in the church sympathised with criticisms of deficiencies in church organisation and practices; but on the other hand, toleration of a plurality of opinions on 'matters indifferent' led ultimately, not to a strengthening of a unified church, but rather to a weakening of authority and dissipation of energies. The complex processes of development of a conditional toleration led less to the desired reform of the church as a whole than to the segregation and passivity of the godly few within a latitudinarian church. This ambiguity was reflected in the history of the church's response to conventicles. Spener had proposed the establishment of conventicles, or *ecclesiola in ecclesia*, for the fostering of lay piety. This proposition had been taken up by Spener's friend Johann Andreas Hochstetter in the Synod in 1692, when he suggested the *collegium pietatis* as a useful means for furthering piety and religious education. But Hochstetter's colleagues had responded with considerable reserve to this suggestion, leaving Hochstetter in a minority of one on this point of the Pietist programme. Nevertheless, there had been a long history of lay conventicles in Württemberg, and there is evidence of active lay gatherings in the 1680s. In the 1690s and 1700s these conventicles posed an increasing problem of order to the church. The Consistorium, which had opposed Hochstetter's suggestion for the introduction of *ecclesiola* under the oversight of the church, now found that it had to face the problem of *de facto* organisation of conventicles, some led by radical pastors, others by lay people.[4]

These conventicles ranged considerably in their nature and composition. At one extreme were the chiliastic separatists, ill-educated but socially and politically concerned men and women who sought solutions to the troubles of their times in the apocalyptic visions of wandering mystics and preachers. Less dramatic were the groups who had specific criticisms of their own particular pastors, or the inadequate church services in their local area. These groups were only partly separatist, seeking a purer religious life by joining together for worship, Bible study, repetition of the sermon and discussion of edificatory literature, either in addition to, or apart from, the regular religious services of the parish. And well within established church life were the conventicles actually run by leading theologians such as Reuchlin in Tübingen, to improve the religious

---

[4] On conventicles, see particularly: Christoph Kolb, 'Die Anfänge des Pietismus und Separatismus in Württemberg', *Württembergische Vierteljahresheft für Landesgeschichte* 9 (1900): 33–93, 368–412; 10 (1901): 201–51, 364–88; 11 (1902): 43–78; and F. Fritz, 'Konventikel in Württemberg von der Reformationszeit bis zum Edikt von 1743', *Blätter für Württembergische Kirchengeschichte* 49 (1949): 99–154; 50 (1950): 65–121; 51 (1951): 78–137; 52 (1952): 28–65; 53 (1953): 82–130; 54 (1954): 75–119. See also Hermelink, *Geschichte der Evangelischen Kirche*, ch. 23 and ch. 24.

education of the people. It was partly because of the existence of the latter that a tolerant attitude was gradually developed towards the former varieties of separatist or potentially separatist conventicle, in an effort to harness their religious energies and retain them for the state church.

The chiliastic, separatist, groups posed the greatest problem for the church. Certain individuals, such as Rosenbach, travelled around the country building on the foundations of Brunnquell and Zimmermann, stimulating lay interest in the mystic and spiritualist traditions of Boehme, the Petersens, and others. Several pastors also developed somewhat heterodox interests in these ideas, and the church decided it would have to take disciplinary action in individual cases. The Pastor of Grossgartach, Christoph Mayer, eventually had to leave Württemberg, despite a petition from part of his congregation pleading for his retention. Gruber, assistant pastor in Grossbottwar, was removed to a post in Hofen, following disruptive splits in the congregation erupting into open conflict after a visit of Rosenbach to Gruber's conventicle. But in Hofen Gruber failed to obtain the support of his congregation, and he was eventually forced to give up service in the church. Sigmund Christian Gmelin, an assistant in Herrenberg, similarly was removed from his post, and later was asked to leave the country entirely because of his continued propagation of what were considered erroneous and dangerous beliefs. In these cases, the church was simply dealing in a disciplinary manner with those of its officers who failed in their pastoral or educational duties. It was less easy to deal with the members of the laity involved in such activities. The most prominent group of radical separatists appears to have been active in Stuttgart, although there were others, in towns and villages outside the capital, which attracted less attention. The Stuttgart group, which centred for a while on the house of Bengel's teacher Spindler, had participants ranging from the wife of a courtier, the *Trabantin* Schneider, and the widow and daughter of Geheimrat von Kulpis, through to a motley collection of tradesmen, artisans, and journeymen. The group was periodically visited by the enthusiast Rock, as well as the heterodox pastors Gruber and Mayer. Meetings were held at night; the church was viewed as Babel, and the group upheld the ideal of an early Christian community. It was investigated a number of times by the church, and was the immediate cause of several of the edicts concerning Pietism and separatism in the early eighteenth century. The wildest activities of the Stuttgart group occurred in 1710; and Bishop Weissmann, who required the protection of the secular authorities to preach without interruption, requested 'Schutz vor diesen fanatischen Leuten, die in ihren Konventikeln Tag und Nacht mit Schreien, Wehklagen, Händeklopfen, die ganze Nachbarschaft alarmieren und die Leute vom Schlaf abhalten. Auch künden sie der weltlichen Obrigkeit allen Gehorsam auf, weil Christus ihr König sei, dem sie zu parieren haben, und als Martyrer bei seiner Offenbarung zu leiden.'[5] One of the group, Schwanfeld, was triumphantly carried on high by his supporters, as on a throne, as they went off to their imprisonment. Within prison, the group indulged in private communion services and unorthodox religious activities: the tobacconist, on God's promptings, rent his clothes and wounded himself with a broken jug until held for dead. Supporters and fellow enthusiasts came from Calw, Göppingen, Leonberg, Schöckingen, Heumaden and other places, to participate from outside the tower where the Stuttgarters were held.[6]

Such activities were evidently not exactly the sort of thing inner-churchly Pietists of the Spenerian variety had in mind when they supported the notion of conventicles. But their response to this type of fanaticism, as they saw it, was tempered by the milder forms of semi-separatist activity. Calw presented the main instance of this. There had been a long tradition of lay conventicles in Calw, and they were heard of again in connection with a Frau Mayer in 1705 and 1706. Although visited by the *Trabantin* Schneider from Stuttgart, by the ex-pastor Mayer from Grossgartach, and others who were in trouble with the church, this group did not begin to separate itself from the church until after the arrival of the new dean, Zeller, in 1710. It was Zeller who reported the group to the Consistorium in the summer of 1712; and in early 1713 the church conducted an official investigation. It transpired that prominent members of the group were socially respectable, wealthy members of the *Calwer Compagnie*, a major trading and manufacturing concern; and that Zeller had contributed to pushing them towards separatism. Not only had he preached sharply against Pietists, causing them embarrassment when attending public worship services; he also fulfilled his own duties inadequately, and indeed actively breached accepted standards of conduct and morality:

In seinen Wochenpredigten legte er die Genesis aus, verirrte sich aber bei den ersten Kapiteln in Erörterungen über ehelichen und ausserehelichen Verkehr der Geschlechter, welche so 'obskur und obscön' herauskamen, dass selbst die weniger zarten Ohren der Mägde beleidigt wurden.[7]

From Calw, the investigative commission moved on to Herrenberg, where it was inclined to see similar deficiencies in the services provided by the church, and thus to be sympathetic to Pietist criticisms.[8]

---

[5] 'Protection against these fanatic people, who in their conventicles alarm the whole neighbourhood and keep people awake night and day with their shrieking, wailing, and clapping. Also they withdraw all obedience from the secular authorities, because Christ is their King, whom they have to follow, and they have to suffer as martyrs at his revelation.' Kolb, 'Anfänge', *Württembergische Vierteljahresheft für Landesgeschichte* 10, p. 212.

[6] Ibid., pp. 201–19; Fritz, 'Konventikel', *Blätter für Württembergische Kirchengeschichte* 51, pp. 113–14.

[7] 'In his weekly sermons he expounded the Book of Genesis, but went astray in the first chapters in discussions of the marital and extramarital intercourse of the sexes, which came out so "obscure and obscene" that even the less delicate ears of the maids were offended.' Kolb, 'Anfänge', *Württembergische Vierteljahresheft für Landesgeschichte*, 10, p. 222.

[8] See also Hartmut Lehmann, 'Pietismus und Wirtschaft in Calw am Anfang des 18. Jahrhunderts', *Zeitschrift für Württembergische Landesgeschichte* 31 (1972): 249–77.

Even less objectionable to leading members of the Württemberg church were the conventicles which corresponded most closely to Spener's model. There was of course still dissension within the church hierarchy, between those Spenerian Pietists such as the Hochstetter family who supported the concept of conventicles, and those orthodox churchmen who were more suspicious of the possible implications for doctrine and unity. But when certain townspeople of Tübingen asked the *Repetenten* of the *Tübinger Stift* for further instruction, it was decided, after some discussion, that this should be permitted under specified conditions. And a theologian at the University, Reuchlin, himself held gatherings for religious education and was loath to see any potential attack on these.[9]

The response of the church to these various activities – ranging from the inner-churchly Pietist groups through to the enthusiast–separatist groups of the Stuttgart variety – was ambivalent but on the whole tolerant. Because of the dissensions among members of the Consistorium, no edict or decree in the period up to 1715 was either completely unambiguous or general in its application. But the thrust of the measures was to make a distinction between 'seducers' and 'seduced'. The former were usually conceived of as 'foreigners' and 'idlers', or vagabonds, entering Württemberg and under the pretence of special piety misleading simple souls into erroneous beliefs. Such 'seducers' were to be dealt with firmly: either made to earn an honest living, or to leave the country. The 'seduced', on the other hand, were to be treated gently: to be informed of the errors in their opinions, to be educated into better ways, and to be enticed back into the fold of the established state church. At the same time, inner-churchly Pietists succeeded in incorporating a number of criticisms of the church itself into the measures concerned to combat separatism. It was pointed out that the clergy themselves must reform their lifestyle and morals, that lay piety must be fostered and given scope within the church, and that the church itself must do its job well if it was not to be open to justified criticism and to pave the way for seduction and alienation. Particular emphasis was put by the Calw investigative commission on the notion of separatism as a *malum utile*, a *nützliches Übel*, which provoked the church into a serious examination of its own deficiencies. The implicit solution in the measures to combat separatism in the Württemberg church was, not that those criticising the church should be punished, but rather that the causes for criticism should themselves be removed: a Pietist solution to the problem of radical Pietism.[10]

---

[9] In addition to Kolb and Fritz, see Martin Leube, *Die Geschichte des Tübinger Stifts*, vol. 2 (Stuttgart: Chr. Scheufele Verlag, 1930), ch. 12.

[10] See A.L. Reyscher (ed.), *Sammlung der Württembergischen Geseze*, vol. 8 (Tübingen: Im Commission bei Ludw. Friedr. Fues, 1834), pp. 470–9; 523–30; 535–9; 539–40;

The measures of 1703, 1706, 1707, and 1711 arose largely in response to specific issues, and the last was valid only for Stuttgart. An attempt was made in 1715 to introduce a more general measure to establish conditions for the toleration of inner-churchly gatherings of the pious; but this attempt was foiled by the machinations of Jäger, in conjunction with Weissmann, both opponents of Pietism. The Pietist Andreas Adam Hochstetter (son of Spener's friend Johann Andreas Hochstetter) was removed from his position as court preacher and sent back to his professorship at Tübingen University; and the draft of a *Generalreskript* to give positive approval to Pietist groups within the church was not approved. But despite this setback in achieving a formal and general statement of toleration, the earlier measures implied a degree of flexibility and tolerance in practice. It was hoped by many in the church that moderation would ensure greater peace and quiet, preferable to severity provoking schism and active dissent; and if people were good, pious, peaceful citizens who posed no threat to public order, then their doctrinal errors should be dealt with gently and they should be given time to reform. This flexible attitude, ambivalent in its combination of disapproval and yet sympathy, had considerable consequences for the development of Pietism in Württemberg in subsequent decades.

The incorporation of Pietism: 1715–1743

After the Treaty of Utrecht, Württemberg was able to enjoy a period of relative peace; and this contributed both to a decline in the haranguing of the ruler by Pietist preachers at court, and to a decline in chiliasm and separatism at the local level. Furthermore, the lenient treatment of dissenters by the established church contributed to the decline of separatism in the years after 1715, as diverse opinions were in one way or another accommodated within the church. In theology, Bengel's interpretation of the scriptures gradually rose to a position of pre-eminence; while through his teaching at Denkendorf Bengel directly influenced the education and outlook of more than three hundred future theologians as well as many others.[11] Pietists held accepted places in a broad church, which tolerated a relatively wide spectrum of Lutheran opinion and which had, right from the time of Müller's attempt to publish his anti-Pietist lecture in 1694, been concerned to avoid getting entangled in vituperative dispute

---

543–4; 546–8, for relevant decrees and edicts. Cf. also Christian Friedrich Sattler, *Geschichte des Herzogthums Würtenberg, Dreyzehnter Theil* (Ulm: bey Aug. Lebr. Stettin, 1783), pp. 45–7 and Beylagen pp. 31–5.

[11] Gottfried Mälzer, *Johann Albrecht Bengel: Leben und Werk* (Stuttgart: Calwer Verlag, 1970); I. Hartmann, 'Das religiöse Leben' in *Herzog Karl Eugen von Württemberg und seine Zeit*, hrsg. vom Württembergischen Geschichts- und Altertums-Verein, vol. 1 (Esslingen a. N.: Paul Neff Verlag (Max Schreiber), 1907), pp. 364–5.

and controversy. For a brief period, during the reign of the Catholic Duke Karl Alexander, the peace of church and state were threatened; but in the years of ducal minority following his death, the status of religion in Württemberg was to some extent resolved, and Pietism formally incorporated into the structures of the church. What then did Pietist activity look like in these years?

In national politics, the early outspokenness of Pietist politicians and preachers declined as in peace-time the pressure was eased in relations with the court. Osiander, the Pietist spokesman for the Estates who took the place of Johann Heinrich Sturm, acted more as a mediator between Duke and Estates than had his strong-willed predecessor. Osiander was inclined to be conciliatory, even weak, in his dealings with the ruler; and he lacked any consistent or energetic support from the Estates to take a firmer line. To some extent Osiander tried to work with the old, seventeenth-century ideal of co-operation between Estates and ruler for the common good, unaware that the court was no longer prepared to abide by what it considered to be outmoded rules.[12] To some extent also, a second generation of Pietists may have been becoming accustomed to the new style at court. Georg Konrad Rieger, whose thundering sermons initially exhorted both ruler and people to reform their ways, gradually turned his major attentions to the latter, as court culture became more firmly established. Rieger's criticisms of the state were by 1741 directed onto the citizenry, as he complained:

Wie sind ... unsere Bürger von der ehemaligen Häuslichkeit, Sparsamkeit und Einfalt in Kleidern, Essen, Trinken, Reden, Handeln in allerhand neue Moden, Eitelkeit, Pracht, Vertuerei, Schlecherei verfallen, dadurch alle gute Mittel unserer Alten vollends verdestilliert werden und nichts übrigbleibt als ein prächtiges Nichts, ein mit holländischen Spitzen und anderen Spenglereien eingehüllter, schwindsüchtiger, verwundeter, verbluteter, verarmter und mit Schulden überhaüfter Staatskörper.[13]

In 1707, by contrast, Hochstetter had in the Synod complained that 'vom Hof komme alles übel', and the Synod had condemned the luxuries of the court and bemoaned the poverty of the people.[14] Despite the opposition of Stuttgart preachers to the hedonistic, Catholic celebration of Carnival, in 1719 when the Duke ordered all court officials, traders and citizens to

---

[12] Grube, *Stuttgarter Landtag*, Book 3, ch. 1.

[13] 'How have ... our citizens fallen, from their former frugality, thrift, and simplicity in dress, food, drink, speech, behaviour, into all manner of new fashions, vanity, luxury, extravagance, pampering, so that all the good ways and means of our elders are quite frittered away and nothing remains except a sumptuous nothing, a body politic muffled in dutch lace and other baubles, consumptive, injured, bleeding to death, impoverished and overwhelmed with debts.' F. Fritz, 'Die evangelische Kirche Württembergs im Zeitalter des Pietismus', Part 1, *Blätter für Württembergische Kirchengeschichte 55* (1955): 68–116, p. 91.

[14] 'All evil comes from the court.' Ibid., p. 79.

participate, the church in general ceased active protest. The *Buss-predigten*, demanding repentance to ease the plight of the land, lost their relevance as conditions improved in a country no longer at war, despite no notable changes in the style of the court.[15]

At the local level, Pietism took two main forms. On the one hand were the private conventicles, in practice tolerated whether led by laymen or pastors, so long as they occasioned no major disturbance of the peace. On the other hand, there was a concern among certain clergymen to increase moral discipline among their congregations, and to impose stricter standards of social and religious behaviour. When disciplinary concerns reached a certain level, major political problems could develop in the local community, necessitating intervention by the church. A further factor complicating these two lines of development was the continued infiltration of the Württemberg church by emissaries from Halle, and later from Zinzendorf's Herrnhut community, with both of which the Württemberg church had ambivalent relations.

Some inner-churchly Pietist conventicles appear to have run quite smoothly during this period; many more may have existed than appear in the historical records, simply because it was generally only when troubles arose that activities were investigated and recorded. We hear quite laconically of Johann Jacob Moser's gatherings, mentioned briefly in his autobiography. He describes the *Erbauungsstunden* of 1733 as follows:

Sonntags nach vollendetem öffentlichen Gottesdienst sammlete sich unvermuthet von selbsten nach und nach ein Häuflein redlicher Seelen in meinem Haus; da wir dann unsere fernere Andacht mit singen, beten und Betrachtung des Wortes GOttes hatten. So bald es die Zahl anfieng starck zu werden, ertheilte ich dem Statt-Superintendenten und *Professori Theologiae*, Herrn D. Hagmaier, Nachricht von der ganzen Sache, und er hatte nichts dagegen: Als auch die Zahl sich mehrete und zwey Fürstliche Consistorial-Befehle desswegen an Herrn D. Hagmaier ergiengen, berichtete er so favorabel, dass wir ungestört gelassen wurden; wie dann niemalen die geringste Unordnung vorgienge, und auch nach meinem Abzug von Tübingen diese Erbauungs-Stunden noch vile Jahre ... fort-gesetzt wurden.[16]

In 1734 Moser became *Regierungsrat* in Stuttgart, where, on the sugges-tion of Rieger, he continued to hold such Pietist gatherings. Less socially

---

[15] Lehmann, *Pietismus und Weltliche Ordnung*, p. 66, p. 58.
[16] 'On Sundays when the public service was over a small group of honest souls would gather, of their own accord, by and by at my house; for we then had our further devotions, with singing, praying, and reflection on the Word of the Lord. As soon as the number began to grow large, I informed the town-superintendent and Professor of Theology, Dr Hagmaier, about the whole thing, and he had nothing against it: Also as the numbers increased, and therefore two royal consistorial orders were sent to Dr Hagmaier, he reported so favourably that we were left undisturbed; as then there was never the least disorder, and also after I had moved away from Tübingen these devotional meetings were continued for many more years...' J.J. Moser, *Lebens-geschichte, von ihme selbst beschriben* (n.p.: 1768), pp. 55–6.

elevated lay people held gatherings also: we hear of 'ein alter lieber Mann' in Freudenstadt, and an 'erweckte Mädchen' in Stuttgart in 1734, who seem to have held *Erbauungsstunden*.[17] It was likely that there were many other such private gatherings: an early argument of Pietists for toleration had been that it would be unreasonable to forbid this kind of gathering when social gatherings for drinking, dancing, games-playing and other secular activities were condoned.

Some of these Pietist meetings were run by pastors, and could serve as a channel of information to the pastor about the more recalcitrant members of the congregation. A Stuttgart pastor's report of 1734 explained that his group would come together on a Sunday evening to pray, read the Gospels, repeat the sermon, and discuss the readings. The pastor could not refrain finally from commenting that the 'Visitator ... will darüber Gottes Gnade preisen, um so mehr, als solche Leute beiderlei Geschlechts des lieben Predigers Augen, Ohren, Zungen, Hände und Füsse in der Gemeinde sein und werden können, manches Nötige von dem Zustand der Häuser offenbaren können u.s.f.'[18] The people of Zainingen, complaining of their Pietist pastor Kuhn, explained that 'der Pfarrer wäre ihnen schon recht, wenn nur die Leute, die alles verschwätzten, nicht zu ihm kämen'.[19]

Pietist pastors were not always content, however, simply to hold *Erbauungsstunden* for the godly few in their congregations; at this time many were concerned to effect major changes in the whole community. The disciplinary technique employed was generally strict exclusion from communion for all but the consistently and deeply pious. This strictness could easily cause rifts in the community which were counter-productive to the more general aims of a state church. The Consistorium then had to investigate, and if necessary discipline, the over-zealous actions of particular Pietist pastors. Here again the church found itself in an ambiguous situation. On the one hand it condemned laxity of morals, drunkenness, swearing, gambling, and disdain of religion, and was concerned to improve social, religious and moral standards. In this task the church seems in the eighteenth century to have lost the support or alliance of the secular authorities. The *Kirchenkonvente*, set up by Andreae in the seventeenth century, had combined religious and secular authorities in an effort to establish a rigorous and effective moral court and moral police.

---

[17] 'A dear old man' and 'an inspired girl.' Fritz, 'Konventikel', *BWKG* 53, p. 121.
[18] 'The Inspector... will praise God's grace in this matter, and all the more so, since such people of both sexes are, and can become, the eyes, ears, tongues, hands and feet of the dear preacher in the congregation, can reveal many necessary things concerning the state of the households, etc.' Christoph Kolb, 'Zur kirchlichen Geschichte Stuttgarts im 18. Jahrhundert', *Blätter für Württembergische Kirchengeschichte* 3 (1899): 34–52, 160–70, p. 169.
[19] 'The pastor would suit them alright, if only the people who gossiped about everything did not go to him.' Fritz, 'Konventikel', *Blätter für Württembergische Kirchengeschichte* 52, p. 43.

But it seems that from about the 1690s or early 1700s onwards, the *Kirchenkonvente* became less effective, largely because of a loss of interest on the part of the secular arm.[20] Unsuccessful attempts were made by the church to revive co-operation with political officials in the local courts in the eighteenth century, but it increasingly became apparent that the church would have to tackle problems of immorality alone. In 1727 a *Generalreskript* was passed by the Synod stressing the importance of preparation for Holy Communion and reminding pastors to warn potential communicants of the dangers of partaking in communion in a sinful and unrepentant state.[21] But on the other hand, too strong an application of this injunction could drive most of the congregation out of the church altogether; and the church had to guard against excesses of zeal on the part of pastors. Again, a delicate balance had to be found, as the Württemberg church sympathised with Pietist aims, but needed to restrain some of the possible implications of Pietist energy in practice.

In 1726, a few like-minded pastors started meeting once a month to discuss means of improving their own and their parishioners' religiosity.[22] Rues from Dürrmenz, Seeger from Lomersheim, Lang from Rosswag and Brotbeck from Mühlhausen on the Enz were participants in this gathering. Rues and Seeger in particular began to take very seriously the instrument of exclusion from communion. In 1727, fifty individuals were excommunicate in Dürrmenz; in 1732 there were eighty; in 1735, 133 were excluded from communion. In Lomersheim, in 1731 twelve were excommunicate; in 1734, twenty-seven; but by 1736, the majority of the congregation had voluntarily excluded themselves, since they had been convinced that, not being numbered among the reborn, they were not worthy to receive communion. Here the church had been reduced to the tiny group of the truly converted.[23] The Consistorium had to intervene firmly in these cases, to resolve the local tensions arising from such rigour. Seeger was removed from Lomersheim to Rietenau, where he developed a milder approach. Rues, ordered in 1727 to be less severe in future, continued his activities in Dürrmenz until the confrontation which occurred in Karl Alexander's reign.

The peace of the church, its established position in Württemberg state and society, and its broad tolerance, were all threatened when the Catholic Duke Karl Alexander succeeded Eberhard Ludwig as ruler. Karl

---

[20] Brecht, *Kirchenordnung und Kirchenzucht*, p. 80; Fritz, 'Die evangelische Kirche Württembergs im Zeitalter des Pietismus', Part 2, *Blätter für Württembergische Kirchengeschichte* 56 (1956): 99–167, pp. 105–6.

[21] Fritz, 'Konventikel', *Blätter für Württembergische Kirchengeschichte* 52, p. 35.

[22] Ibid., pp. 34ff.

[23] Ibid.; see also Fritz, 'Gottlieb Seeger (1683–1743), Leben und Wirken eines altwürttembergischen Pietisten', *Blätter für Württembergische Kirchengeschichte* 39 (1935): 51–64; and Fritz, 'Johann Jakob Rues (1681–1754), ein pietistischer Seelsorger und seine Schicksale unter Herzog Karl Alexander', *Blätter für Württembergische Kirchengeschichte* 28 (1924): 130–43.

Alexander, with the help of General von Remchingen and the Jew Süss Oppenheimer, had plans to overthrow the Protestant constitution of Württemberg and ignore the provisions of the *Tübinger Vertrag*. Karl Alexander's policies included the unconstitutional raising of revenues to support troops and dispense with the co-operation of the Estates; and another aspect of his programme was a reduction in the powers of the church, which was such a fundamental bulwark of the Estates. In conjunction with the Bishop of Würzburg and Bamberg, Karl Alexander considered plans for the introduction of equal status for Catholicism in Württemberg. The court chapel in Ludwigsburg was transformed into a Catholic chapel, a centre for Catholic propaganda. Catholic priests were appointed for the army, and Catholic military services were introduced.[24] And the *Konsistorialdirektor* Scheffer reported that Karl Alexander 'habe mit Ungnaden vernommen, dass so viele sogenannten Pietisten und Schwärmer im Lande wären, und dahero befohlen, dass man so viel möglich hierunter remedieren solle'.[25] The most direct victims of Karl Alexander's anti-Pietist policies were Rues in Dürrmenz, and Kuhn in Zainingen.

Despite the Consistorium's earlier pleas for moderation on the part of Rues, he had managed to get involved in a dispute with the *Amtmann* Fischer, whom he accused of immorality, Sabbath-breaking, drunkenness and dishonesty. Fischer appealed directly to the Duke, alleging that Rues had spread false doctrines, misused his power to excommunicate, and had spoken disrespectfully of the ruler. On 3 November 1736, a cavalry captain and twenty hussars were sent to interrogate Rues, search his house, and take evidence from members of the congregation. Despite overwhelming support for Rues from most of his parishioners, Rues and his wife and daughter and nine citizens were arrested and imprisoned. A similar fate befell pastor Kuhn in Zainingen. After receiving little satisfaction following complaints to the Consistorium, a disaffected tailor appealed directly to the Duke, also asserting that Kuhn had been publicly disrespectful of the Duke from the pulpit. On 31 October 1736 Kuhn and a few others were arrested. The Consistorium tried to intercede with the Duke, requesting mildness and asking to set up its own commission to investigate these cases. This request was granted, the Duke perhaps feeling that he had already made his point, and by early December all the prisoners were freed on the recommendation of the investigative commission. Kuhn and Rues remained however suspended from duty.[26]

---

[24] Cf. Chapter 3, above; and Julius Schall, 'Zur kirchlichen Lage Württembergs unter Karl Alexander', *Blätter für Württembergische Geschichte* 4 (1900): 123–43.

[25] 'Had heard with displeasure that there were so many so-called Pietists and enthusiasts in the land, and had therefore given orders that this situation should be remedied as far as possible.' Quoted in Fritz, 'Konventikel', *Blätter für Württembergische Kirchengeschichte* 53, p. 123.

[26] Ibid., pp. 125ff.; and Fritz, 'Johann Jakob Rues', pp. 137ff.

The response to Karl Alexander's policies, threatening as they were to Württemberg's constitution and religion, was divided and irresolute. This was true in particular of the response of Pietists. There were those who agreed with Pfaff's doctrine of legitimate resistance to an ungodly ruler. In tones reminiscent of Calybute Downing in England in 1640, Pfaff asserted that

Derjenige ist kein Rebelle, der um sein Gewissen, Freyheit und Leben sich in defensions-stand setzet und um sich von der unendlichen Unterdruckung zu retten wehren muss.[27]

This was hardly the sort of sentiment normally associated with the Lutheran doctrine of obedience to authority. On the Small Committee of the Estates (the *Engerer Ausschuss*), valiant defenders of the old constitution included the Maulbronn prelate Augustin Hochstetter, maintaining the Hochstetter family tradition, and Johann Heinrich Sturm the younger, son of the earlier protagonist of the Estates' cause.[28] But Pietists were not united in their approach: most notably, Bishop Weissensee, a close friend of Bengel, was suspected of subversive dealings with the court and the Jew Süss Oppenheimer. At the very least, it seems that Weissensee was politically naive and easily led into betraying the secret discussions of the *Engerer Ausschuss* to the Duke, through the skilful manipulations of Süss Oppenheimer.[29] The Duke was thus enabled to exploit dissensions voiced in the private meetings of the Estates' Committee. At the same time other Pietists remained politically quite passive, waiting on the will of the Lord. It is possible that, had Karl Alexander lived longer, an effective resistance to his policies might have been developed; but coherent opposition had not been organised by the time of his sudden death in March 1737.

This event was the cause of much rejoicing among Pietists and others, more particularly after the danger of a military coup led by General von Remchingen had been averted. In the period of minority administration which followed, a General Diet was called for the first time in forty years, and measures were taken to ensure the future safety of the constitution. The Enlightenment thinker and politician Bilfinger and his associates were concerned to tighten up Württemberg's laws and regulations, and the *Pietistenreskript* of 1743 arose partly out of this impetus to achieve a formal legal status for certain accepted religious and social practices

[27] 'That person is no rebel, who for the sake of conscience, freedom, and life defends himself, and in order to save himself from endless oppression must take up arms.' Quoted in Martin Hasselhorn, *Der Altwürttembergische Pfarrstand im 18. Jahrhundert* (Stuttgart: W. Kohlhammer Verlag, 1958), p. 70.

[28] Grube, *Stuttgarter Landtag*, p. 393.

[29] See Eduard Lempp, 'Philipp Heinrich Weissensee', *Blätter für Württembergische Kirchengeschichte* 31 (1927): 114–67; and Lempp, 'Weissensees Sturz: Nachtrag zur Biographie Ph. H. Weissensees', *Blätter für Württembergische Kirchengeschichte* 32 (1928): 234–53.

which had so recently been threatened.³⁰ It arose also because of the church's need to define more precisely the limits of what was permissible, in response both to the activities of 'missionaries' from Zinzendorf's ever less orthodox Herrnhut community, and to the continued activities of Pietist pastors and laity in organising gatherings separate from the public services of the established church.

Many of the Württemberg Pietist gatherings were in the tradition of those which had in practice been tolerated by the church since 1715. Bengel, by now perhaps Württemberg's leading theologian, had influenced a large number of those who held *Erbauungsstunden*. These included Beckh in Ludwigsburg, Sigel in Kirchheim, Autenrieth in Dettingen, and the *Repetent* Christoph Schmidlin in Tübingen. Members of the laity also held conventicles: the schoolmaster in Balingen, the *Amtmann* in Laichingen, the *Bürgermeister* in Heidenheim, and a member of the *Magistrat* in Freudenstadt were among those respectable citizens of Württemberg who held peaceful Pietist gatherings. But there were also continuing problems when conventicles were held at socially suspicious times – late into the night – and the participants were believed to hold unorthodox opinions. Köstlin in Blaubeuren was investigated, for example, for holding night-time gatherings and propagating mystic and spiritualist beliefs. It was also clear that there was an active network of Pietists with their own organisation and activities separate from those of the all-embracing state church. Many of these Pietists were former pupils of Bengel, who had ties of friendship with each other formed in their student days at Tübingen. On 14 and 15 August 1742 there was a large meeting of Pietists in the independent imperial city of Esslingen, geographically right next to Württemberg's capital Stuttgart, yet outside the jurisdiction of the Duchy. *Geheimrat* Bilfinger was sufficiently concerned about the political implications of such a gathering to obtain protocols concerning the participants.³¹

A more pressing concern, however, was that of the continued infiltration of the Württemberg church by emissaries from Zinzendorf's less than orthodox Herrnhut community. 'Missionaries', including the Graf von Zinzendorf himself, came in the guise of orthodox Lutherans, establishing contacts with the more radical Pietist wing of the Württemberg church. But after a while they would split the communities they had entered, to win over members for a more heterodox, separatist approach. Earlier, Zinzendorf had been accepted by Württemberg theologians as orthodox in his opinions, but by the late 1730s it was beginning to be agreed, even by Pietists in the upper ranks of the church, that the nature

³⁰ Cf. Lehmann, *Pietismus und Weltliche Ordnung*, pp. 82–94. On Bilfinger, see Heinz Liebing, *Zwischen Orthodoxie und Aufklärung. Das philosophische und theologische Denken Georg Bernhard Bilfingers* (Tübingen: J.C.B. Mohr (Paul Siebeck), 1961).
³¹ Fritz, 'Konventikel', *Blätter für Württembergische Kirchengeschichte* 54, pp. 75–119.

and implications of Herrnhut religion had changed. Zinzendorf's workers, however, were having some success at the local level, particularly in the Black Forest and in the Enz region, both areas with long traditions of heterodox activity. In Freudenstadt, where inner-churchly Pietism had been developing quite peaceably over a number of years, the advent of the Herrnhuters provoked political disturbances and the formation of opposing factions in the community. In Nagold, a 'brother' and 'sister' found more success: both secular authorities and pastors were favourable towards them. Subtle emotional pressures were put on those leading or prominent Pietists who retained an ambivalent affection for Zinzendorf's project. Oetinger, for example, who had reconverted to Württemberg Lutheranism and held a pastorate in Hirsau, was nevertheless dissuaded by the Herrnhuters Meisner and Gradin from publishing an anti-Herrnhut tract he had written. Freiherr Christoph Karl Ludwig von Pfeil – always somewhat of an exception among Württemberg Pietists, not least for his aristocratic status – even went ahead with plans for buying land on which to establish a new Herrnhut community in Württemberg, until as a result of continued disputes Zinzendorf gave up this plan in 1741.[32] The Württemberg church faced what might be seen as a problem of 'entryism', as individuals with other affiliations entered an organisation with similar aspirations, and used the sympathy they encountered to subvert that organisation, acting to dissolve the vehicle entered.

Accordingly, the Synod repeatedly discussed the questions of conventicles, Pietism, and separatism, and by 1743 the combined efforts of the Enlightenment-influenced Bilfinger and the Pietist lawyer Johann Jakob Moser had produced the *Generalreskript* on Pietism.[33] Building on Moser's recommendations of 1734 concerning conventicles in Reutlingen, this measure was exceptionally mild in tone. It began by reminding Württembergers that they should not stay away from public worship services, nor neglect their private household devotions, and suggested that these provisions should in fact suffice. Nevertheless, private gatherings for pious purposes with neighbours and friends should not be forbidden, so long as these did not lead to factionalism within the church. These gatherings should be limited in size, and kept under the oversight of a pastor. Apart from reading the Bible in Luther's translation, along with aids to understanding the scriptures, it was permitted to read other 'erbauliche Schrifften Evangelischer, alter und neuer Gottes-Gelehrten, die geprüft, und von der Kirche gebilliget, auch Gott Lob! in grosser Anzahl, und nach allen Arten vorhanden sind'.[34] But books, letters, and

---

[32] Ibid., pp. 88ff.
[33] Reprinted in Reyscher (ed.), *Württembergische Geseze*, pp. 641–52.
[34] 'Devotional writings by old and new godly Protestant scholars, that have been examined and approved by the Church, and also – praise God! – are available in great quantity and variety.' Ibid., p. 649.

pamphlets which were considered to be mystical, dark, suspicious, ambiguous, sectarian, syncretistic, were forbidden, as was the singing of 'dark' and 'mysterious' hymns. It was thus hoped that 'die allgemeine und besondere Erbauung begieriger Seelen keineswegs gehemmet und gehindert, anbey aber gleichwohlen alle Abweege, welche einzelnen Personen, oder der Kirche, gefährlich und schädlich seyn können, nach Möglichkeit verhütet werden'.[35] Inner-churchly Pietism was now officially and formally defined and accepted.

Pietism in mid-century Württemberg: political pluralism and passivity

Already after the demise of Karl Alexander Pietists were disunited politically. Those active on the Small Committee of the Estates disagreed with Pfaff's criticisms of this in comparison with a fully representative Diet; and at the other end of the political spectrum stood Weissensee, disgraced by his close relations with the court and bitterly opposed by Pfaff. This lack of unity on secular political affairs at the national level continued in subsequent decades, while at the local level, after the formal incorporation of conventicles in the church, the laity became more passive under pastoral supervision.

Bengel, for most of his life devoted to educational and scholarly work, became in old age a member of the Small Committee and hence directly involved in national politics. He recognised himself that he was suited by neither temperament nor experience to play an active political role: 'Zu Herbrechtingen glaubte ich am Ende der Welt zu seyn, zu Stuttgart bin ich mitten in ihrem sumpfigen Gewühle, und dazu muss ich als einer, der sein Leben in lauter geistlichen Beschäftigungen zugebracht, noch im Alter einen Lehrling im Weltlichen abgeben.'[36] Bengel was a deeply committed, conscientious person who attempted to fulfil his duties and honestly speak his mind on issues of conscience; but his age, ill-health, and lack of political experience combined with his eschatology to render him relatively passive and ineffectual in the face of things he considered to be wrong. Bengel upheld the old Estates' ideal of co-operation with the ruler; but he was prepared to interpret ungodly, absolutist rule as an aspect of the reign of Anti-Christ, part of God's plan for the World prior to the Second Coming. This view was not shared by other Pietists in national politics. Christoph Karl Ludwig von Pfeil, who had been

[35] 'The general and particular edification of eager souls will in no way be limited or hindered, but at the same time all the wrong turnings, which can be dangerous and injurious to individuals or to the Church, will as far as possible be guarded against.' Ibid., p. 651.
[36] 'In Herbrechtingen I felt I was at the end of the world, in Stuttgart I am in the midst of its quagmire and tumult, and on top of this I, who have spent my life in nothing but spiritual affairs, must in my old age become an apprentice in worldly matters.' Quoted in Mälzer, *Bengel*, p. 296.

strongly attracted to Zinzendorf and the Herrnhuters, actively supported Duke Karl Eugen in his absolutist projects. Pfeil even played a prominent role in the violent appropriation of money from the Estates' Chest in 1759.[37] Other Pietists had never entirely trusted the aristocratic von Pfeil, and they now turned against him. In 1763, partly regretting his earlier actions, Pfeil left Württemberg for Prussia. A number of Pietists held high positions in the church, and preached the need for patience, faith, and prayer; political activity was regarded by many as indicative of impatience, disobedience, and lack of faith. Philipp Friedrich Rieger, Storr, the Reuss brothers, Oetinger and others, whatever their varied personal opinions and criticisms of Duke Karl Eugen's rule, preached the importance of conscientious fulfilment of worldly duties.[38] Karl Eugen was quite cunning in relation to religious politics: by tolerating Pietist preachers in high positions, he succeeded in ensuring that no active ideologically unified opposition would emerge from this quarter. Karl Eugen could never hope to take over and use the machinery of the state church; it was therefore better to ensure that it was not united against him.

One Pietist, Johann Jakob Moser, did become a martyr to the cause of the Estates against the Duke, but in what can only be described as an isolated and idiosyncratic fashion. On returning to Württemberg in 1751, Moser incurred the suspicions of his colleagues when he found the Duke more sympathetic to his innovative plans for reform than were the conservative representatives of the Estates. As Moser puts it in his autobiography:

So bald ich ferner anfing, in- und ausser der Landschafft von Verbesserung des Policey- Manufactur- Handlungs- und Oeconomie-Wesens zu sprechen, gienge der Handel an, und ich würde darüber von vilen sonst patriotischen Leuten in- und ausser der Landschafft für weis nicht was für einen schädlichen Mann angesehen; aus einem national-Vorurtheil, als wären die bereits vorhandene Geseze und Anstalten schon hinlänglich genug, oder doch eine Verbesserung derselbigen hier zu Land nicht möglich, oder doch der Landes-Verfassung entgegen, und mit allerley besorglichen Missbräuchen verbunden.[39]

At the start of the troubles arising from the onset of war, the need to raise money and troops, and the revelations of the Duke's secret subsidy agreement with France – 'die betrübte jezige Landes-Irrungen', as Moser

---

[37] Lehmann, *Pietismus und Weltliche Ordnung*, pp. 104–5.

[38] Ibid., pp. 106–12. See also Albrecht Ritschl, *Geschichte des Pietismus*, vol. 3 (Bonn: Adolph Marcus, 1886), chs. 45 and 46.

[39] 'As soon as I began further to talk, inside and outside the Estates, about improvements in policy, manufacturing, trading and economic affairs, the whole business would start up, and I would be considered, by many otherwise patriotic people in and outside the Estates, as I don't know what sort of dangerous man; from national prejudice, as though the already existing laws and institutions were already quite adequate, or that after all any improvement of these would not be possible in this country, or that it would after all be contrary to the constitution, and connected with all sorts of alarming abuses.' Moser, *Lebensgeschichte*, p. 110.

puts it[40] – the Estates made a number of false accusations against Moser. But at the same time, Moser acted as the spokesman for the Estates against absolutist rule, and found himself becoming a scapegoat for the Estates in the battle with the Duke. Again, it is worth quoting his autobiography at some length, for what it indicates of the political processes as perceived by Moser himself:

Weil...ich bey allen in den Geheimen Rath erforderten Landschaftlichen Deputationen das Wort führen musste; so fiele der ganze Hass des Hofes und des Herrn Grafens allein auf mich, ich sollte Dinge gethan haben, daran ich nicht den geringsten Antheil hatte, und der Herr Graf glaubte, dass ich nicht allein gegen seine *Principia* sondern auch gegen seine Person agire, äusserte sich auch: Wer ihn attaquire, musse auf den Boden, und sollte er gleich mit darauf müssen: Und obgleich in denen Herzoglichen Resolutionen (welche immer schärffer gefasst und darinn von begangenem *crimine laesae Majestatis divinae humanae* gesprochen wurde,) weder den Consulenten, noch meiner, namentlich gedacht ware: so konnte ich doch mit Händen greiffen, dass ich entweder gehen und das Land im Stich lassen müsste, oder ein Opfer für dasselbige werden würde: Das erstere konnte und wollte ich Gewissens halber nicht; also erfolgte das letztere.[41]

On 12 July 1759 Moser was arrested and imprisoned.

During the course of Moser's imprisonment, neither the Estates in general nor Pietists in particular made much effort to support him, improve his conditions, or obtain his release. Moser was finally freed when the war, which had been the immediate occasion of the constitutional struggles, ended in 1764, and international powers put pressure on the Duke to resolve his internal difficulties. On Moser's release, a few Pietists or sympathisers – Oetinger, Jeremias Friedrich Reuss, Jakob Heinrich Dann, and Johann Gottlieb Faber – made efforts to get him reinstated on the Small Committee. But Moser failed to resolve his differences with this body: disagreements on organisation, policy, and principle were complicated by personal animosities and rivalry with the Stockmeyer family. The Small Committee excluded Dann; in 1770 Oetinger gave up his participation on the committee; and Moser never realised his plans for reform of what he considered to be a corrupt, incompetent, and unrepresentative institution. Thus the one truly active

---

[40] 'The present sad state of affairs into which the country has strayed.' Ibid., p. 177.

[41] 'Because I had to act as spokesman for all the deputations of the Estates called for in the Privy Council; so therefore the whole hatred of the court and the Count fell on me alone, I was supposed to have done things in which I had not taken the slightest part, and the Count believed that I was acting not only against his principles but also against his person, and expressed his opinion also: Whoever attacks him must be brought down, and straightaway: And although in those ducal resolutions (which were increasingly sharply expressed, and in which he spoke of committed *crimine laesae majestatis divinae humanae*), neither the *Consulent* nor myself was mentioned by name; yet it was as clear as daylight to me that either I must go, and leave the country in the lurch, or that I would become a martyr for the country. The former, for reasons of conscience, I would not and could not do; so the latter ensued.' Ibid., p. 120.

Pietist in national politics lacked adequate and united support to make an appreciable impact.[42]

At the local level, too, it appears that the general tendency of mid-century Pietism was towards pluralism and passivity. Increasingly, it seems, as conventicles were tolerated, even encouraged, by the church, they were instituted by pastors or schoolmasters and organised from above for a quietistic minority of the laity. While a considerable number of pastors and theology students were influenced by inner-churchly Pietism, separatist numbers had diminished from the levels at the beginning of the century.[43] Lay Pietists had become more inward-turning, subdued, and complaisant members of the congregation; favoured by the pastor in a passive piety, rather than rebelling against authority and engaging in clandestine organisation. They had lost the effervescence and activism of their predecessors who had fought against established structures to meet and worship in their own ways. Lay Pietists by now had become a distinctive and accepted subculture, with a peculiar mode of dress, set of gestures and expressions.[44] Weckherlin, an Enlightenment critic, has an acute characterisation of later Pietists, as perceived by their fellow citizens:

Pietisten sind demnach, wenn man den Wirtemberger fragt, blose Andächtige, Eiferer im Dienste Luthers, stille Enthusiasten im öffentlichen und gesellschaftlichen Gottesdienste, und im Privat Religionsexerzis büssende Seufzer. Lieblosigkeit oder laxer genommen, Unzufriedenheit mit der Singularitätssucht dieser Leute ist es wann sie unter dem allegemeinen Namen, Kopfhenker, übrigens mehr Begrif als Name, bezeichnet werden.[45]

Weckherlin evokes the strange appearance, gestures, expressions, clothing and gait of Pietists, the peculiar forms of speech (such as the frequent use of the adjective 'liebe', qualifying several nouns in each sentence), and even the particular style, tone or manner of speaking: 'weinerlich, sanft und leise wimmert oder seufzt vielmehr der arme Pietiste sein Anliegen hervor'.[46] From Seybold's contemporary novel, *Hartmann: Eine Wirtem-*

---

[42] Reinhard Rürup, *Johann Jacob Moser: Pietismus und Reform* (Wiesbaden: Franz Steiner Verlag, 1965); Grube, *Stuttgarter Landtag*; Alb. Eugen Adam, 'Herzog Karl und die Landschaft' in *Herzog Karl Eugen... und seine Zeit*; and Lehmann, *Pietismus und Weltliche Ordnung*.

[43] Fritz, 'Die evangelische Kirche Württembergs', Part 1, pp. 115–16.

[44] Cf. Martin Scharfe, *Die Religion des Volkes. Kleine Kultur- und Sozialgeschichte des Pietismus* (Gütersloh: Gütersloher Verlagshaus Gerd Mohn, 1980).

[45] 'Pietists are accordingly, if one asks the Wirtemberger, merely devout people, zealots in the service of Luther, quiet enthusiasts in public and societal worship services, and in private devotions penitent sighers. It is uncharitableness, or, more loosely, dissatisfaction with these people's urge to be peculiar, when they are characterised by the general name, headhangers, anyway more a concept than a name.' F.A. Weckherlin, *Wirtemberg. Pietismus. Schreiber. Schulen. Und Erziehung und Aufklärung überhaupt* (n.p.: 1787), pp. 13–14.

[46] 'Whining, meekly and faintly the poor Pietist whimpers or rather sighs out his concerns.' Ibid., p. 24.

bergische Klostergeschichte (1778) we obtain a similar picture: Seybold, describing how one youth was able to fake piety to achieve more nefarious ends, explains that 'niemand konnte den Kopf besser hängen, niemand die Augen andächtiger verdrehen, niemand rührender seufzen, als dieser kleine Heuchler'.[47] The characteristic Pietist stances are reproduced in their portraits, eyes turned to heaven, and the fortitude in suffering the ills of this world is highlighted in the pious biographies.[48]

What sort of citizens were these people? While some Pietist gatherings may have caused disturbances of the peace, it does not appear that these other-worldly souls were very active politically.[49] They may have used Pietist contacts for business purposes, as being trustworthy, but politically they appear to have stood rather apart from the world. We lack any detailed village studies which could tell us how Pietists related to the *Amtsversammlungen* which according to Grube were growing in importance in the course of the eighteenth century, putting increasing democratic pressures on the Estates.[50] But Weckherlin's picture – admittedly a picture drawn by an unsympathetic observer – does not suggest that these Pietists played an active role in local politics:

Man sah, dass des Pietisten Grundzug ist: Schleichen, (nicht eben kriechen) Dulden, Seufzen. Er ist ehrlich, er mag wahrer oder blos heuchlerischer Andächtiger seyn. Er hat den Hass seiner Mitbürger; dennoch das Zutrauen derselben. Sein Wandel ist abgezogen, einsiedlerisch.[51]

The 'Dulden', the patient suffering of Pietists, was a way of failing to answer the criticisms and mockery of the world. In separating from the world, according to Weckherlin, Pietists were bad citizens, unconcerned about the well-being of the whole community.[52]

A circular correspondence of Pietist pastors in the period 1760 to 1810 gives a direct insight into the concerns of some at least of the clergy.[53] From this it appears that in the relevant period, apocalyptic and chiliastic beliefs were not central concerns. The stress in the correspondence was

---

[47] 'No-one could hang his head better, no-one roll his eyes more devoutly, no-one sigh more stirringly, than this little hypocrite.' David Christian Seybold, *Hartmann: Eine Wirtembergische Klostergeschichte* (Leipzig: In der Weygandschen Buchhandlung, 1778), pp. 104–5.

[48] Cf. Scharfe, *Religion des Volkes*.

[49] Cf. for example Christoph Kolb, 'Strenge Handhabung des Edikts von 1743', *Blätter für Württembergische Kirchengeschichte* 6 (1902): 90–2.

[50] Cf. Chapter 3, above.

[51] 'It has been seen that the characteristic of the Pietist is: slinking (not quite creeping), enduring, sighing. He is honourable, whether he be a genuine or a purely hypocritical devout person. He is hated by his fellow citizens; but trusted by them nevertheless. His conduct is withdrawn, reclusive.' Weckerlin, *Wirtemberg. Pietismus. Schreiber. Schulen.*, p. 33.

[52] Ibid., pp. 40–6.

[53] See C. Hoffmann, 'Aus einer altpietistischen Zirkularkorrespondenz', *Blätter für Württembergische Kirchengeschichte* 4 (1900): 1–35.

on carrying out the clerical vocation, on the conduct of gatherings, and improvement of morals in the congregation. Although the numbers attending gatherings seem from these reports to have been large, and although separatism and heterodoxy were mentioned as problems, the initiative seems to have remained with the pastors rather than the people. In many cases, it appears that *Erbauungsstunden* ended when the pastor who had run them left the locality.[54]

Changes were to take place in the Württemberg Pietist tradition in the closing decades of the eighteenth century. In changing social and political conditions, a lower-class lay Pietism arose in tension with the incorporated, passive form of Pietism of the mid-century.[55] But in the crucial period of the constitutional struggles between Duke and Estates, when the issue of absolutist rule was in the balance, Pietists presented a passive, disunited picture of pluralism and retreat. While Puritans at a comparable moment provided the ideological rallying-cry for battle and the organisational network for effective opposition, Pietists in Württemberg withdrew into quietistic disapproval. Incorporated into the state church, tolerated in their religious orientations and organisation, Pietists were not provoked into political action. Structural circumstances were such that, unlike in England, no unity of purpose was forged in adversity. Pietism in Württemberg was safe in its tolerant retreat.

How does this narrative of the politics of Württemberg Pietists compare with that presented for English Puritans in the preceding chapter? It is worth very briefly reiterating the points of similarity and difference in structure as these affected patterns of agency. In both cases, precisionists had a relatively strong societal base against a relatively weak absolutism. In both cases, they tended to develop an antipathy against the hedonism and immorality of a would-be absolutist court. State/society relationships were in many ways comparable, as analysed in Chapter 3. But state/church relationships were rather different, as recounted in Chapter 4, and this had crucial consequences for the politicisation or otherwise of the movements. In England, the ambiguous, politically contested location of the state church meant that, when the state tried to use the established church for certain political ends, then the Puritans, whose religious programme had very different implications, were inevitably roused to political action. In Württemberg, the church was politically, economically, and socially too strong for the ruler to be able to make any serious use of it for his own ends. The relative independence of the Württemberg church gave it a certain freedom to determine its own response to the precisionist movement for religious reform. Since this movement appeared not to pose a political threat, it was tolerated and incorporated.

---

[54] Lehmann, *Pietismus und Weltliche Ordnung*, p. 119.
[55] See ibid., passim, for details of the further development of Pietism in Württemberg.

This defused the initial political activism of the Pietists. They shared the anti-absolutist attitudes of Puritans, but because of the different church/state relations they tended, in a period of political crisis for absolutism, to remain quiescent and marginal actors on the historical stage. Let us turn now to the very different pattern of developments in the Prussian case.

7

From reform to state religion: Pietism in Prussia

Those who followed the call of Spener to reform and renew the Christianity of their Protestant state churches represented initially a challenge to the established order of things. In Württemberg, as we have seen, this challenge was responded to with tolerance and incorporated into the life of the established church; one consequence of this toleration was that Württemberg Pietism lost its political dynamism and failed to develop into an effective, organised political force in national affairs. A different pattern of development took place in contemporaneous Prussia. Rather than being accepted by and incorporated into the church, Pietism was here opposed by orthodoxy. But the dynamics of the situation were such that the Pietist movement, rejected by orthodoxy, was not, as in England, rejected also by the state, but was rather, over time, absorbed by the state and transformed into a new form of orthodoxy, a new style of state religion.

Spener had left Frankfurt, the scene of the first Pietist gatherings and the place where he wrote his influential *Pia Desideria*, to take up a position in Dresden. But the Electorate of Saxony, where the orthodox church was closely allied with the state, soon became ill-disposed towards Pietism. The social disturbances occasioned by Pietist meetings in Leipzig, and the threats to the monopoly status of orthodoxy, aroused governmental disfavour; and the ruler found listening to Spener's outspoken preaching against the immorality of court life quite unbearable. Spener himself tended to passivity, even fatalism, in his personal affairs; but when in 1691 a call came from Berlin offering him an influential position at the Nicolaikirche, the Saxon state was not unwilling to release Spener from its services and Spener was glad to accept the new position in Prussia.[1]

Spener made use of his new position in Berlin to aid the cause of Pietism in Brandenburg-Prussia. The location and the moment were both opportune. The Prussian state, for reasons described in Chapters 3 and 4

---

[1] See particularly Kurt Aland, 'Philipp Jakob Spener. Sein Lebensweg von Frankfurt nach Berlin (1666–1705), dargestellt an Hand seiner Briefe nach Frankfurt' in Aland, *Kirchengeschichtliche Entwürfe* (Gütersloh: Gütersloher Verlagshaus Gerd Mohn, 1960); Paul Grünberg, *Philipp Jakob Spener* (Göttingen: Vandenhoek und Ruprecht, 3 vols., 1893–1906); also Erich Beyreuther, *Geschichte des Pietismus* (Stuttgart: J.F. Steinkopf Verlag, 1978), ch. 2.

above, favoured policies of religious toleration and welcomed religious minorities which seemed to offer political or economic rewards. More specifically, the 1690s were a propitious moment for the introduction of Pietism in the religious and intellectual life of Prussia. The new University of Halle was founded as a Prussian counterbalance to the strongly orthodox Lutheran universities of Wittenberg and Leipzig. Partly through Spener's influence, two notable young Pietists, rejected by Saxony for their activities in Leipzig, were able to take up professorships at Halle: J. J. Breithaupt and August Hermann Francke. Francke, as well as holding the chair of oriental languages, became the pastor of the parish of Glaucha, a suburb of Halle just on the outskirts of the town. It was here that the Prussian Pietist movement developed its first great centre of dynamism and influence. And it was here that the first troubles occurred which occasioned the mutual working out of positions and relationships among orthodoxy, Pietists, and the state. At the same time, however, the Pietist movement was gaining adherents in Berlin and in Königsberg, far over in East Prussia.

This chapter will look, first, at the early development of relationships between Pietists and the state in each area under Friedrich III (I); and then at the later partnership of Pietism and the state, or incorporation of Pietism in the service of Prussian absolutism, under Friedrich Wilhelm I. It will focus on the ways in which the different aims and interests of the various protagonists combined to produce the peculiar development of an oppositional, individualistic religious minority into a state religion under absolutism.

The initial establishment of Pietism in Prussia

The town of Halle, south-west of Berlin in the province of Magdeburg-Halberstadt, had suffered badly during the Thirty Years War; it had been further devastated by plague in 1681–2 and by fires in 1683 and 1684. The population had suffered great physical losses and people were psychologically demoralised. When Francke arrived, his parish of Glaucha had no less than thirty-seven taverns for two hundred houses. Drunkenness and immorality were the norm, and even Francke's predecessor as pastor had been a notable drunkard. Standards of religious education and practice were minimal. Francke, with his zeal for conversion and for the establishment of the Kingdom of God upon Earth through the regeneration of the individual, immediately set about trying to remedy this disordered state of affairs.[2]

---

[2] See particularly: Klaus Deppermann, *Der Hallesche Pietismus und der Preussische Staat unter Friedrich III. (I.)* (Göttingen: Vandenhoek und Ruprecht, 1961); Erich Beyreuther, *August Hermann Francke 1663–1727: Zeuge des Lebendigen Gottes* (Marburg an der Lahn: Verlag der Francke-Buchhandlung GmbH, 1956); Gustav Kramer, *August Her-*

Francke's initial instrument for the enforcement of social and moral order was exclusion from communion until the individual had shown a genuine change in life-style, rather than merely expressed a verbal formula of repentance with no meaning during the rest of the week. Francke's strict use of excommunication was applied without consideration of the social standing of the potential communicant: an early local controversy arose from Francke's refusal to admit the cantor to communion because of his excessive smoking, gambling, and drinking. Francke also preached on such problems as the 'sehr verwildete Jugend', the 'schlechte Kinder-zucht' and the 'grosse entheiligung des Sontages und sonst grosse Unordnung Tages und Nachts in der Gemeinde'.[3] Francke's strong church discipline and outspoken preaching against the general life-style of his congregation soon aroused antagonism from a number of quarters; not least was the complaint that 'man die Wirthe umb ihre Nahrung bringen wolte'.[4] Tavern-keepers may have been concerned for their material livelihood; their clientele, not entirely unconcerned for the spiritual state of their souls but unwilling to follow the straight and narrow path prescribed by Pietists, fled from Francke's strict discipline to receive communion from more lenient pastors in the town parishes of Halle. This led Francke into making both implicit and explicit criticisms of orthodox pastors, who in his opinion were lulling people into a false sense of security while confirming them in their ungodly ways. Orthodoxy, particularly in the shape of Roth, archdeacon of the St Ulrich church, had for its part long been ready to criticise Pietists. Roth's 1691 anti-Pietist pamphlet, *Imago Pietismi*, had been forbidden publication in Prussia, but had been published instead in Leipzig; it was soon responded to by Veit Ludwig von Seckendorff, and a flurry of theological polemics and pamphleteering complemented the social disturbances aroused by Pietist activities in Halle.[5]

There were many strands to the controversies. At a theological level, Pietists accused orthodoxy of withholding the real means of salvation through internal understanding and genuinely experienced conversion leading to a new and fully Christian life. Orthodoxy accused Pietists of dissolving correct doctrine, which alone was the true means of salvation, of devaluing God's word by arguing that its efficacy was dependent on the state of grace of the preacher proclaiming it. At the social level, the

---

mann Francke: Ein Lebensbild (Halle: Verlag der Buchhandlung des Waisenhauses, 1880), Part 1.
[3] 'The youth which has run wild', the 'bad child-rearing', and the 'great profanation of the Sabbath and otherwise great disorders day and night in the parish.' Excerpts from Francke's diary, reprinted in G. Kramer (ed.), *Beiträge zur Geschichte August Hermann Franckes* (Halle: Verlag der Buchhandlung des Waisenhauses, 1861), pp. 187–91.
[4] 'They wanted to deprive publicans of their livelihood.' Ibid., p. 192.
[5] On Francke's troubles with Halle orthodoxy, see the discussion and documents reprinted in G. Kramer (ed.), *Neue Beiträge zur Geschichte A.H. Franckes* (Halle: Verlag der Buchhandlung des Waisenhauses, 1875), Part 2; see also references cited in n. 2, above.

collegia pietatis held by Breithaupt, and the evening prayer meeting held by Francke, occasioned suspicion; and splits developed among Pietists and non-Pietists in the congregation. The anti-Pietist polemics of orthodox pastors led to members of the laity ridiculing Pietists openly on the streets, and a variety of accusations were made against those who frequented Pietist gatherings. After only a few months of Pietist activity in Halle, theological polemics and social unrest had reached major proportions.

Francke chose a direct way to attempt to resolve this unrest. He asked von Schweinitz, a Pietistically inclined old noble member of the Berlin government, to set up a lay commission to investigate the troubles, which by now posed a problem for secular authorities. This appeal to the laity to resolve what was at least in origin a theological dispute did not meet with the approval of all Pietists; von Seckendorff, for example, who had answered Roth's *Imago Pietismi*, was against the involvement of the government in theological controversy.[6] Nevertheless, a commission was duly set up, composed generally of individuals favourable to the Pietist cause. By the time it made its investigations, Roth had left Halle for Leipzig, and the evidence presented by orthodoxy was weak and unsubstantiated.[7] The commission, which had started meeting on 17 November 1692, soon found in favour of the Pietists, and ordered that they should no longer be denounced as heretical:

Was von der Wiedergeburt, Erleuchtung, Heiligung, Verläugnung seiner selbst, innerlichem Menschen und dergleichen Stücken dem Worte Gottes und den symbolischen Büchern gemäss gepredigt oder in Privatdiscursen gemeldet wird, ist keineswegs für schwärmerei oder Neuerung zu halten, sondern als göttliche Wahrheit anzunehmen und in Kraft Gottes aller Fleiss dahin anzuwenden, dass solche göttliche Lehren in lebendiger Erkenntniss von einem Jeden gefasst werden mögen.[8]

This statement was to be read from all pulpits in December, much against the wishes of orthodoxy. But as part of the compromise solution for peace, Breithaupt was to exclude townspeople from his *collegia* when students were undertaking exegeses, and Francke was to hold his prayer meetings before, rather than after, the evening meal, thus avoiding suspicions of holding a 'nocturnal conventicle'. (One consequence of this publicity was that participation in Francke's gathering rose from twenty to 250 people, and it had to be moved from a room in his own house to

---

[6] Deppermann, *Hallesche Pietismus*, p. 78.
[7] Kramer, *Neue Beiträge*, pp. 66–77.
[8] 'Whatever is preached or imparted in private discussions according to the Word of God and the symbolic Books, concerning rebirth, enlightenment, self-denial, the inner man, and such-like matters, is in no way to be considered fanaticism or innovation, but is rather to be accepted as godly truth, and with the power of God pains are to be taken that such godly teachings may be grasped with true understanding by everyone.' Ibid., p. 76.

take place in the church.) During the course of 1693, Francke also became more wary of supporting a variety of enthusiasts, prophetesses, and *Schwärmer*, removing other causes for orthodox suspicion.[9]

Despite ostensible external resolution of the controversies, tensions between Pietists and orthodoxy continued during the 1690s. Theological differences were augmented by more practical grounds for opposition to Pietist activities and institutions. Francke relates the development of his world-renowned orphanage, schools, and associated enterprises, in his masterpiece of publicity and propaganda, the *Segens-volle Fussstapfen des noch lebenden und waltenden liebreichen und getreuen Gottes, zur Beschämung des Unglaubens und Stärckung des Glaubens, entdecket durch eine Wahrhafte und umständliche Nachricht von dem Waysen-Hause und übrigen Anstalten zu Glaucha vor Halle...*[10] In 1694 Francke started catechising the beggars who came on Thursdays for alms; in 1695 he instituted a donations box for the poor, and at Easter started a small school for poor children. After a while, Francke also took on children of wealthier citizens and nobles, at their own expense. In the summer of 1695 there were one or two extremely generous donations, and Francke, seeing this as a sign of God's providence, expanded his school, rented rooms in a neighbouring house, and divided the school into separate classes. He also started taking in orphans, paying foster parents to look after them, and then decided to run a full-scale orphanage. More money was coming in from donations, some of them very large, and in 1696 Francke bought the neighbouring house outright. He set up *Studententische*, at which poor students from the university could receive free board in return for giving some lessons, and began to develop his pedagogical ideas about streaming according to ability rather than social background and training for different future careers. In 1697 Francke's assistant, Georg Heinrich Neubauer, was sent to Holland to look at the latest orphanages there, to develop ideas and models for a new building in Halle. The following year the foundation stone was laid for the Halle orphanage, which in the course of a few years was built up into a majestic five-storey stone building with numerous additional houses and associated concerns.[11]

Francke makes much in his account of the providential way in which God provided for every need of the orphanage and schools as they developed, God's providence acting through the worldly instruments of well-meaning individuals who made crucial donations of exactly the

---

[9] Deppermann, *Hallesche Pietismus*, pp. 81–6; see also Beyreuther, *Francke*, and Grünberg, *Spener*.

[10] August Hermann Francke, *Segens-volle Fussstapfen...* (Halle: In Verlegung des Waysenhauses, 1709).

[11] Francke, 'Wahrhafte und umständliche Nachricht von dem Wäysen-hause und übrigen Anstalten zu Glaucha vor Halle. I. Vom Ursprung und Veranlassung, auch Fortgang und Zunehmen der Anstalten', in Francke, *Segens-volle Fussstapfen*.

required amounts at times of particular need. But Francke was a shrewd businessman, with a keen eye for secular ways of furthering God's work in any conceivable manner. During the course of establishing the orphanage and schools, Francke developed a number of associated economic enterprises which helped to give financial independence, and explored a variety of tax concessions and means of obtaining a steady income additional to unpredictable private donations. The economic enterprises included a book printing and publishing business, a chemist for the production and selling of medicines, and a variety of long-distance trading ventures, which dealt not only in such Christian products as the Bible in various foreign languages but also in items of luxury consumption of which Pietists generally disapproved. Tax concessions included freedom from excise duties on food intended for the consumption of poor children and orphans, and later franking privileges for the postage and distribution of a newspaper. Francke also won from the ruler rights to a steady income from a 'Kirchentaler' – an annual contribution from all solvent churches in Magdeburg-Halberstadt – and one-tenth of all fine payments under fifty talers (later increased to five hundred talers) in the province. And, against guild regulations, Francke obtained the right to give children of unknown parentage (hence illegitimate) a certificate of honour to allow them to take up apprenticeships, learn a trade and gain honest employment. Not surprisingly, these related aspects of Francke's primarily religious and educational institutions – their economic underpinnings – aroused antagonism from a variety of affected quarters.[12] The churches of Magdeburg-Halberstadt were reluctant to pay their yearly contribution; and the secular authorities were markedly unwilling to hand over a tithe of their income from fines. The early complaints of tavern-keepers in Glaucha that Francke was robbing them of their livelihood were soon augmented by the complaints of other craftsmen and traders against the competition posed by Francke's various economic endeavours. The provincial tax-officials were unwilling to make it easy for Francke to obtain his agreed tax rebates. The local guilds developed strong opposition to Francke's providing certificates for illegitimate children. In all sorts of ways, Francke's activities provoked the hostility of established organisations and interests. This hostility was only heightened by the high-handed and self-righteous manner in which Francke went about pursuing his goals, as when he tried to misinterpret the law to appropriate church funds to which he was not entitled, in the case of the Schulkirche, or when he forcibly put through his own plans for buying and building on a controversial piece of property.[13] These practical controversies ran

[12] See particularly Deppermann, *Hallesche Pietismus*, on which these paragraphs are based.

[13] See ibid., pp. 126–8, for the story of the Schulkirche affair, in which Francke exhibited a singular lack of charity and honesty. Spener and Paul von Fuchs disapproved of Francke's dealings in this matter.

alongside the continuing theological polemics between Pietists and orthodox pastors.

In the course of these antagonisms the partnership between Pietism and the absolutist state was formed. Where the state could see potential economic and political benefits for itself, it supported Francke and his concerns, against provincial Estates' and orthodox opposition. Where the local opposition proved too strong, and it appeared politically prudent to withdraw, the state dropped its support of parts of Pietist activities. This was the case, for example, with the opposition of the guilds to accepting illegitimate children as apprentices; Francke was forced to return to accepted social standards and conform to the guild codes of conduct. The payment of a tithe of all fines proved impracticable, and what income was dredged in from this source was in relative terms negligible, so that Francke was himself finally prepared to forgo it. But on other matters Francke had his way, eventually, and in the early years of the eighteenth century Halle Pietism appeared well-established. At least until about 1705, there seemed to be a certain parallelism between the aims of ruler and government in Berlin, and those of the Pietists in Halle. This parallelism, in which the religious and educational endeavours of Francke performed certain useful political and economic functions for the state – reducing local Estates' and guild powers, stimulating manufactures and trade – led to ideological as well as practical legal and financial support by the state.

In 1698 Francke delivered his outspoken sermon about false prophets, in which he identified orthodoxy as prime examples of wolves in sheep's clothing; on 2 February 1699 he made an even more specific attack on certain Halle pastors in particular.[14] The ministry of Halle not surprisingly complained about this; and Francke responded unrepentantly to orthodoxy's complaints. Even if it were true that he had attacked orthodoxy, the reverse was even more true: he had himself been under attack for over seven years, 'continuirlich mit Schelten und Schmähen'. Francke continued his criticisms of the way in which orthodoxy confirmed and condoned worldly lusts and sins, failed to exercise adequate church discipline, and preached in a manner which served 'offenbarlich mehr zum Gespötte und Aergerniss, als zur Erbauung'. Orthodox sermons could never offer the way to true repentance and conversion: 'den Leuten nicht recht, noch zulänglich die Mittel angezeiget werden, wie sie aus ihrem innerlichen Elende und verderbten Zustande in einen rechten neuen und bessern Zustand versetzt werden können ... Wenn ich dann und wann ihre Predigten gehöret, bin ich sehr niedergeschlagen und

---

[14] The sermon on false prophets is reprinted in Erhard Peschke (ed.), *August Hermann Francke: Werke in Auswahl* (Evangelische Verlagsanstalt Berlin: Luther-Verlag, 1969), pp. 305–35; see also Kramer, *Neue Beiträge*, pp. 66–118; an extract of the sermon of 2/2/1699 is reprinted on pp. 87–8.

betrübet wieder herausgegangen weil ich allemal überzeugt gewesen, dass daraus ohnmöglich eine wahre Erbauung gehoffet werden könne ...'[15] Not only were orthodox pastors not offering the means of edification; they were also trying to hinder the work of others – the Pietists – who did make efforts to achieve true conversions. Pietists were even made fun of in the streets by children, as a result of anti-Pietist campaigns. And these same pastors, themselves unregenerate, allowed people to continue drinking, gambling, profaning the Sabbath and living in sin... Francke's tone throughout was one of self-righteous indignation: it was not he who was 'Zankhaft', but rather his opponents, who refused to keep quiet when Francke himself was conciliatory, patient, tolerant, and concerned only for the greater glory of God.

Whatever the righteousness or otherwise of Francke's case, the controversies were bad for the wider reputation of the young University of Halle in which both the ruler and the local Estates, who paid taxes for its support, had an interest. In 1700 accordingly another secular investigative commission was set up to consider the theological issues; subsequently, the running of the orphanage and associated enterprises in Glaucha was also investigated. As in 1692, the findings of the investigations were generally favourable towards the Pietists, who appeared to be doing much for the standards of morality, social control, and economic activity of the area. Theological polemics were quelled, and in 1702 Francke easily obtained from the newly crowned king a renewal of the electoral privileges for the Pietist institutions. The state confirmed its support for Pietist activities, insofar as these seemed to operate for the good of the state as perceived by the ruler.

In Berlin in the 1690s Pietism was gathering adherents under the influence of Spener and his followers outside court circles. And in Berlin, as in Halle, Pietist attitudes and activities occasioned social unrest and theological controversy. One particular episode, the so-called 'Berliner Beichtstuhlstreit', neatly illustrates the parallelism between the aims of the state and the aims of certain Pietists, however different, ultimately, these aims might be.[16]

Johann Caspar Schade, one of Spener's three assistants at the Nicolaikirche, was a highly conscientious, sensitive, somewhat melancholic individual of delicate health. He began to develop extreme scruples about the

---

[15] 'Continually with abuses and insults', 'evidently more for mockery and vexation than for edification', 'people are neither correctly nor sufficiently shown the means by which they can be removed from their inner misery and depravity into a new and better condition... When I now and then heard their sermons, I left very downcast and distressed, because I was continually convinced that it was impossible that a true edification could be hoped for from this.' Kramer, *Neue Beiträge*, pp. 81, 90, 93.

[16] See particularly Helmut Obst, *Der Berliner Beichtstuhlstreit* (Witten: Luther-Verlag, 1972), on which this account is largely based.

carrying out of his duties, and in particular became concerned about the efficacy of the routine methods of confession and absolution before receiving Holy Communion. Fearful lest confession should become, or be considered, a purely mechanical act, and that absolution should be viewed as a purchasable commodity related to the amount a would-be communicant could pay, Schade drove himself to a mental and physical breakdown in the process of a more thorough carrying out of his confessional duties. This alone might have remained a purely personal crisis, assuaged somewhat by the willingness of Schade's colleagues to relieve him for a while of part of his work-load; but Schade's excessive concern with spiritual discipline provoked, through one particular incident, a more general controversy. Schade had a reputation for achieving notable effects on the religiosity of adolescent girls: it was proudly proclaimed by Pietists that Schade could teach teenage girls to extemporise the most beautiful, heart-rending spiritual prayers. But Schade's frequent visits to the female members of the congregation aroused suspicions on the part of many less well-disposed towards Pietism. When Schade disciplined two pubescent girls by giving them a beating on bare flesh, a full-scale row broke out. In retrospect, it is impossible to determine the precise details of Schade's particular case, which was at the very least highly embarrassing for the sober, aging leader of the Pietist movement, Spener. The incident provoked public debate about a wider set of controversies, which in relation to theological issues focussed on the question of whether communicants should be allowed freedom of choice between private or general confession and absolution before receiving communion. Sides were taken; the populace of Berlin was violently divided, with Schade amassing a personal following of enthusiasts (*Schwärmer*); growing dangers of separatism and the disturbance of public order through incidents leading to riots necessitated eventually the intervention of the Elector and the setting up of an investigative commission.

Friedrich's decision, finally, was in favour of the Pietist position supporting personal freedom to choose between private or general confession. This meant that pastors could more effectively employ the instruments of confession and participation in Holy Communion in the interests of real church discipline, taking time over individual problematic cases and, with a change in the financing procedures, not needing to worry about the number of fees collected or the wealth or poverty of communicants. But at the same time the change loosened the compulsory nature of the ties of individuals to the institutional church. Pietists were in favour for the former reasons; the state for the latter, since it represented a move towards the potential union of the Lutheran and Reformed faiths and towards the religious toleration favoured by the state for political and economic reasons. Orthodox Lutherans, not surprisingly, viewed this as a considerable blow to the institutional monopoly of the established church over the means of salvation. Yet even in this case, where the parallelism between the aims of the state and the aims of Pietists, against the interests of the established church, appeared quite clear, there were some ambiguities. Spener, while trying to protect and excuse his young friend and colleague Schade, had great misgivings about the issues, and disapproved of Francke's vociferous support of Schade's position. The younger generation of Pietists were readier to throw themselves into battle against orthodoxy with the aid of the state than was the elderly leader of a movement which was escaping his control.[17]

East Prussia in the 1680s and '90s was a province far from the seat of government in Berlin, its religious life characterised by syncretism and sectarianism in Königsberg, superstition and ignorance in the country areas.[18] There were fears of the recatholicisation of Königsberg, as large numbers were converted in the 1680s. In 1689 a *Holzkämmerer*, Theodor Gehr, arrived in Königsberg, imbued with a piety akin to that of Spener. Gehr set up his own private house meetings for prayer and religious edification. In 1693, after a visit to Berlin in the course of which he met Spener, Gehr remodelled his devotional sessions along the lines of Spener's *collegia pietatis*, finding a number of willing participants in Königsberg. Already by 1695 these modest beginnings had provoked anti-Pietist polemics in the city, as orthodox pastors denounced Pietism as a hidden papism; but the Elector issued a pro-Pietist edict. In 1697 Gehr made a trip to Halle, where he met Francke and gained ideas for educational activities. In August 1698 Gehr started a small school with four boys; in January 1699 he opened a school for the poor. Pietism in East Prussia thus evolved out of indigenous initiatives stimulated by contacts with Spener and Francke in Berlin and Halle.

These early developments met with great opposition on the part of orthodoxy. There were vitriolic polemics about 'unberuffenen Winckelprediger' and 'Winckelschulen' depriving trained teachers and pastors of their rightful livelihood; there were complaints about syncretism, religious innovation, and heresy. Gehr adopted what had become the recourse of Pietists in Halle: in 1699 he appealed to the ruler, Elector Friedrich III, for a commission of inquiry. The opponents of Pietism

---

[17] Grünberg, *Spener*, p. 332; see also Francke, 'Kurtzer und Einfältiger Entwurff / Von den Missbräuchen Des Beichtstuhls...', reprinted in Peschke, *Francke: Werke*, pp. 92–107.

[18] See generally: Walter Hubatsch, *Geschichte der evangelischen Kirche Ostpreussens*, 3 vols. (Göttingen: Vandenhoek und Ruprecht, 1968); Walter Borrmann, *Das Eindringen des Pietismus in die Ostpreussische Landeskirche* (Königsberg: Kommissionsverlag Ferd. Beyers Buchhandlung, Thomas und Oppermann, 1913); Erich Riedesel, *Pietismus und Orthodoxie in Ostpreussen* (Königsberg und Berlin: Ost-Europa-Verlag, 1937); Albert Nietzki, *Bilder aus dem evangelischen Pfarrhause Ostpreussens im achtzehnten Jahrhundert* (Königsberg: Kommissionsverlag Ferd. Beyers Buchhandlung, Thomas und Oppermann, 1909).

failed to prove that Gehr taught heretical doctrines, and the commission's findings were favourable to the Pietists. Polemics did not abate, however, and on the instigation of anti-Pietist ministers the Estates' *Gravamina* of 1699–70 complained about the 'new sect' of Pietism and the disturbance of the public peace. Nevertheless, the Elector remained well-disposed towards Pietist activities, as he continued in his attempts to reduce the local powers of Estates and orthodoxy.

In 1701 Elector Friedrich III crowned himself King Friedrich I in Prussia. As King, he took over the summepiscopacy of the church in East Prussia, and made moves to increase his control over its activities. In future the consistoria, under the King, had to ratify the nomination of pastors even under private noble patronage; and there were edicts for the introduction of stronger church discipline and better religious education.[19] Friedrich also founded an orphanage, on the Halle model, on his coronation day. These religious policies were of course very much in line with Pietist activities, which Friedrich was not loath to support. In March 1701 he took over Gehr's school, renaming it eventually the Collegium Fridericianum, and giving it a privileged status. Gehr, while possessing great personal motivation and religious inspiration, had no formal qualifications for teaching; so a Pietist associate, Lysius, was appointed Director of the school alongside his other positions. Lysius transformed the school from a 'Winckelschule' into an important educational institution offering the study of classical languages and natural sciences, a curriculum soon to be copied by other Königsberg schools. The school was influential not only in educating future Pietist ministers, but also in training people for lay professions and impregnating them with Pietist attitudes and goals. Part of the school buildings (the kitchen and woodstall) were converted into a small church, where Pietist preaching drew huge audiences from the Königsberg population, attracted by the unintended publicity given by anti-Pietist preaching elsewhere. The Estates' *Gravamen* of 1703 made strong complaints about the school, which it held responsible for widespread sectarianism and chiliasm, and demanded its closure. The complaints had to be toned down before being sent to the King, who did not give up his support for the Pietists' work. By 1707 an anti-Pietist coalition had developed among the ministry, the Consistorium, the secular magistrates, and the academic senate of the University, as a result of Lysius' and other Pietists' criticisms of orthodox preaching and teaching. Public disorders and the loss of authority by ministers over members of their congregations led to yet another official governmental inquiry; and again Berlin reaffirmed the rectitude of Pietist ideas, choosing to disregard the provocative nature of Pietist attacks on orthodoxy. Internally, however, the disputes remained unresolved, and began to spread into the surrounding countryside. With the deaths from

[19] Hubatsch, *Evangelische Kirche Ostpreussens*. Cf. Chapter 4, above.

plague in 1709 of two orthodox professors at the University, the King proposed Lysius for a better position. Despite strong opposition, Lysius finally was installed, thus obtaining increased influence over the developing minds of theology students. By the time of Friedrich's death in 1713, Pietism had an established, if hotly contested, foothold in East Prussian religious and educational life.[20]

The incorporation of Pietism under Friedrich Wilhelm I (1713–40)

The developing partnership between Pietism and the state under Friedrich III (I) was not entirely smooth. From 1705 onwards, Halle Pietism fell into some disfavour at court. This partly resulted from the deaths of some of the main supporters of Pietism in Berlin. (Paul von Fuchs, minister for school and church affairs, died in 1704; Spener died in 1705, leaving Pietists without a moderating influence and respected theological spokesman; Samuel von Chwalkowski died in 1705, and Georg Rudolf von Schweinitz committed suicide in a fit of religious depression in 1707.) It took some time for Francke to strengthen and develop other links to the King, most importantly through Canstein and General von Natzmer. It was partly because of conflicts over specific religious policies – Pietists never became purely puppets of Prussian absolutism – particularly concerning the proposed introduction of a Professor of the Reformed Faith at the University of Halle. And it was partly because of the religious fanaticism of Friedrich's young, third, wife, Sophie Luise, who under the influence of her mystic pastor Porst fled into religious fantasies and eventual madness. A high point of Sophie Luise's mental illness coincided with a visit of Francke to Berlin in 1709. Despite Francke's opposition to Porst's mysticism, and his attempts to instil more practical elements into the young Queen's religiosity, Francke was generally held responsible for Sophie Luise's orientations and was expelled from Berlin, forbidden to return. These developments were hardly conducive to the fostering of a sympathetic attitude towards Pietism on the part of the Crown Prince, Friedrich Wilhelm.[21]

Nevertheless, Francke was a shrewd operator in public relations; the Pietist institutions at Halle were well-established and widely renowned; and Friedrich Wilhelm was developing strong ideas and interests of his own concerning the state he was to inherit. After viewing the outside of the Halle buildings in the course of journey in 1711, Friedrich Wilhelm received conflicting reports on Pietist activities which aroused his interest. Later in the same year, Francke composed a detailed memorandum

---

[20] See particularly Borrmann, *Eindringen des Pietismus*, ch. 3.
[21] Deppermann, *Hallesche Pietismus*, ch. 13; Carl Hinrichs, *Friedrich Wilhelm I. König in Preussen* (Hamburg: Hanseatische Verlagsanstalt, 1941), Book 4, ch. 2.

for the heir to the throne, pointing out the economic and political advantages of his various enterprises for the state. Not only were there mercantilistic justifications for the manufacturing and trading activities; there were basic political justifications for Pietist educational activities. As Francke pointed out to the Crown Prince, a Pietist education laid 'einen guten Grund in der Gottesfurcht; so hat davon die hohe Obrigkeit redliche Unterthanen und treue Bediente in allen Ständen zu gewarten: gleichwie man sich im gegentheil zu einem Menschen keiner Treue versehen kann, wenn keine Furcht Gottes bei ihm ist'.[22] Shortly after his accession to the throne, Friedrich Wilhelm I came to see the Halle institutions for himself.

On the occasion of his visit on 12 April 1713, Friedrich Wilhelm I was twenty-five years old, and had been King for two months; August Hermann Francke was fifty, had established his institutions against strong opposition, and was experienced in gaining support for his cause. An eye-witness report reveals how adeptly Francke was able to display his institutions to the young King, taking him around the various buildings and explaining the different areas of activity. The most difficult part of the encounter was the final discussion about Pietist attitudes towards war and military activities. Francke's replies were highly diplomatic: 'Ew. Königl. Majestät muss das Land schützen, ich aber bin berufen zu predigen: Selig sind die Friedfertigen.'[23] The visit was rapidly followed up, three days later, by a letter from Francke to the king; and within a month Friedrich Wilhelm had reconfirmed in full the 1702 privileges of the Halle Pietist institutions.[24]

There has been some debate as to whether Friedrich Wilhelm I was himself personally inclined towards Pietist religiosity. He was in fact a committed Calvinist, but had little time for theological controversies: in his *Instruktion ... für seinen Nachfolger* of 1722, Friedrich Wilhelm I asserted that he was 'versicherdt das ein Lutterischer der dar Gottsehlich wandelt eben so guht seylich werde als die Reformirte und der unter[sch]-eidt nur herrühre von die Prediger Zenckereien'.[25] It seems clear that

---

[22] 'A good foundation in the fear of God; so the ruler can expect to have honest subjects and faithful servants in all ranks of society: just as in contrast one cannot trust a person who has no fear of God.' Quoted in Deppermann, *Hallesche Pietismus*, p. 166.

[23] 'His Royal Highness must defend the country, but I have been called to preach: blessed are the peacemakers.' The eye-witness account is reprinted in Kramer, *Neue Beiträge*, and in J. Klepper (ed.), *Der Soldatenkönig und die Stillen im Lande* (Berlin – Steglitz: Eckart-Verlag, 1938), pp. 21–38; the quoted sentence is on p. 37.

[24] Parts of the letter are reprinted in Deppermann, *Hallesche Pietismus*, pp. 169–70.

[25] 'Convinced that a Lutheran with godly ways could just as well attain salvation as those of the Reformed faith, and that the differences only arose out of the bickerings of the preachers.' 'Instruktion König Friedrich Wilhelms I. für seinen Nachfolger', Jan.–Feb. 1722, in G. Schmoller, D. Krauske and D. Loewe (eds.), *Acta Borussica. Die Behörden-organisation und die allgemeine Staatsverwaltung Preussens im 18. Jahrhundert*, vol. 3 (Berlin: Verlag von Paul Parey, 1901), p. 457.

what he was most interested in were the practical consequences for the Prussian state of the active Christianity of the Pietists.[26] The incorporation of Pietism into the Prussian state under Friedrich Wilhelm I demanded more compromises on the part of the former than the latter. The King, an astute ruler, realised the potential usefulness of aspects of Pietist activities for the development of centralised rule; it was these aspects that he fostered, at the expense of other ideals of the early Pietists, transforming the nature of Prussian Pietism in the process.

The Halle Pietists were themselves ready to enter into a closer relationship with the Prussian state, not only because they needed governmental support against orthodox opposition, but also because, in a specific way, particularly after 1713 Prussia differed from other absolutist states. The usual method employed by absolutisms to reward 'domesticated' nobles for loss of political autonomy through service to the centralised state was to develop the cultural apparatus of court society, with associated status privileges. It was this flowering of baroque court culture and conspicuous consumption which precisionists in England and Württemberg generally found distasteful. The Pietists in Prussia, too, disliked the frivolity and hedonism of aristocratic court life. But with the reign of the soldier king, Prussian absolutism became distinctively different. The major proportion of state revenues was henceforward devoted exclusively to military expenditure; at the end of the reign, in 1740–1, it was as much as eighty per cent. All other expenditure was pared to a minimum: baroque court culture as a technique for attracting the nobility through a created social/cultural need was discarded in favour of an emphasis on military service, commitment to the army, the virtues of discipline and obedience.[27]

Pietists appeared to be initially unaware of the power-political motives behind the change in style; instead, they welcomed the new 'puritanism' and asceticism of the Prussian court. In this way, a major attitudinal obstacle to the development of a close relationship between precisionism and absolutism was removed.

Friedrich Wilhelm I made use of Pietism in a number of ways. The most difficult, and least in harmony with the Pietists' own goals, was in relation to military activities. The King was much impressed by the conscientiousness implanted by a Pietist education; and when Francke

---

[26] Cf. Wilhelm Stolze, 'Friedrich Wilhelm I. und der Pietismus', *Jahrbuch für Brandenburgische Kirchengeschichte* 5 (1908): 172–205; Karl Wolff, 'Ist der Glaube Friedrich Wilhelms I. von A.H. Francke beeinflusst?', *Jahrbuch für Brandenburgische Kirchengeschichte* 33 (1938): 70–102; Walter Wendland, *Siebenhundert Jahre Kirchengeschichte Berlins* (Berlin und Leipzig: Walter de Gruyter and Co., 1930), pp. 116–17.
[27] Cf. Chapter 3, above. See also Jürgen von Kruedener, *Die Rolle des Hofes im Absolutismus* (Stuttgart: Gustav Fischer Verlag, 1973); Gordon Craig, *The Politics of the Prussian Army, 1640–1945* (Oxford: Clarendon Press, 1964), ch. 1.

refused to accept two soldiers' sons in his orphanage at Halle, the King employed Pietists to establish and run a military orphanage at Potsdam. Halle-trained Pietists were also employed to staff the new Berlin *Kadettenhaus*. Many Pietists were chosen as *Feldprediger*, or army preachers, who were an elite of pastors directly appointed by the King and destined for considerable advancement in their later careers. Pietist *Feldprediger* took very seriously their religious and educational duties among soldiers, whose levels of morality, literacy, and religious knowledge were in Pietist eyes abysmally low. As the officers of the army were being converted into a service nobility owing primary allegiance to the centralised state, so the common soldiers were transformed from illiterate, ill-educated and unwilling forced recruits into Bible-reading, God-fearing, conscientious and obedient troops, easily disciplined and organised for motivated combat. Pietists may have helped to make some soldiers into better Christians; they certainly contributed to making them better servants of the King.[28]

Pietist education had comparable consequences in non-military life. A number of historians have pointed out the 'defeudalisation' of nobles affected by Pietism, and the nobility was sending more and more of its sons to receive a Pietist education at Halle. In place of the old aristocratic virtues relating to notions of rank and honour, with licentious attitudes towards money, women, gambling, drinking, pretentiousness and pomposity, worldliness and so on, there were new 'bourgeois' virtues of frugality and self-control. Hinrichs, for example, comments thus on the implications of General von Natzmer's advice to his son: 'Es ist das Bild eines rechnenden, ökonomischen, auf gewissenhafte Berufserfüllung gerichteten, unauffälligen, diskreten, selbstbeherrschten, von Überheblichkeit und Dünkel freien, stoisch auf die Genüsse und Reize der Welt verzichtenden adligen Menschen, das hier aufgerichtet wird, ein "entfeudalisiertes" Bild, in das bürgerliche Züge einzudringen beginnen.'[29] In 1717, the King introduced compulsory schooling for all his subjects and, in theory at least, founded two thousand schools on the model of Halle.[30] The lower orders, too, were to be imbued with Pietism.

[28] Carl Hinrichs, *Preussentum und Pietismus* (Göttingen: Vandenhoek und Ruprecht, 1971), particularly the essay on 'Pietismus und Militarismus im alten Preussen'; Erich Schild, *Der Preussische Feldprediger* (Part 1: Eisleben: Verlag von Otto Maehnert, 1888; Part 2: Halle: Verlag von Eugen Strien, 1890).

[29] 'It is the picture of a noble person who stoically renounces the pleasures and enticements of the world, oriented to conscientious fulfilment of his vocation, calculating, economic, inconspicuous, discreet, self-controlled, free of arrogance and presumption, that is painted here, a "defeudalised" picture, in which bourgeois traits are beginning to enter.' Hinrichs, *Preussentum und Pietismus*, p. 215; for figures on the rising proportions of aristocratic pupils at Halle, see ibid., p. 216; for similar comments on 'defeudalisation', cf. Beyreuther, *Francke*, p. 188; Deppermann, *Hallesche Pietismus*, p. 176.

[30] Beyreuther, *Francke*, p. 187.

The cultural colonisation of the eastern provinces of Brandenburg-Prussia was particularly important in this respect. Here the religious and educational aspirations of Pietists, who were willing to convert the heathen at home if they lacked the support to travel to the heathen abroad, harmonised well with the political aims of the centralising state. The King supported the activities of the Pietists Lysius, Abraham Wolf, Rogall, and later Schultz, against the combined opposition of orthodoxy, the Consistorium, the Königsberg magistracy and the provincial Estates, as well as individual nobles.[31] In 1715 Lysius was appointed court preacher; in 1721 he became the Löbenitsche town pastor, and a full Professor at the university. In 1724, on Francke's suggestion, the King appointed two young Pietists, Rogall and Wolf, to positions at the university; in 1727 Wolf gained the pastorate of the Altstadt, and in 1732 Rogall took over the Domgemeinde. Pietists thus held key positions in the main churches of Königsberg and in the training of future theologians at the university. They were to use these positions to influence political as well as religious and moral attitudes in Königsberg and surrounding provinces.

The visitations of 1714 and 1715 had revealed miserable conditions in East Prussia. Following his appointment as Inspector of Schools and Churches in 1717, Lysius produced plans for practical reforms, including the introduction of *Pfarrkonferenzen* for the further education of pastors already in livings. Pastors were to be trained specially for work among non-German-speaking peoples: after some controversy, a Lithuanian seminar was introduced at the university, to which later a Polish seminar was added. These activities were not purely Pietist endeavours: the leader of orthodoxy, Quandt, vied with the Pietists for the support of the King, and in 1721 he took over the Inspectorate of Schools and Churches.[32] The King was prepared to support whichever party seemed most energetic in implementing his policies of cultural colonisation, and in the course of the 1720s and early 1730s there was considerable oscillation in the balance of power between Quandt and the Pietists. But the latter proved the more hard-working both at the university and in the churches. In 1727 the Lithuanian seminar was transferred from the care of the somewhat lazy Quandt to the committed leadership of Wolf. Pietist credentials now became essential for entering state service: the King decreed that all theologians must have studied at least one year in Halle, and in 1729 this was extended to a minimum of two years. The East Prussian Pietists were given monopoly powers over the selection of candidates for

[31] See generally the references cited in n. 18, above.
[32] On Quandt, see the over-favourable account in Albert Nietzki, *D. Johann Jakob Quandt. Generalsuperintendent und Oberhofprediger in Königsberg, 1686–1772. Ein Bild seines Lebens und seiner Zeit, insbesondere der Herrschaft des Pietismus in Preussen* (Königsberg: Kommissionsverlag Ferd. Beyers Buchhandlung, Thomas und Oppermann, 1905).

the ministry, which included detailed investigations of personal morality, life-style, and state of regeneracy or salvation. No-one could take up a position without a Pietist testimonial. The following year this *Zeugnis-pflicht* was extended to cover even pastors under private noble patronage, representing a considerable assault on the local powers of nobles. In 1732 Friedrich Wilhelm set up the 'Perpetuierliche Kirchen- und Schulkommission', extended in 1734 under the 'Erneuerte und erweiterte Verordnung über das Kirchen- und Schulwesen in Preussen...'. This has been described by one commentator as 'die grösste innere Kolonisationstat der Neuzeit in Deutschland'. Pietists and state together used educational reform for sociocultural transformation, though with very different aims in mind: 'Den letzten Untertanen nicht nur zum Staat, sondern auch zur christlichen Gemeinschaft heranzuziehen, war das mühevoll angestrebte Ziel.'[33] Wolf had died in 1731, and Rogall in 1733; but Schultz, who had arrived in Königsberg on 1731, took over the leadership of the Pietist movement. In 1737 the decree requiring a period of study at Halle was amended to except those who had studied at Königsberg: the latter had come to equal Halle as a centre of Pietism.[34]

By the 1730s, Pietism had become firmly established as the new orthodoxy of Brandenburg-Prussia. In a number of controversies old orthodoxy had been losing ground against Pietists, supported as they generally were by the central government of the state. Valentin Ernst Löscher, an orthodox theologian who struggled for reconciliation with Pietists in the interests of church unity against atheism and rationalism, was finally defeated in a debate at Merseburg in 1719. The self-righteousness of the second generation of Pietists in Prussia would admit of no compromise, only victory. In 1725, after Königsberg Pietists had complained to Francke about the rationalist Fischer, the latter was expelled by order of the King. Königsberg Pietists were somewhat shocked by the speed and severity of this action, and resolved not to make such complaints in future; but the secular demolition of opposition to Pietists certainly aided their ascendance to a position of ideological and institutional supremacy. In 1725, orthodoxy were characterising themselves as 'das arme Häuflein der Rechtgläubigen'.[35]

[33] 'The greatest act of internal colonisation of modern times in Germany'; 'the arduously pursued goal was to draw every last subject not only into the state but also into the Christian community.' Hubatsch, *Evangelische Kirche Ostpreussens*, vol. 1, p. 188, p. 210. In ibid., vol. 3, Documents, are reprinted the 1729 'Verordnung über die Theologische Kandidatenprüfung...' (pp. 208–10) and the 1734 'Erneuerte und erweiterte Verordnung über das Kirchen- und Schulwesen in Preussen' (pp. 211–23).
[34] See the references cited in n. 18, above. Letters of Königsberg Pietists are reprinted in: Theodor Wotschke, *Georg Friedrich Rogalls Lebensarbeit nach seinen Briefen* (Königsberg: Kommissionsverlag Ferd. Beyers Buchhandlung, Thomas und Oppermann, 1928); and Theodor Wotschke, *Der Pietismus in Königsberg nach Rogalls Tode in Briefen* (Königsberg: Kommissionsverlag Ferd. Beyers Buchhandlung, Thomas und Oppermann, 1929–30).
[35] 'The poor little group of the orthodox.' Martin Greschat, *Zwischen Tradition und*

This supremacy led in a number of ways to the transformation of Prussian Pietism. For the genuinely committed leadership, it implied a change from being religious visionaries with world-wide aims and missionary ambitions into being loyal servants of the Prussian state. Hinrichs describes this process both for the early work of Francke in Halle and for the activities of Pietists in East Prussia. As he comments, Rogall and Schultz 'wirken in ihrer Eigenschaft als Professoren, Pfarrer und Kirchenbeamter schon wie preussische Staatsdiener, die ganz in der Arbeit für das ihnen anvertraute Gebiet aufgehen und sich für internationale Verbindungen und Tätigkeiten nicht mehr interessieren'.[36] For others, the ascendancy of Pietism meant a less committed, less genuine profession of Pietist attitudes to gain political and personal advancement. Nietzki suggests that 'Es hatte sich auch, je offenkundiger der Einfluss der Pietisten in der Staatsverwaltung wurde, eine Anzahl von Leuten in die Reihen der Pietisten gedrängt, denen es nur auf den äusseren Schein ankam und deren heuchlerisches Gebaren nur schlecht die eigennützigsten Bestrebungen verhüllte.'[37] An anti-Pietist sermon of 1736 commented on the outward asceticism of Pietism, making Pietists easily recognisable to others, in the process looking 'ganz scheusslich'.[38] The need for Pietist testimonials to obtain positions in church and state led to superficial professions of conversion and regeneration according to the routinised general stages of Pietist experience. Pietism, conceived as a spontaneous religion of the heart, had become rationalised and mechanical as the orthodoxy of the state.

At the same time, however, the picture is slightly more complex. Even for those who could neither genuinely accept nor outwardly profess Pietist religiosity, there were sociocultural consequences. It is worth looking in some detail at the autobiography of an eighteenth-century rationalist, Johann Salomo Semler, for what it reveals of the implications of later Pietism in north-eastern Germany.[39] Born in 1725, son of a non-Pietist pastor, Semler makes many critical comments about Pietists as he

neuem Anfang. Valentin Ernst Löscher und der Ausgang der Lutherischen Orthodoxie (Witten: Luther-Verlag, 1971); Riedesel, *Pietismus und Orthodoxie*, pp. 40ff.; Albrecht Ritschl, *Geschichte des Pietismus*, vol. 2 (Bonn: Adolph Marcus, 1884), pp. 421–3.

[36] 'Already work, in their capacities of Professor, pastor, and church official, as servants of the Prussian state, completely involved in the work for their allotted area and no longer interested in international connections and activities.' Hinrichs, *Preussentum und Pietismus*, p. 289.

[37] 'As the influence of Pietism in the government became more apparent, a number of people had pushed themselves into the ranks of the Pietists, who were concerned only about outward appearances and whose hypocritical behaviour only thinly disguised the most self-serving aspirations.' Nietzki, *Quandt*, p. 78.

[38] 'Quite ghastly.' Sermon reprinted in ibid., pp. 75–7; the quotation is from p. 75.

[39] Johann Salomo Semler, *Lebensbeschreibung von ihm selbst abgefasst* (Part 1: Halle: 1781; Part 2: Halle: 1782). Semler in fact grew up in Salfeld, outside the Prussian state, but at this time close to and much under the influence of later Prussian Pietism. Many small courts, and particularly the tiny independent imperial knights, took up Pietism once it became fashionable in Prussia.

experienced them in his childhood. Professions of piety replaced hard work and intellectual achievement as a means to advancement. Once Pietism had become the fashion, people were pressured to join in as a matter of social survival: even Semler's father had to soften towards Pietism and later, for career reasons, to join in with Pietists and persuade his son also to participate. Semler speaks of the various reasons why the townspeople flocked to Pietist gatherings:

man hatte schon am Früh- Vor- und Nachmittags-predigten, wozu jetzt auch gar noch von 1 bis 2 eine Betstunde kam, viele Jahre lang genug gehabt. Aber nun sollten die Leute auf einmal alle durchaus from, oder Wiedergeborne werden; diese vorgegebene Absicht ist unmöglich, wenn nicht alle Schwärmerey und Heucheley eingerechnet wird. Die wahre Absicht war, sich gros Ansehen zu geben, ohne Arbeit und Gelehrsamkeit, und sich des Herzogs und Hofes zu bemächtigen.

A further advantage was that one could get on intimate terms with members of the opposite sex, in the course of the emotional, soul-searching Pietist sessions; and a marriage with a Pietist could be fairly certain of bright prospects:

Aus der angeblich geistlichen Vereinigung in solchen Erbauungsstunden, entstunden sehr viel menschliche sinliche Verbindungen; und sehr leichte Heiraten, weil solche Personen ganz unfelbar, vor allen andern ihres Standes und Berufes, den Vorzug bekamen.

Semler's brother became involved in a Pietist circle at university, where Pietist conversions had become a matter of routine:

Eine Historie der eigenen Erfarung und Erbauung wurde die Regel für andere, es ja eben so zu machen; gerade wie zur Zeit der Mönchsorden. Ueber den Seelenzustand fürten manche Prediger ein grosses Stadtregister; die Vorsteher der einzelnen Erbauungsstunden hatten ebenfals dergleichen Calender eingefüret, woraus jeder seinen Seelenzustand in der vorigen ganzen Woche, wieder hersagte. Dieses war für sehr viele ein recht sicherer Weg, sich nun bei allen hohen und vornemen Personen so zu empfehlen, dass sie ihre häuslichen und bürgerlichen Endzwecke aufs aller unselbarste hiermit erreichten.[40]

[40] '... for many years it had been quite enough to have early sermons, morning sermons, and sermons in the afternoon, to which was now added, on top of this, an hour of prayer from 1 to 2. But now suddenly people were all supposed to become pious, or re-born; this alleged aim is impossible, if one doesn't count in all the hypocrisy and fanaticism. The true purpose was, to give oneself great airs, without work or scholarship, and to get in with the Duke and the court.'
  'Out of the ostensibly spiritual union in such conventicles arose very many human sensual connections; and very easy marriages, because without fail such persons, above all others of their station and calling, were given preference and privileges.'
  'The story of one's own experience and edification became the rule for others to follow exactly; just as at the time of the monastic orders. Many preachers kept a great town register on the state of people's souls; those in charge of particular conventicles had similarly introduced such diaries, from which each recounted the state of his soul in the whole previous week. Now this was for many a sure means by which to recommend themselves to all high and eminent people, so that they could in this way attain their

Semler's brother was unfortunately too honest to be able to reproduce or find appropriate symptoms of conversion in himself, and fell into a severe depression, weeping and praying all night. Semler's family made great efforts to help and comfort him, although taking care not to offend local Pietists; but his spiritual struggles were cut short by a premature death.

The interesting development in Semler's autobiography is the way in which he was himself unintentionally affected by Pietist attitudes. He eventually gave in to social pressures to participate in a Pietist group; and while he failed to experience any form of conversion or regeneration, he nevertheless developed a markedly Pietist form of conscience about minor sins and transgressions. Later, as a student at Halle, where he rented a room in the orphanage buildings, Semler again combined disapproval of the falsity and pretentiousness of much of Pietism with a number of strongly impregnated Pietist attitudes. He was, for example, overcome with feelings of remorse and guilt about his initial overwhelming delight at having obtained a copy of a book he had long been looking for. He felt a conflict between his intellectual curiosity and his religious purity. Semler's generally critical opinions about the 'Idiotismus der Erbauung' which had spread over Germany in the previous decades are strangely counterbalanced by certain internalised aspects of the new Pietist culture. Other secular rationalists of the later eighteenth century were similarly affected by experience of Pietism in their youth.

Initially a persecuted minority movement attracting the genuinely committed alone, by the time of the accession of Friedrich II (Frederick the Great) in 1740, Pietism was a religious and cultural movement officially supported by the Prussian state and attracting the socially aspiring and politically ambitious. At the same time, it had effected major changes in the nature of Prussian social and political processes. Francke's work in Halle, continued by his son and followers after his death in 1727, and the work of Pietists in East Prussia, had transformed the educational experience of all classes in Brandenburg-Prussia. The takeover of the orthodox Lutheran church by the Prussian state through the sponsorship of the heterodox Pietist movement had broken the powers of patronage of the old nobility and transformed the foci of political identification and obedience. The support given to Pietism in its battles with the Estates had aided in reducing the powers of the Estates to the benefit of centralised rule. The spread of Pietism across all the scattered provinces of Brandenburg-Prussia had developed a unity of cultural orientations and concerns, a uniformity of educational background and experience, a shared language helping to break down provincial isolation and political decentralisation. Whatever the numbers of those who pretended Pietism only,

domestic and civic goals in the most unspiritual fashion.' Semler, *Lebensbeschreibung*, pp. 32, 33, 48.

Pietism had wide implications for motives and attitudes. Even those who remained the creatures, rather than the creators, of political life, had their focus of identity transformed. As Oberkonsistorialrat Süssmilch reported in 1756 on the effects of Pietist education in the province of Lithuania:

Der alte eigensinniger Litauer ist durch den Unterricht fast ein ganz anderer Mensch in der bürgerlichen Gesellschaft geworden und übt jetzt auch die Pflichten gegen die Obrigkeit ... Welch schöne Belohnung der darauf gewandten Kosten und Mühen.[41]

Once the energies of Pietists were harnessed to those of the centralising state, in the common fight against local Estates and local power structures on which orthodox Lutheranism was dependent, there was much that could be achieved, socially, politically, and culturally. That this achievement did not represent the Kingdom of God upon Earth, but merely the construction of Prussian absolutism, was something the early Pietists had not foreseen. Yet it resulted from the logic of the situation in which they had sought the impossible.

What, very simply, are the structural similarities and differences with the cases of England and Württemberg which account for the different pattern of Pietist political activities in Prussia? The dependent, ambiguous status of the established church in Prussia meant that, as in England, a movement for religious reform would inevitably have political implications. This was in contrast to the independence of the church in Württemberg, which ultimately made possible the marginal political status of Württemberg Pietism. But the sociopolitical links of the church were rather different in Prussia from those in England, as were relations between ruler and key sociopolitical groups. These different state/society relationships, combining with the different social location of the church meant that, while Prussian Pietism would become as politically important as English Puritanism, the force of its efforts would develop in a very different direction. The following chapter seeks to bring together systematically the similarities and differences across the three cases which in combination account for the different patterns of development; it summarises and reflects on the argument unfolded above.

---

[41] 'The old obstinate Litauer has, through education, virtually become a quite different person in civil society, and now also fulfils his duties towards authority... What a nice reward for the cost and trouble expended.' Quoted in Nietzki, *Quandt*, p. 60.

8

Conclusions and implications

Puritanism in England, Pietism in Württemberg, Pietism in Prussia: these were three similar religious movements for the further reform of their Protestant state churches. Yet, as they evolved, they made very different contributions to the dynamics of absolutist rule in each state. The different political trajectories of the movements cannot be explained simply in terms of certain ideas or class bases. They can be adequately understood only when certain structural features are taken into account. In particular, it is the intersection of two related sets of variables which is important. One set has to do with church/state relations, in a particular form of society; the other has to do with degrees and sources of religious toleration. Together, these variables help to determine whether or not the religious movement will be politicised; and in what direction its political sympathies and alliances will lie.

The structural argument developed in the preceding chapters may be summarised as in the table on p.175. This is intended to present, in condensed form, the features which were discussed in some detail in Chapters 3 and 4, and to indicate the logic of the different outcomes in each case. It is not intended to imply any sort of mechanical determinism to the course of history, and in this concluding chapter I shall discuss more generally the nature and implications of the argument presented in this study.

Puritanism and Pietism both arose as movements within European Protestant churches agitating for the completion of the Reformation. In the case of English Puritanism, the reformation of the English Church was quite obviously only partly accomplished by Elizabeth's settlement of 1559; and Puritans were those who were not prepared to accept a pragmatic *via media* as theologically justifiable or practically tolerable. A similar incompleteness of reformation was perceived by Pietists in a Lutheran context a century or so later; it became clear that Luther's reform of church doctrine had not been accompanied by a corresponding reformation of life, and that practical measures were required to bring about a complete reformation. In both Puritanism and Pietism similar measures were evolved to further the processes of reformation: Pietists and Puritans stressed the importance of the Bible; of a clear, simple and

Structural contexts, toleration, and political outcomes

	England 1560–1640	Württemberg 1680–1780	Prussia 1690–1740
	Puritan and Pietist movements for religious reform: essentially similar aims and ideals across cases		

Structural contexts

Society	Domesticated aristocracy; increasing commercialisation	No indigenous aristocracy; small peasant and burgher property-ownership	Feudal aristocracy; enserfed peasantry, declining towns
State	Unitary nation-state Parliament Decentralised local government	Unitary state Single Diet Decentralised local government	Composite state Regional Estates Centralised state bureaucracy
Church	Economically weak: Crown and lay patronage Reduced but rising social status	Economically strong: centrally salaried pastorate High social status	Economically weak: Crown and lay patronage Very low social status
Inter-relations	Church linked with ruler; but lay interventions and ambiguities	Church independent, but allied with Estates and upper social ranks	Church dependent on regional Estates and local nobles; but ruler seeking control

Toleration of precisionists

Society	Considerable lay support	General toleration	Estates and guild opposition
State	Ambivalent/hostile	Tolerant/opposed	Active support
Church	Ambivalent/hostile	General toleration	Hostile

Political outcomes: Precisionist responses to absolutist rule

Degree	Active	Passive	Active
Direction	Anti-absolutist	Anti-absolutist	Pro-absolutist

effective preaching ministry, oriented to conversion and a new life; of the extension of church discipline; and of the meeting together in small groups for further edification, as the 'church within the Church'. Pietists and Puritans were concerned to institutionalise their programmes for reform: to transform society through the moral arm of the church, and not simply to abdicate responsibility for building the Holy Commonwealth on earth.

These precisionist projects for further reformation worked themselves out in various practical directions which are systematically related to the specific configurations of society, church and state in the context of which they attempted to achieve their religious goals. That is, precisionist projects coincided or clashed with the projects of other groups as affected by varying aims, interests, and sociopolitical locations.

In England, Puritanism became involved with a number of other social and political pressures. Puritanism became firmly embedded in the structure and outlook of Elizabethan and early Stuart society: it had a foothold, through the economic power of the laity, and the peculiar structure of the post-Reformation English church, in educational institutions, in lectureships, in certain parishes and at different levels of the church hierarchy itself. But the state church in England was intimately linked with the state. The ruler of England was the supreme governor of the church, and made use of its machinery for a variety of administrative, political and ideological purposes. Conversely, the church was in many ways economically and politically dependent on the state for its support, maintenance and prestige. Anyone wanting to reform the church would necessarily be seen as having designs in relation to the state; conversely, any use made by the state of the state church was political as well as religious in intent.

Hence, Puritanism was inevitably politically active; and, in a situation of revolution against absolutist rule, when that rule made use of the church in certain ways, Puritanism was inevitably revolutionary. It was so, not because of specific ideas about the role of individual conscience, the direct relationship of man to God, the importance of Bible-reading by every individual, however lowly in the social order, but because of the peculiar structure of the society and state in which it arose and flourished. When Charles and Laud succeeded in alienating large numbers and crucial sections of the population; when the Scottish and Irish troubles precipitated the impending crisis for English absolutism; then those Puritans who were concerned to reform the church allied with all those antagonised by other aspects of personal rule to turn their attentions to the nature of government. A multiplicity of alliances were united in their opposition to a regime of which a variety of groups disapproved; the rapid passing of this early unity rendered evident the few bases for positive agreement once the crisis had erupted and developed. The Civil Wars in England cannot simply be reduced to a 'Puritan Revolution'; but Puritanism became involved, and made important ideological and organisational contributions, because of the particular structure of the regime in which it had been able to develop in shifting and ambiguous ways.

This argument can be substantiated by comparison with the course of developments in the German cases. Pietists too had notions of the individual conscience, the direct relationship of man to God, the importance of the Bible, of group organisation and discussion, of church discipline and social and moral regeneration. Pietists were no less activist in their missionary and educational endeavours than Puritans. Yet their strivings worked themselves out rather differently.

The Württemberg case is particularly interesting in comparison with England, because of the considerable similarities across the two cases. In the first phase of Württemberg Pietism, from the 1680s to the 1720s, the similarities are particularly striking: Württemberg Pietists organised for reform, and took up an active stance against court morality, absolutist politics, and social disorganisation, stressing by contrast the importance of personal transformation, an adequate and living Christianity sustained by an educated, preaching ministry. In Württemberg too there existed a parliamentary tradition, of an oligarchical nature, representing independent property-holding classes, and a decentralised form of local government. There were of course numerous differences between the socioeconomic and political life of England and Württemberg in the relevant periods, having consequences for the dynamics of absolutism in each case; but in Württemberg, as in England, Pietism took hold as a form of culture and morality opposed to an absolutist, hedonistic style of life at court – particularly when the latter was Catholic in inclination or practice. Further, in the mid-eighteenth century there were constitutional struggles in Württemberg which were in many ways analogous to those of mid-seventeenth-century England. Yet Pietism, as an organised movement, or a rallying cry for opposition, a source of emotional energy, leadership, justification of revolt, played no active part. Why not? The crucial difference distinguishing the Pietists at this time from the English Puritans appears to be that, to a large extent, Pietists had achieved their religious aims: Pietist ideas, and organisation in conventicles, had in 1743 been accepted and incorporated into the established church in Württemberg. And the latter, the church, was allied with (indeed part of) the Estates in their opposition to absolutist rule. Pietists, in their political orientation, were spoken for by both commoners in the Estates and bishops, representatives of the church, which was relatively independent of and opposed to the policies of the ruler. In their religious role, Pietists no longer had a need to fight; their own aims and activities were no longer threatened; and Pietism in Württemberg ceased to be a politically active movement, much less a leading revolutionary force. Toleration was accompanied by quietism.

Prussian Pietists were, in a sense, as revolutionary as Puritans; but in a different direction. The Lutheran church in Prussia preached the Lutheran doctrine of obedience to authority; but the 'authority' to which Lutheran orthodoxy referred was that of provincial nobles, the feudal aristocrats who were patrons of the church in the scattered provinces of the emerging, composite Hohenzollern state. Yet, as in England, the church was in a politically ambiguous situation, the battle-ground for different conceptions of the political and social order. The ruler was seeking to gain control of the church through sponsorship of a movement which was not so tied to local political interests. Because of this different structural configuration, Pietists in Prussia entered into a quite different alliance, while being similarly politicised: Pietists entered an alliance with the centralising state itself, with Prussian absolutism. The political projects of the state coincided to a considerable degree with the religious, moral and social projects of the Pietists. Lutheran orthodoxy and the provincial nobility were the 'conservative' defenders of the old order; Pietists, in the attempt to achieve the religious reformation and social transformation they desired, became co-opted into the battle of the state to rework the old order into a new, centralised and militarised regime. But the partners in battle were unequal, and Pietist goals were submerged under secular pressures and priorities. The energies and activism of Pietism here came to support absolutism because it seemed to Pietists that this was the only feasible route to achieving their own goals; in the end, these goals were subverted as Pietist energies were employed for quite different mundane ends.

Apart from suggesting that it is extremely difficult to bring about anything approaching anyone's conception of the perfect religious, moral and social community, let alone the Holy Commonwealth on earth, these tales of the different secular fates of the Puritan and Pietist movements suggest more general historical conclusions.

The main implication is that the particular historical role of a religious movement will depend on the combination of circumstances in which it emerges and acts. The content of the role may be limited by certain internal aspects of a particular idea system; but these limits still allow a considerable range of variation for external expression. Theories of history or society which appeal purely to specific cultural orientations or values are inadequate by themselves – as are those which fail entirely to take non-rational values into account.

Certain substantive conclusions may be drawn about the sorts of circumstances under which particular orientations are likely (at least to appear) to enjoy considerable autonomy in affecting the course of events. For the problem posed in this study, the following seems to be the case. First, the overall context is important. Puritanism and Pietism arose in an age when the 'metaphor' of political thought was religious. This is not to imply anything about a possible process of 'secularisation', but rather to point out that, whatever long-term trends about the social location and individual meaning of religion might or might not exist, religious movements cannot become powerful political forces except in a context where the ideas involved are, for whatever reasons, taken seriously by large numbers of people. These people are not only those who positively support the movement in question; they include also those who oppose it, perceive it as potentially dangerous and to be suppressed. The case of Württemberg to some extent illustrates this point. Although the German *Aufklärung* retained a more religious complexion than the Enlightenment of eighteenth-century France, ideas of religious toleration, and the irrelevance of doctrinal or credal differences, had begun to permeate eighteenth-century German thought. Lutheran orthodoxy in Prussia was threatened by the ruler's attempts to institutionalise religious toleration, and hence strongly opposed the Pietist movement which was sponsored by the state as part of its general religious policies. The church in Württemberg was however in no such threatened situation, and was able to join with Enlightenment pressures (represented by Bilfinger) to allow a greater freedom of religious opinion within the bounds of Lutheranism. It was partly because of this that the Pietist movement in mid-eighteenth-century Württemberg declined as a political force. A similar point might be made in relation to post-1689 Dissent or Nonconformity in England: religion and politics had become separate spheres of endeavour, and movements for religious revival were no longer *intrinsically* movements for overall political change.

The causes of the 'metaphor', or overlapping of religion and politics, in a specific phase of European development, are complex. Partly the change is related to movements of thought, as indicated above with reference to the Enlightenment. But this is not a sufficient explanation: ideas of religious toleration were readily available for a long time, without people deciding that it would be a good idea to implement them; and such implementation took place in different states at different times, irrespective of the availability of the ideas as such. The problem has much more to do with the political uses made of religious institutions, and the relative benefits to any given ruler or state of policies of religious uniformity or toleration in given circumstances. Viewed in a long-term perspective, it appears that there was something about the emergence of unified nation states out of the feudal system which eventually, when consolidated, set the seal of doom on the notion that political and religious units must be coterminous. There are also the questions of the sources of toleration, and the limits of toleration: the Prussian state was in favour of toleration, the Lutheran church was not; the Württemberg rulers frequently favoured some forms of toleration (such as of Catholics) which the Lutheran church opposed, while it was prepared, unlike the Prussian church, to tolerate Pietists. The picture is more complicated than would be suggested by notions of a 'rise' of toleration in the passage to 'modernity', fuelled by the Enlightenment.

Because of the nature of internal developments in Prussia, despite the ruler's support of toleration, Pietism was able to achieve considerable effect. This arose out of the opposition of orthodoxy, and the state's recognition that Pietism was a force capable of revolutionising both local power structures and the status ethics of important social groups; of centralising loyalties and transforming the character-type of Prussian Junkerdom. The state supported Pietism in pursuit of these aims; once societal and political transformation had been achieved, the state withdrew from active support and left its flailing protégé to fend for itself against the pressures of orthodoxy and Enlightenment. Elsewhere, the impact of Pietism could be of a quieter nature: a cultural tradition stressing the feelings of the heart, emotionalism, the piety of 'simple folk', the importance of the nation, and so on. These orientations were inherent, or latent, in English Puritanism also; but Puritanism was activated in its revolutionary situation. In many German areas, including later Württemberg, where Pietism was tolerated it was the quieter traditions that were to feed into the German heritage, laying the basis for cultural developments quite separate from the facts of political power and this-worldly battle.

The second substantive conclusion has to do with the nature of state power, and the relationships between state and society. It will be helpful to reflect for a moment on the cases of England and Prussia. England produced only a 'weak' form of absolutism, effectively terminated in the English Revolution. Prussia, by contrast, produced in the eighteenth century a highly efficient militarised absolutism with a centralised state bureaucracy. One aspect of the weakness of English absolutism, which had important consequences for the Puritan movement, was the sale of church properties under the Tudors. Had this not occurred, there would have been two crucial consequences: the laity would have lacked the economic foothold in the church which allowed Puritanism to develop with a certain independence; and the Crown would in the long term have had a stronger economic base, decreasing royal reliance on Parliament for revenues. In that case, Puritanism might have been in as weak a position as was Pietism in Prussia, and would have had to rely on state support of such religious goals as the maintenance of a preaching ministry. Given the different nature of church/state relations in England, however, it is unlikely that Puritanism would have received the kind of support accorded to Pietism in Prussia; it is more likely that, like Pietism in certain other German states, Puritanism would have been effectively persecuted out of existence.

This mental experiment indicates not only that the nature of the state is important in affecting the degree of leverage of the precisionist movement; but also that church/state relations provide a crucial switch deflecting a movement in one direction or another. Given the sort of sociopolitical foundations for absolutism in England, had the church been allied with parliamentarian opposition as in Württemberg, the Puritan movement might have been absorbed within the framework of the established church, and, like Württemberg Pietism, not become a revolutionary force. As it was, the combination of two facts – the economic power of the laity in the Church of England, and the use of the church by the state – meant that political and religious conflict in England overlapped to a considerable degree.

These conclusions should not be viewed as in some sense a simple, additive list of unrelated 'factors'. They are in fact all interrelated; and it is the nature of the interrelationships which conditions the ultimate outcomes. As indicated, degrees and sources of religious toleration are intimately related to particular sets of church/state relations in particular forms of society. Relations between 'state' and 'civil society', or ruler (with associated apparatus of rule) and crucial sociopolitical groups, do not simply affect the politics of precisionism, but rather their effect is mediated and refracted by the location of the church. It is the way in which the church is involved in the struggles among groups which determines the particular political implications of a movement for religious reform. Thus it is the specific combination of the different variables detailed in the table at the beginning of this chapter which explains the relationships between precisionism and absolutism in any given set of historical circumstances. Nevertheless, it is possible to give a brief and general answer to the question posed at the beginning of this study, as follows:

Given an overall context where the metaphor of political processes was religious, unless a precisionist movement had a strong societal base against a weak absolutism, and unless church/state relations were such that religious heterodoxy was directly a political issue, a precisionist movement was not likely to be an important political force against absolutism.

Let me now consider the theoretical implications of the argument. What, in particular, is implied by the 'structural approach' presented here? This can best be considered in relation to the problem of structure and change. There are two main aspects, relevant here, to this problem. One is the question of structural change itself, and the difficulty of describing unambiguously some form of static picture of the structural features of a given state and society. The other is the question of the relationships between structural constraints and possibilities, on the one hand, which help to determine what is or is not likely to happen, and the freedom and openness of social action, on the other hand, as men and women make their own history. As Marx succinctly put it, 'Men make their own history, but they do not make it just as they please; they do not make it under circumstances chosen by themselves, but under circumstances directly encountered, given and transmitted from the past.'[1] Despite Marx's sage comment, much recent philosophy of the social sciences has concerned itself with lengthy discussions of relationships between structure and action; and different theoretical approaches over the decades have tended to fall on one side or other of the divide between a structuralist determinism and a voluntarist idealism. To discuss where the pre-

---

[1] Karl Marx, 'The Eighteenth Brumaire of Louis Bonaparte' in *Marx and Engels: Selected Works* (London: Lawrence and Wishart, 1970), p. 96.

sent study stands in relation to these issues is to locate it within a wider framework of questions about the relations between sociology and history.

It is evident that in the three cases considered here there were certain dynamics of structural change, such as processes of demographic expansion and socioeconomic differentiation. There were also changes in the relationships among church, state, and social groups over the periods considered in each case. Yet certain broad features stand out which, with qualifications, can be summarised as constituting, for analytic purposes, the 'structural contexts' of action in relation to the religious movements under investigation. Although abstracted out as 'contexts', it still remains true that the contexts were neither static, nor unaffected by the activities of the religious movements which were part of the developing political, social, and cultural relationships. At different points in time, however, one may (again, for analytic rather than descriptive purposes) separate what might be termed specific historical circumstances from more enduring structural features. Thus for example, the defeat of the Spanish Armada in 1588 weakened the apparent threat of Catholicism in England and rendered Puritanism the greater perceived danger to the stability of the state. This influenced the increased intensity of the anti-Puritan campaigns of the late 1580s and early 1590s. This question becomes important in relation to the translation of what might be called 'structural potentialities' into action. It was only in a given set of historical circumstances – a unique historical configuration – that Puritanism would become a 'revolutionary' movement. It required a combination of factors to produce the particular breakdown of the English state in the 1640s. But, given this particular constellation of circumstances (a constellation about which historians are still arguing), it was the peculiar set of structural relationships among society, state, and church that determined the side on which Puritan energies would lie. Puritanism in England would not have been revolutionary had there not been, for a variety of other reasons, a revolutionary situation. But conversely, it was not the mere fact of occurrence of constitutional crisis which rendered Puritanism revolutionary. For in a comparable situation of constitutional crisis in Württemberg (which, for a variety of reasons, took a different course), Pietism was not goaded into a politically active stance. The implications of the structural configuration in Württemberg were different, and thus in a similar political position, Württemberg Pietists remained politically passive.

In many ways, the stark contrasts which have been drawn across cases can be repeated by comparisons across time and place within each case, focussing on finer differences and ambiguities within each movement and state. There were different degrees of activity or passivity, different political opinions and attitudes, within each movement at different times and in different circumstances. A more general picture has been drawn in this study, highlighting certain features for comparison across larger units of time and space. But at a more micro-level of social analysis, a similar approach could help to explain why there was an active, radical presbyterian movement in England, which yet did not command widespread support, in the 1570s and '80s, but not in the early seventeenth century; why Francke and his colleagues were politically active in the 1690s in Prussia, and his successors less so in the 1730s; why Pfaff had a doctrine of legitimate rebellion against ungodly rule under Karl Alexander in Württemberg, whereas later Pietists preached the virtues of obedience. To some extent, these differences over time within each case have been indicated in each of the narrative chapters. The fact of taking a sharp, static photograph at given points in time may perhaps over-emphasise certain characteristics of each case at the expense of others. But the focus of interest of the study as a whole was the crucial, historically significant contributions made by the movements to the dynamics of absolutist rule in each case: and for this, certain periods were more significant than others.

The second question concerning structure is that of the relationship between structural determinism and creative social action. This has plagued sociologists and historians who are sensitive to the existence of historical regularities, general patterns of structure and change. By analysing long-term relationships and regularities, and focussing on features of which participants in the process may have been unaware, sociological approaches of this sort have appeared to imply some form of determinism. Against such approaches, others have placed great theoretical emphasis on historical uniqueness, creativity, and the unpredictability of individual human action. Anti-determinist approaches have frequently fallen into the opposite trap of over-stressing the intentions and motives of particular actors in historical explanations. This sort of approach is highly prevalent among certain professional historians, who are concerned with the unique characteristics and significance of individual personalities, particular details, decisions, coincidences, mistakes, in the idiographic mode of analysis.

In this study, an attempt has been made to steer a delicate course between these two sorts of approach. It has sought to show that there are certain patterns of relationships among analytically separable variables, and that what may be termed structural features or contexts have certain implications for likely historical developments. At the same time, it has not intended to imply any form of structural determinism. At any given time, it is an open question whether humans will choose to act in one way or another; and there is no way of reducing, in any fundamental sense, the non-rational choices, values, and ethical conceptions of people to 'more basic' societal features. This study has developed a strong theory about the particular sets of variables which explain the different outcomes in the three cases under analysis. It is strong in the sense that it is partially predictive: given certain facts about other early modern Protestant states, for example, it would be possible to have a very good guess at the probable responses of authorities and the probable political alliances and activities of pietistic groups in the area. This does not mean that people could not, remarkably, have chosen to do things differently; it does mean that, given knowledge of certain general constraints and of the positions and interests of certain groups, the sociologist can suggest what developments are most likely in any particular set of circumstances.

It is worth briefly clarifying this point by comparing the status of structural analysis in this study with its use in two other recent comparative-historical structural analyses. Perry Anderson's *Lineages of the Absolutist State* and Theda Skocpol's *States and Social Revolutions* served as provocative models in the light of which, and against which, the present argument was developed.[2] These stimulating works were highly suggestive in attempting to construct a more adequate approach to the politics of Puritanism and Pietism than the rather one-dimensional prevalent approaches reviewed at the start of this study. Nevertheless, in the end, the argument presented here differs methodologically and substantively from the (quite different) approaches of Anderson and Skocpol, in relation to the question of structure and agency.

Methodologically, the greatest difference is with the work of Anderson. Skocpol's method is what she and Somers have termed 'macro-causal analysis': by systematically comparing and contrasting analytically separable variables on a selected range of cases, Skocpol seeks to isolate those aspects which have causal significance. It is this macro-causal approach which has been practised in the present study; and this is rather different from Anderson's use of comparative history. Anderson treats his historical cases in terms of their similarity with, or deviation from, theoretically conceived pure types. These theoretical concepts are holistic in nature: they constitute long-term synthetic wholes, in which the parts gain significance both by virtue of their role in relation to the structural whole, and by virtue of their particular 'lineage', their historical pedigree. Although this is not the only way in which Anderson uses comparative history, the thrust of his analysis in *Lineages* is to evoke the 'pure' path of evolutionary advance, based on presuppositions about the telos of history, and to delineate the ways in which 'deviant' cases have strayed from the privileged path of historical progress. The theoretical framework is illustrated by case studies, rather than extracted from detailed comparisons of combinations of variables. One of the problems

---

[2] Perry Anderson, *Lineages of the Absolutist State* (London: New Left Books, 1974); Theda Skocpol, *States and Social Revolutions* (Cambridge: Cambridge University Press, 1979).

which is related to this methodology is that Anderson cannot adequately deal with the actors' perceptions of their interests (which are sometimes contrary to those dictated by the telos of history), or with the historical ideas, capacities, wishes and idiosyncrasies of particular individuals. These appear and disappear in the case sketches, but are not integrated theoretically with the general explanatory framework. Thus there is a disjuncture between Anderson's general motor of history, and the particular ways in which the patterns are played out in each case. Anderson has, in effect, not satisfactorily integrated structural analysis and the role of agency.[3]

Skocpol's work is an admirable interplay of history and theory, of analysis and interpretation of evidence: there is a full integration of general and particular as she derives the explanatory framework out of, and in terms of, the cases studied. But despite the difference in methodology, Skocpol perhaps shares with Anderson a certain over-emphasis on the role of structure in explanation. In Skocpol's work, this arises for substantive reasons. Skocpol is, rightly, concerned to argue against motive explanations of social revolutions. She presents instead a strong case for explanation in terms of particular structural relationships in particular world-historical conditions, the combination of which together explain the patterns of occurrence and outcome of successful social revolutions. But, leaving aside in this context the historical force of her argument, it seems to me that there are two related weaknesses in her understanding of the nature of the argument she has presented so well. First, she operates implicitly with certain social-psychological theories about the sorts of sociopolitical conditions under which certain forms of consciousness will be fostered, eventuating in perception of certain political interests and capacity for action on those perceived interests. She may well be right that peasants have a perpetual grievance against the extractors of surplus value, and the assumption of relatively constant motives varying only in space for expression and communal organisation may be warranted in this case. But the position of the 'organised, revolutionary leaderships (recruited from the ranks of previously marginal, educated elites)' is a good deal more ambiguous. It was these groups who seized the opportunities presented by the military-administrative breakdown of the state in the context of external pressures and revolts from below. Skocpol's emphasis is on the pressures of the situation, and she pays too little attention to the ways in which these are mediated and translated into purposeful political action. (Such translations are glossed over lin-

[3] See: Theda Skocpol and Margaret Somers, 'The Uses of Comparative History in Macro-Social Inquiry', *Comparative Studies in Society and History* 22 (1980): 174–97; and Mary Fulbrook and Theda Skocpol, 'Destined Pathways: The Historical Sociology of Perry Anderson' in Theda Skocpol (ed.), *Vision and Method in Historical Sociology* (Cambridge: Cambridge University Press, forthcoming).

guistically: for example, 'the exigencies of revolutionary consolidation *helped ensure* that leaderships willing and able to build up centralized coercive and administrative organizations would come to the fore during the Revolutions, and that their handiwork would create a permanent base of power for state cadres within the revolutionised social orders'.)[4] Related to this is the second point: Skocpol underemphasises (or misinterprets) the role of the narrative of action in her accounts. The structural analysis delineates the historical *conditions* within which certain eventuations were possible or not possible: it defines and delimits the range of possibilities. But outcomes were not entirely predetermined by particular relationships in particular conditions, both internal and international; they depended also on the skills, perceptions, and fortunes of certain political actors. It is these which Skocpol in fact relates in the narrative sections, giving the reader a sense of completeness in the account; but the role of the narrative of agency is not explicitly accorded the importance it in fact enjoys in Skocpol's account of her 'structural approach'.[5]

It is less easy to ignore actors' perceptions, motives, and the difference these made to the course of events, when the focus is not on macro-transformations of the social and political order (as in Anderson's and Skocpol's work) but rather on the non-rational goals of religious movements. The focus of analysis in this work has been on the formation and transformation of political activities, attitudes and alliances of groups whose aims had little to do with obvious material or political interests. And their activities did make a difference to the course of events. What I have attempted to argue above is that religious ideas must be taken seriously as causal factors in historical analysis; but that these ideas do not have simple effects arising directly out of either the idea system itself or the social groups acting as carriers of the ideas. The structural analysis presented above has been intended to explicate what features of state and society help to deflect and refract the implications of certain religious goals, conditioning and pressuring religious movements into one or another political position. The structural analysis clarifies the conditions within which certain action was possible, given certain ultimate ends. It suggests what outcomes were or were not likely in given circumstances. It delineates certain regularities, certain patterns of relationship. But it cannot explain the different aims held by the actors, nor their perceptions of their interests, nor the actual skills with which they operated in certain conditions: and all of these might make a difference to the actual patterns

---

[4] Skocpol, *States and Social Revolutions*, p. 286, emphasis added. The quotation about elites is from p. 287.
[5] See also the review essay by Peter T. Manicas in *History and Theory* 20 (1981): 204–18. Skocpol has subsequently developed her approach to take more account of cultural traditions: see Skocpol, 'Rentier State and Shi'a Islam in the Iranian Revolution', *Theory and Society* 11 (3) (1982): 265–83.

of historical change, as circumscribed by given structural constraints and possibilities. At any particular time, in the stories recounted above, there was a certain (limited) openness to possible future histories. Retrospectively, we can see what features appear to have been most important in pushing the patterns of eventuation into one direction or another, given the existence of the particular historical actors.

Thus, in a sense, the comparative-historical structural analysis presented in this study is claiming slightly less for itself than the structural determinism of Anderson, or the structural explanation of Skocpol. It analyses conditions and constraints which tend to push action in one direction or another; but the actual perceptions and ideas of actors retain a (vastly reduced, compared with some approaches) limited causal force and autonomy.

This raises, finally, the question of the scope of the theory presented in this study. In some ways, it is quite limited in scope; in others, more extensive in implication. In the limited sense, it simply serves as a systematic, selective redescription of what we know already about three particular historical cases. But by summarising certain features in certain ways — by focussing on particular variables and the relationships among them — it helps to make sense of what initially appears as a problem, a question with no adequate solution. In this limited sense, the theory is a purely historical theory: a particular explanation of a particular historical problem.

At a slightly less specific level, the theory developed in this study provides suggestions for the analysis of other reforming religious movements within the overall historical context of early modern European states with established Protestant state churches. Many other permutations and combinations of the variables could be played with. There is nothing which in principle would preclude a wider set of comparisons: there were other rulers who attempted absolutism, other precisionist movements for religious reform. An analysis of other cases would in fact constitute some sort of test for the theory developed in relation to the initial three, perhaps indicating where the theory requires extension or modification.

At a more general level, the study has certain wider theoretical implications. If it is correct, it implies two broader conclusions. One is, that the most fruitful way out of the 'materialist/idealist' debate is to re-focus analysis on the conditions under which certain ideas are able to be historically effective, and the directions in which they will achieve their effects. Any sociology of religion must therefore also be a political sociology — but not one which does not take seriously the object of analysis. The second has to do with the questions of transitions from one 'historical stage' to another. Many sociological approaches to history,

which are typological and concerned with regularities of social organisation (rather than ordered by strict chronology and idiographic reconstruction of unique historical individuals), tend to derive certain features
of development from the nature of the relevant 'stage'. This may be
conceived in terms of political development (absolutism, bourgeois
democracy, and so on), 'mode of production' (feudal, capitalist), technology (agrarian, industrial), culture (Renaissance, Reformation,
Enlightenment), or even abstract criteria such as degree of differentiation
and specialisation (traditional, intermediate, modern; simple, complex;
and so on). While the present study has adopted one form of typological
approach, it has sought to escape from the evolutionism generally present, whether implicitly or explicitly, in such approaches. In particular, it
was not anything about the 'historical stage' as such which determined
the different responses of Pietists and Puritans (emergence of capitalism,
the nature of absolutism, baroque culture, 'early modernity', 'experience
of rapid social change', to mention some of the more frequently invoked
principles). Rather it was certain historically unique sets of circumstances, such as the different patterns of church/state relations resulting
from different Reformation legacies in each area, acting as crucial
switches determining the political direction each religious movement
would take.

Theoretical debate is only useful if we do not forget what it is about:
ways of understanding what actually happened, of answering culturally
relevant questions about the actual course of history. We are interested in
Puritanism and Pietism not simply as conceptual tools, theoretical variables, but for the parts these committed Protestants played, in an alien
cultural context, in the making of the world in which we live. What,
generally, can we conclude from this study?

Neither Puritanism nor Pietism can be reduced entirely to other factors: the religious beliefs and aspirations of Puritans and Pietists, while
perhaps more easily adopted by certain groups with certain forms of
social experience than by others, do not correspond neatly with specific
material interests, whether political or economic. Puritanism and Pietism
were essentially *religious* movements, and attempts to correlate them
directly with other factors can do no more than indicate 'elective affinities'. The vitality of religious ideas of earlier centuries may sometimes be
difficult to comprehend; but to attempt to deny a reality to these ideas by
dismissing them in terms of other factors or ignoring their relevance to
patterns of social and political change is to do an injustice to the facts of
human history.

It may be that cultural factors will not take us very far in explaining
different political developments. The 'course of German history' has less
to do with the Lutheran doctrine of obedience to authority than with

specific social, economic, and political developments. It is on the latter that the direction of obedience postulated in Lutheran doctrines depends; the substantive content given to the emotions evoked by religious ideas is formulated in specific political circumstances. Similarly, 'Calvinism' will not go far to explain the English Revolution; it is only in a particular situation of alliance and opposition that certain forms of Calvinist belief may provide a motivating force and rallying cry for battle. It is on the circumstances that the specific content and power of religious orientations depend.

But in 'favourable' circumstances, such orientations may have considerable power to influence the course of events in one direction or another. Puritanism cannot be ignored in the genesis of the English resistance to absolutist rule; nor Pietism in the successful establishment of absolutism in Prussia. What is required is analysis of the patterns of combination of elements: of the ways in which different projects, with different resources, and different goals and interests, interrelate in specific historical situations.

The diversity of historical patterns can be adequately comprehended only by focussing both on the active 'making' of history and on the structural contexts of action. Men and women seek to interpret and act on experience in accordance with internal standards and socioculturally conditioned notions of ideal and material interests. The obstacles groups face in pursuit of particular goals affect the practical directions their efforts will take and the consequences these may have for historical change. A systematic investigation of the ways in which 'unchosen circumstances' affect the 'making' of history can help to elucidate both the varying patterns of the past and the social and cultural legacies bequeathed by past generations to the context of the present. In this way we can understand how, by differing paths, Puritans and Pietists contributed to the formation of the world which we see and to the ways in which we see it.

Bibliography

Adam, A.E., 'Herzog Karl und die Landschaft' in *Herzog Karl Eugen von Württemberg und seine Zeit*, hrsg. vom Württembergischen Geschichts- und Altertumsverein, Esslingen, Paul Neff Verlag (Max Schreiber), vol. 1, 1907.

Aland, Kurt, *Kirchengeschichtliche Entwürfe*, Gütersloh, Gütersloher Verlagshaus Gerd Mohn, 1960.

(ed.), *Pietismus und Moderne Welt*, Witten, Luther-Verlag, 1974.

Alexander, H.G., *Religion in England 1558–1662*, London, University of London Press, 1968.

Anderson, M.S., *Europe in the Eighteenth Century*, 2nd edn, London, Longman, 1976.

Anderson, Perry, *Lineages of the Absolutist State*, London, New Left Books, 1974.

Angermann, Erich, 'Einführung: Religion – Politik – Gesellschaft im 17. und 18. Jahrhundert. Ein Versuch in vergleichender Sozialgeschichte', *Historische Zeitschrift* 214 (1972), 26–9.

[Anon.], *Christliche und Bescheidene Antwort auf die sogenannte aufrichtige und wohlmeynende REISE-Gedanken eines ANONYMI A.M.Z.P.C.I. vom dem heutigen so genannten PIETISMO...*, Halle, 1699.

Ashton, Robert, *The City and the Court 1603–1643*, Cambridge, Cambridge University Press, 1979.

The English Civil War, London, Weidenfeld and Nicolson, 1978.

Ashton, Trevor (ed.), *Crisis in Europe, 1560–1660*, London, Routledge and Kegan Paul, 1965.

Aubrey, John, *Brief Lives*, ed. Oliver Lawson Dick, Harmondsworth, Penguin, 1972.

Aylmer, G.E., *A Short History of Seventeenth-Century England*, New York, Mentor Books, 1963.

Babbage, S.B., *Puritanism and Richard Bancroft*, London, S.P.C.K., 1962.

Bahlmann, Dudley W.R., *The Moral Revolution of 1688*, New Haven, Yale University Press, 1957.

Bainton, Roland, *The Reformation of the Sixteenth Century*, Boston, Beacon Press, 1952.

Barbour, Hugh, *The Quakers in Puritan England*, New Haven, Yale University Press, 1964.

Barnes, John, 'The Righthand and Lefthand Kingdoms of God. A Dilemma of Pietist Politics' in T.O. Beidelman (ed.), *The Translation of Culture*, London, Tavistock Publications, 1971.

Barnes, T.G., *Somerset 1625–1640: A County's Government during the 'Personal Rule'*, London, Oxford University Press, 1961.

Bassler (Pfarrer), 'Die Ersten Jahre nach dem Dreissigjährigen Krieg im Bezirk Maulbronn', *Blätter für Württembergische Kirchengeschichte* 2 (1898), 119–28, 166–73.

Baumgart, P., 'Leibniz und der Pietismus: Universale Reformbestrebungen um 1700', *Archiv für Kulturgeschichte* 48 (1966), 364–86.

Baxter, Richard, *The Autobiography of Richard Baxter*, ed. J.M.L. Thomas, London, J.M. Dent and Sons Ltd, 1931.

Bebb, E.D., *Nonconformity and Social and Economic Life 1600–1800*, London, The Epworth Press, 1935.

Bechtel, Heinrich, *Wirtschaftsgeschichte Deutschlands, 2: Vom Beginn des 16. bis zum Ende des 18. Jahrhunderts*, München, Verlag Georg D.W. Callwey, 1952.

Wirtschafts- und Sozialgeschichte Deutschlands. Wirtschaftsstile und Lebensformen von der Vorzeit bis zur Gegenwart, München, Verlag Georg D.W. Callwey, 1967.

Becker, Carl, *The Heavenly City of the Eighteenth-Century Philosophers*, New Haven, Yale University Press, 1932.

Bendix, R., *Kings or People*, Berkeley, University of California Press, 1978.

(ed.), *State and Society*, Berkeley, University of California Press, 1968.

Bergner, Dieter, 'Bemerkungen zur Geschichtlichen Stellung des Halleschen Pietismus und zur Bedeutung A.H. Franckes' in *August Hermann Francke: Festreden und Kolloquium*, Halle–Wittenberg, Martin-Luther-Universität, 1964.

Beyreuther, Erich, *August Hermann Francke 1663–1727. Zeuge des Lebendigen Gottes*, Marburg an der Lahn, Verlag der Francke-Buchhandlung GmbH, 1956.

August Hermann Francke und die Anfänge der Ökumenischen Bewegung, Leipzig, Koehler und Amelang, 1957.

Geschichte des Pietismus, Stuttgart, J.F. Steinkopf Verlag, 1978.

Bigler, R.M., *The Politics of German Protestantism*, Berkeley, University of California Press, 1972.

Bindoff, S., et al. (eds.), *Elizabethan Government and Society: Essays Presented to Sir John Neale*, London, Athlone Press, 1961.

Blackwood, B.G., *The Lancashire Gentry and the Great Rebellion, 1640–1660*, Manchester, Chetham Society, 1978.

Blaufuss, D., (ed.), *Orthodoxie und Pietismus*, Bielefeld, Luther-Verlag, 1975.

Born, K.E., (ed.), *Historische Forschungen und Probleme: Peter Rassow zum 70. Geburtstag*, Wiesbaden, Franz Steiner Verlag, 1961.

Bornkamm, H., F. Heyer and A. Schindler (eds.), *Der Pietismus in Gestalten und Wirkungen*, Bielefeld, Luther-Verlag, 1975.

Borrmann, Walther, *Das Eindringen des Pietismus in die Ostpreussische Landeskirche*, Königsberg i. Pr., Kommissionsverlag Ferd. Beyers Buchhandlung, Thomas und Oppermann, 1913. (Schriften der Synodalkommission für Ostpreussische Kirchengeschichte, Heft 15.)

Bosl, Karl, and Karl Möckl (eds.), *Der Moderne Parlamentarismus und seine Grundlagen in der Ständischen Repräsentation*, Berlin, Duncker and Humblot, 1977.

Brauer, Jerald, 'Reflections on the Nature of English Puritanism', *Church History* 23 (1954), 99–108.

Brecht, Martin, 'Die Anfänge der historischen Darstellung des Württembergischen Pietismus', *Blätter für Württembergische Kirchengeschichte* 66/7 (1966–7), 44–51.

Kirchenordnung und Kirchenzucht in Württemberg vom 16. bis zum 18. Jahrhundert, Stuttgart, Calwer Verlag, 1967.

F. de Boor, K. Deppermann, H. Lehmann, A. Lindt and J. Wallmann (eds.), *Pietismus und Neuzeit*, vol. 4, 'Die Anfänge des Pietismus', Göttingen, Vandenhoek und Ruprecht, 1979.

Breining, F., 'Die Hausbibliothek des gemeinen Mannes vor 100 und mehr Jahren', *Blätter für Württembergische Kirchengeschichte*, 13 (1909), 48–63.

'Züge aus dem kirchlich-sittlichen Leben des 17. und 18. Jahrhunderts', *Blätter für Württembergische Kirchengeschichte*, 33 (1929), 141–59.

Bridenbaugh, Carl, *Vexed and Troubled Englishmen, 1590–1642*, Oxford, Clarendon Press, 1968.

Bruford, W.H., *Germany in the Eighteenth Century: The Social Background of the Literary Revival*, Cambridge, Cambridge University Press, 1935.

Brunschwig, Henri, *Enlightenment and Romanticism in Eighteenth-Century Prussia*, Chicago, University of Chicago Press, 1974 (orig. 1947).

Burrell, Sidney, 'Calvinism, Capitalism, and the Middle Classes: Some Afterthoughts on an old Problem', *Journal of Modern History*, 32 (1960), 129–41.

Büsch, Otto, *Militärsystem und Sozialleben im alten Preussen 1713–1807. Die Anfänge der Militarisierung der preussisch-deutschen Gesellschaft*, Berlin, Walter de Gruyter and Co., 1962.

Calder, I.M., *Activities of the Puritan Faction of the Church of England 1625–1633*, London, S.P.C.K., 1957.

Carsten, F.L., 'The Great Elector and the Foundation of Hohenzollern Despotism', *English Historical Review*, 65 (1950), 175–202.

The Origins of Prussia, Oxford, Clarendon Press, 1954.

Princes and Parliaments in Germany, Oxford, Clarendon Press, 1959.

'Prussian Despotism at its Height', *History* 40 (1955), 42–67.

'Die Ursachen des Niedergangs der deutschen Landstände', *Historische Zeitschrift* 192 (1961), 273–81.

Cassirer, Ernst, *The Philosophy of the Englightenment*, Princeton, N.J., Princeton University Press, 1951.

Christianson, Paul, 'The Causes of the English Revolution: A Reappraisal', *Journal of British Studies* 15 (1976), 40–75.

'The Peers, the People, and Parliamentary Management in the First Six Months of the Long Parliament', *Journal of Modern History* 49 (1977), 575–99.

Reformers and Babylon: English Apocalyptic Visions from the Reformation to the Eve of the Civil War, Toronto, University of Toronto Press, 1978.

Clark, G.N., *The Seventeenth Century*, 2nd edn, London, Oxford University Press, 1961.

Clark, Peter, *English Provincial Society from the Reformation to the Revolution: Religion, Politics and Society in Kent, 1500–1640*, Sussex, Harvester Press, 1977.

'Thomas Scott and the Growth of Urban Opposition to the Early Stuart Regime', *The Historical Journal* 21 (1978), 1–26.

Cliffe, J.T., *The Yorkshire Gentry from the Reformation to the Civil War*, London, Athlone Press, 1969.

Coleman, D.C., *The Economy of England, 1450–1750*, London, Oxford University Press, 1977.

Collinson, Patrick, *The Elizabethan Puritan Movement*, London, Jonathan Cape, 1967.

'John Field and Elizabethan Puritanism' in S. Bindoff et al. (eds.), *Elizabethan Government and Society: Essays Presented to Sir John Neale*, London, Athlone Press, 1961.

Mirror of Elizabethan Puritanism: The Life and Letters of 'Godly Master Dering', London, Dr Williams's Trust, 1964.

Cooper, J.P., 'Differences between English and Continental Governments in the Early Seventeenth Century' in J.S. Bromley and E.H. Kossmann (eds.), *Britain and the Netherlands*, London, Chatto and Windus, 1960.

'The Fall of the Stuart Monarchy' in J.P. Cooper (ed.), *The New Cambridge Modern History*, vol. 4, Cambridge, Cambridge University Press, 1970.

Coward, Barry, *The Stuart Age*, London, Longman, 1980.

Cragg, G.R., *The Church and the Age of Reason, 1648–1789*, Grand Rapids, Wm. B. Eerdmans Publishing Co., 1960.

Freedom and Authority, Philadelphia, The Westminster Press, 1975.

From Puritanism to the Age of Reason, Cambridge, Cambridge University Press, 1950.

Craig, Gordon, *The Politics of the Prussian Army, 1640–1945*, Oxford, Clarendon Press, 1964.

Cross, Claire, *Church and People, 1450–1660*, Glasgow, Collins (Fontana), 1976.

The Royal Supremacy in the Elizabethan Church, London, George Allen and Unwin, 1969.

Crowley, Robert, *A Briefe Discourse against the Outwarde Apparell and Ministring Garmentes of the Popishe Church*, n.p., 1566.

Cuming, G.L. (ed.), *Studies in Church History*, vol. 2, London, Nelson, 1965, and vol. 4, Leiden, E.J. Brill, 1967.

Curtis, Mark, 'The Alienated Intellectuals of Early Stuart England', *Past and Present* 23 (1962), 25–43.

'Hampton Court Conference and its Aftermath', *History* 46 (1961), 1–16.

Daly, James, 'The Idea of Absolute Monarchy in Seventeenth-Century England', *The Historical Journal*, 21 (1978), 227–50.

Davies, Horton, *The Worship of the English Puritans*, Glasgow, The University Press, 1948.

Deppermann, Klaus, *Der Hallesche Pietismus und der Preussische Staat unter Friedrich III. (I.)*, Göttingen, Vandenhoek und Ruprecht, 1961.

'Pietismus und moderne Staat' in K. Aland (ed.), *Pietismus und Moderne Welt*, Witten, Luther-Verlag, 1974.

Dering, E., *WORKES More at large then ever hath heere-to-fore been printed in any one Volume*, London, 1597.

Dickens, A.G., 'The Early English Protestants: A Social Survey', Neale Lecture, University of London, 1977.

The English Reformation, New York, Schocken Books, 1964.

The German Nation and Martin Luther, Glasgow, Collins (Fontana), 1976.

Martin Luther and the Reformation, London, Hodder and Stoughton, 1967.

Reformation and Society in Sixteenth-Century Europe, London, Thames and Hudson, 1966.

Dobb, Maurice, *Studies in the Development of Capitalism*, New York, International Publishers, 1947.

Dorn, Walter, 'The Prussian Bureaucracy in the Eighteenth Century', *Political Science Quarterly*, 46 (1931), 403–23; 47 (1932), 75–94 and 259–73.

Dorwart, R.A., *The Administrative Reforms of Frederick William I of Prussia*, Cambridge, Mass., Harvard University Press, 1953.

'Church Organization in Brandenburg-Prussia from the Reformation to 1740', *Harvard Theological Review*, 31 (1938), 275–90.

The Prussian Welfare State before 1740, Cambridge, Mass., Harvard University Press, 1971.

Drummond, A.L., *German Protestantism since Luther*, London, The Epworth Press, 1951.

Ehemann (Pfarrer), 'Aus Amt und Leben der evangelischen Geistlichkeit zwischen 1680 und 1780', *Blätter für Württembergische Kirchengeschichte*, 5 (1901), 178–90.

Eisenstadt, S.N. (ed.), *The Protestant Ethic and Modernization*, New York, Basic Books, 1968.

Elias, Norbert, *The Civilising Process*, vol. 1, Oxford, Basil Blackwell, 1978 (orig. 1939).

Elton, G.R., 'A High Road to Civil War?' in Charles Carter (ed.), *From the Renaissance to the Counter-Reformation. Essays in Honour of Garrett Mattingley*, London, Jonathan Cape, 1966.

'Parliament under the Tudors: Functions and Fortunes', Neale Lecture, University of London, 1978.

Reformation Europe, Glasgow, Collins (Fontana), 1963.

The Tudor Constitution. Documents and Commentary, Cambridge, Cambridge University Press, 1960.

Epstein, Klaus, *The Genesis of German Conservatism*, Princeton, N.J., Princeton University Press, 1966.

Eusden, J.D., *Puritans, Lawyers and Politics in Early Seventeenth-Century England*, New Haven, Yale University Press, 1958.

Everitt, Alan, *Change in the Provinces: The Seventeenth Century*, Leicester, Leicester University Press, 1969.

Suffolk and the Great Rebellion 1640–1660, Suffolk Records Society, vol. 3, 1960.

Fauchier-Magnan, Adrien, *The Small German Courts in the Eighteenth Century*, London, Methuen, 1958 (orig. 1947).

Fausel, Heinrich, 'Von Altlutherischer Orthodoxie zum Frühpietismus in Württemberg', *Zeitschrift für Württembergische Landesgeschichte*, 24 (1965), 309–28.

Fay, Sidney B., and Klaus Epstein, *The Rise of Brandenburg-Prussia to 1786*, revised edn, New York, Holt, Rinehart and Winston, 1964.

Firth, Katherine, *The Apocalyptic Tradition in Reformation Britain, 1530–1645*, Oxford, Oxford University Press, 1979.

Fleischhauer, Werner, *Barock im Herzogtum Württemberg*, Stuttgart, W. Kohlhammer Verlag, 1958.

Fletcher, Anthony, *A County Community in Peace and War: Sussex 1600–1660*, London, Longman, 1975.

[Francke, A.H.], *August Hermann Francke: Festreden und Kolloquium*, Hallesche Universitätsreden, Neue Folge, Heft 6; Halle–Wittenberg, Martin-Luther-Universität, 1964.

Francke, A.H., *Einrichtung des Paedagogii zu Glaucha an Halle*, Halle, 1699.

Erläuterung Der 1699 edirten Einrichtung Des Paedagogii Zu Glaucha an Halle, Halle, 1700.

Glauchische Hauss- Kirch-Ordnung / Oder Christliche Unterricht / wie ein Hauss-Vater mit seinen Kindern und Gesinde das Wort Gottes und das Gebet in seinem Hause üben und Ihnen mit gutem Exempel vorleuchten soll..., Halle, 1699.

Glauchische Schulordnung ..., Halle, 1699.

'A Letter to a Friend Concerning the most useful Way of Preaching', 25 May 1725, in John Jennings, *Two Discourses: The First, of Preaching Christ; the Second, of Particular and Experimental Preaching*, 4th edn, Boston, 1740.

Nutzen So aus denen zur Erziehung der Jugend und Verpflegung der Armen zu Glaucha an Halle gemachten Anstalten entstehen, 1698.

Ordnung So unter denen Studiosis, die in dem Wäysen-Hause zu Glaucha an Halle der Freyen Kost geniessen / zu beobachten ist, Halle, 1699.

Schrifftmässige Lebens-Regeln. Wie man so wohl bey als ausser der Gesellschaft die Liebe und Freundligkeit gegen den Nechsten / und Freudigkeit eines guten Gewissens für Gott bewahren / und im Christenthum zunehmen soll, Bremen, 1696.

Segens-Volle Fussstapfen des noch Liebenden und Waltenden Liebreichen und Getreuen Gottes, zur Beschämung des Unglaubens und Stärckung des Glaubens, entdecket durch eine Wahrhafte und Umständliche Nachricht von dem Waysen-Hause und übrigen Anstalten zu Glaucha vor Halle, Welche im Jahr 1701 zum Druck befördet, ietzo aber zum dritten Mal ediret, und bis auf gegenwärtiges Jahr fortgesetzet, Halle, 1709.

Specification, derer Sachen welche zu der für die Glauchische Anstalten angefangenen Naturalien-Kammer bis anhero verehret worden, n.p., n.d.

Wohlgemeynte Erinnerungen an die Wertheste Eltern / So ihre Kinder in dem Paedagogio zu Glaucha an Halle Erziehen lassen, Halle, n.d.

Frere, W.H. and C.E. Douglas (eds.), *Puritan Manifestoes*, London, S.P.C.K., 1954.

Friedrich Wilhelm I, König in Preussen, 'Erneuerte und erweiterte Verordnung über das Kirchen- und Schulwesen in Preussen' and "Instruktion König Friedrich Wilhelms I. an die Königsberger Professoren D. Wolf und D. Rogall' in Walter Hubatsch, *Geschichte der Evangelischen Kirche Ostpreussens*, vol. 3, Göttingen, Vandenhoek und Ruprecht, 1968.

'Instruktion König Friedrich Wilhelms I. für seinen Nachfolger (22. Jan.–17. Feb. 1722)' in G. Schmoller, D. Krauske and D. Loewe (eds.), *Acta Borussica. Die Behördenorganization und die allgemeine Staatsverwaltung Preussens im 18. Jahrhundert*, vol. 3 (Jan. 1718–Jan. 1723), Berlin, Verlag von Paul Parey, 1901.

Fritz, Friedrich, *Altwürttembergische Pietisten*, Stuttgart, Im Quell-Verlag der Evangelischen Gesellschaft, 1950.

'Die evangelische Kirche Württembergs im Zeitalter des Pietismus', *Blätter für Württembergische Kirchengeschichte*, 55 (1955), 68–116 and 56 (1956), 99–167.

'Georg David Zorer (1673–1735), ein Bekenner der Wahrheit aus den Tagen Eberhard Ludwigs und der Grävenitz', *Blätter für Württembergische Kirchengeschichte*, 29 (1925), 108–16.

'Geschichte des Stundenwesens im Amtsoberamt Stuttgart', *Blätter für Württembergische Kirchengeschichte*, 26 (1922), 98–129.

'Gottlieb Seeger (1683–1743), Leben und Wirken eines altwürttembergischen Pietisten', *Blätter für Württembergische Kirchengeschichte*, 39 (1935), 51–64.

'Hedinger und der Württembergische Hof', *Blätter für Württembergische Kirchengeschichte*, 40 (1936), 244–53.

'Johann Jakob Rues (1681–1754), ein pietistischer Seelsorger und seine Schicksale unter Herzog Karl Alexander', *Blätter für Württembergische Kirchengeschichte*, 28 (1924), 130–43.

'Konsistorium und Synodus in Württemberg am Vorabend der pietistischen Zeit', *Blätter für Württembergische Kirchengeschichte* 39 (1935), 100–31 and 40 (1936), 33–106.

'Konventikel in Württemberg von der Reformationszeit bis zum Edikt von 1743', *Blätter für Württembergische Kirchengeschichte* 49 (1949), 99–154; 50 (1950), 65–121; 51 (1951), 78–137; 52 (1952), 28–65; 53 (1953), 82–130; 54 (1954), 75–119.

'Die Liebestätigkeit des altwürttembergischen Pfarrhauses', *Blätter für Württembergische Kirchengeschichte*, 25 (1921), 213–45.

Fulbrook, Mary, 'The English Revolution and the Revisionist Revolt', *Social History*, 7 (1982), 249–64.

'Max Weber's "Interpretive Sociology": A Comparison of Conception and Practice', *British Journal of Sociology* 29 (1978), 71–82.

and Theda Skocpol, 'Destined Pathways: The Historical Sociology of Perry Anderson' in Theda Skocpol (ed.), *Vision and Method in Historical Sociology*, Cambridge, Cambridge University Press, forthcoming.

Gardiner, S.R., *History of England from the Accession of James I to the Outbreak of the Civil War, 1603–1642*, 10 vols., New York, A.M.S. Press Inc., 1965 (orig. 1883–4).

(ed.), *The Constitutional Documents of the Puritan Revolution, 1625–1660*, Oxford, Clarendon Press, 1979 from 3rd edn of 1906.

Gay, Peter, *The Enlightenment: An Interpretation*, New York, Random House, 1966.

and R.K. Webb, *Modern Europe*, New York, Harper and Row, 1973.

Gee, H., and W.J. Hardy (eds.), *Documents Illustrative of English Church History*, London, Macmillan and Co. Ltd, 1896.

Geiges, R., 'Die Auseinandersetzung zwischen Chr. Fr. Oetinger und Zinzendorf', *Blätter für Württembergische Kirchengeschichte* 39 (1935), 131–48.

George, C.H., 'Puritanism as History and Historiography', *Past and Present* 41 (1968), 77–104.

'Review article: Hill's century: Fragments of a lost revolution', *Science and Society*, 40 (1976/7), 479–86.

and K. George, *The Protestant Mind of the English Reformation 1570–1640*, Princeton, N.J., Princeton University Press, 1961.

and K. George, 'Protestantism and Capitalism in Pre-revolutionary England' in S.N. Eisenstadt (ed.), *The Protestant Ethic and Modernization*, New York, Basic Books, 1968.

Gerhard, Dietrich, 'Regionalismus und ständisches Wesen als ein Grundthema Europäischer Geschichte', *Historische Zeitschrift*, 174 (1952), 307–37.

(ed.), *Ständische Vertretungen in Europa im 17. und 18. Jahrhundert*, Göttingen, Vandenhoek und Ruprecht, 1969.

Gerth, H.H., and C.W. Mills (eds.), *From Max Weber*, New York, Oxford University Press, 1958.

Geuss, Raymond, *The Idea of a Critical Theory*, Cambridge, Cambridge University Press, 1981.

Gilby, Antony, *A Pleasaunt Dialogue conteining a large discourse betweene a Souldier of Barwick, and an English Chaplain, who of a late souldier, was made a Parson, and had gotten a pluralitie of Benefices, and yet had but one eye, and no learning: but he was priestly apparailed in al points, and stoutely maintained his popish attire, by the authoritie of a booke, lately written against London Ministers*, n.p., 1581.

Girouard, Mark, *Life in the English Country House*, New Haven, Yale University Press, 1978.

Gladigow, Burkhard (ed.), *Religion und Moral*, Düsseldorf, Patmos Verlag, 1976.

Godfroid, Michel, 'Gab es den deutschen Pietismus?' in M. Greschat (ed.), *Zur Neueren Pietismusforschung*, Darmstadt, Wissenschaftliche Buchgesellschaft, 1977.

Goodwin, A. (ed.), *The European Nobility in the Eighteenth Century*, London, Adam and Charles Black, 1953.

Green, Ian, 'Career Prospects and Clerical Conformity in the Early Stuart Church', *Past and Present*, 90 (1981), 71–115.

Green, Lowell C., 'Duke Ernest the Pious of Saxe-Gotha and his relationship to Pietism' in Bornkamm et al. (eds.), *Der Pietismus in Gestalten und Wirkungen*, Bielefeld, Luther-Verlag, 1975.

Greenham, Richard, 'The Apologie or aunswere of Maister Grenham, Minister of Dreaton, unto the Bishop of Ely, being commaunded to subscribe, and to use the Romish habite, with allowance of the Com. booke' in *A Parte of a register, contayninge sundrie memorable matters, written by divers godly and learned in our time, which stande for, and desire the reformation of our Church, in Discipline and Ceremonies, according to the pure Worde of God, and the Lawe of our Lande*, n.p., 1593.

The Workes of the Reverend and Faithful Servant of Iesus Christ... Revised, corrected, and published, for the further building of all such as love the truth, and desire to know the power of godlinesse..., 5th edn, London, 1612.

Greschat, Martin, *Zwischen Tradition und neuem Anfang: Valentin Ernst Löscher und der Ausgang der Lutherischen Orthodoxie*, Witten, Luther-Verlag, 1971.

(ed.), *Zur Neueren Pietismusforschung*, Darmstadt, Wissenschaftliche Buchgesellschaft, 1977.

Grotz, Heinrich, 'Das höhere Schulwesen' in *Herzog Karl Eugen...und seine Zeit*, vol. 2.

Grube, Walter, 'Altwürttembergische Kloster vor und nach der Reformation', *Blätter für Deutsche Landesgeschichte*, 109 (1973), 139–50.

'Dorfgemeinde und Amtsversammlung in Altwürttemberg', *Zeitschrift für Württembergische Landesgeschichte*, 13 (1954), 194–219.

'Israel Hartmann. Lebensbild eines altwürttembergischen Pietisten', *Zeitschrift für Württembergische Landesgeschichte* 12 (1953), 250–70.

Der Stuttgarter Landtag 1457–1957, Stuttgart, Ernst Klett Verlag, 1957.

and Ernst Schaude, *Der Kreisverband Nürtingen*, Würzburg, Konrad Tiltsch Druck- und Verlagsanstalt, 1953.

Grünberg, Paul, *Philipp Jakob Spener*, 3 vols., Göttingen, Vandenhoek und Ruprecht, 1893–1906.

Haigh, Christopher, *Reformation and Resistance in Tudor Lancashire*, Cambridge, Cambridge University Press, 1975.

Hall, Basil, 'Puritanism: The Problem of Definition' in G.J. Cuming (ed.), *Studies in Church History*, vol. 2, London, Nelson, 1965.

Haller, William, *Liberty and Reformation in the Puritan Revolution*, New York, Columbia University Press, 1955.

The Rise of Puritanism, Philadelphia, University of Pennsylvania Press, 1972 (orig. 1938).

Haltern, Utz, 'Bürgerliche Gesellschaft. Probleme der Forschung', *Archiv für Sozialgeschichte*, 18 (1978), 524–35.

Hamerow, Theodore, *Restoration, Revolution, Reaction*, Princeton, N.J., Princeton University Press, 1966.

Hampson, Norman, *The Enlightenment*, Harmondsworth, Penguin, 1968.

Hart, A. Tindal, *Clergy and Society 1600–1800*, London, S.P.C.K., 1968.

Hartmann, I., 'Das religiöse Leben', in *Herzog Karl Eugen. . . und seine Zeit*, vol. 1.

Hartung, Fritz, and Roland Mousnier, 'Quelques Problèmes concernant la Monarchie Absolue', X. *Congresso Internazionale di Scienze Storiche, Relazione*, vol. 4, Storia Moderna, Rome, 1955.

Hasselhorn, Martin, *Der Altwürttembergische Pfarrstand im 18. Jahrhundert*, Stuttgart, W. Kohlhammer Verlag, 1958.

Hazard, Paul, *The European Mind 1680–1715*, New York, Meridian Books, 1963 (orig. 1935).

Heal, Felicity, *Of Prelates and Princes: A Study of the Economic and Social Position of the Tudor Episcopate*, Cambridge, Cambridge University Press, 1980.

and Rosemary O'Day (eds.), *Church and Society in England: Henry VIII to James I*, London, Macmillan, 1977.

Heer, Friedrich, *The Intellectual History of Europe*, London, Weidenfeld and Nicolson, 1966 (orig. 1953).

Hermelink, Heinrich, *Geschichte der Evangelischen Kirche in Württemberg von der Reformation bis zur Gegenwart*, Stuttgart und Tübingen, Rainer Wunderlich Verlag Hermann Leins, 1949.

'Das Hochschulwesen: Universität', and 'Die Wissenschaften' in *Herzog Karl Eugen. . . und siene Zeit*, vol. 2.

Herzog Karl Eugen von Württemberg und seine Zeit, ed. Württembergische Geschichts- und Altertumsverein, 2 vols., Esslingen a. N., Paul Neff Verlag (Max Schreiber), 1907–9.

Hexter, J.H., 'Power Struggle, Parliament and Liberty in Early Stuart England', *Journal of Modern History*, 50 (1978), 1–50.

Reappraisals in History, London, Longman, 1961.

The Reign of King Pym, Cambridge, Mass., Harvard University Press, 1941.

Hey, David, *An English Rural Community: Myddle under the Tudors and Stuarts*, Leicester, Leicester University Press, 1974.

Hill, Christopher, *Antichrist in Seventeenth-Century England*, London, Oxford University Press, 1971.

The Century of Revolution, New York, W.W. Norton, 1966.

Change and Continuity in Seventeenth-Century England, London, Weidenfeld and Nicolson, 1974.

Economic Problems of the Church, Oxford, Clarendon Press, 1956.

The English Revolution 1640, London, Lawrence and Wishart, 1940.

God's Englishman: Oliver Cromwell and the English Revolution, Harmondsworth, Penguin Books, 1970.

Intellectual Origins of the English Revolution, Oxford, Clarendon Press, 1965.
'Parliament and People in Early Seventeenth-Century England', *Past and Present*, 92 (1981), 100–24.
Puritanism and Revolution, London, Secker and Warburg, 1958.
'Puritans and the Poor', *Past and Present*, 2 (1952), 32–50.
Reformation to Industrial Revolution, Harmondsworth, Penguin, 1969.
Society and Puritanism in Pre-revolutionary England, New York, Schocken, 1967.
Some Intellectual Consequences of the English Revolution, London, Weidenfeld and Nicolson, 1980.
The World Turned Upside Down, Harmondsworth, Penguin, 1975.
Hillerbrand, H.J. (ed.), *The Protestant Reformation*, London, Macmillan, 1968.
Hinrichs, Carl, *Friedrich Wilhelm I. König in Preussen*, Hamburg, Hanseatische Verlagsanstalt, 1941.
Preussentum und Pietismus, Göttingen, Vandenhoek und Ruprecht, 1971.
Hinton, R.W.K., 'The Decline of Parliamentary Government under Elizabeth I and the Early Stuarts', *Cambridge Historical Journal*, 13 (1957), 116–32.
'English constitutional theories from Sir John Fortescue to Sir John Eliot', *English Historical Review*, 75 (1960), 410–25.
Hintze, Otto, 'Die Epochen des evangelischen Kirchenregiments in Preussen', *Historische Zeitschrift*, 97 (1906), 67–118.
The Historical Essays of Otto Hintze, ed. Felix Gilbert, New York, Oxford University Press, 1975.
Hirst, Derek, 'The Defection of Sir Edward Dering, 1640–1641', *The Historical Journal*, 15 (1972), 193–208.
'The Place of Principle', *Past and Present*, 92 (1981), 79–99.
The Representative of the People?, Cambridge, Cambridge University Press, 1975.
'Unanimity in the Commons', *Journal of Modern History*, 50 (1978), 51–71.
Hobbes, Thomas, *Behemoth*, London, Simpkin, Marshall and Co., 1889 edn.
Hoffmann, C., 'Aus einer altpietistischen Zirkularkorrespondenz', *Blätter für Württembergische Kirchengeschichte*, 3 (1899), 1–34 and 4 (1900), 1–35.
Holborn, Hajo, *A History of Modern Germany*, vol. 2, New York, Alfred Knopf, 1964.
Holmes, Geoffrey (ed.), *Britain after the Glorious Revolution, 1689–1714*, London, Macmillan, 1969.
Hoskins, W.G., *The Making of the English Landscape*, Harmondsworth, Pelican, 1970.
Houlbrooke, Ralph, *Church Courts and the People during the English Reformation, 1520–1570*, Oxford, Oxford University Press, 1979.
Howell, Roger, *Newcastle-upon-Tyne and the Puritan Revolution*, Oxford, Clarendon Press, 1967.
Hubatsch, Walter, *Geschichte der Evangelischen Kirche Ostpreussens*, 3 vols., Göttingen, Vandenhoek und Ruprecht, 1968.
Hurstfield, Joel, *Elizabeth I and the Unity of England*, Harmondsworth, Penguin, 1971.
and Alan Smith (eds.), *Elizabethan People: State and Society*, London, Edward Arnold, 1972.
Hutchinson, Lucy, *Memoirs of the Life of Colonel Hutchinson*, ed. James Sutherland, London, Oxford University Press, 1973.

Ives, E.W. (ed.), *The English Revolution, 1600–1660*, London, Edward Arnold, 1968.

James, Mervyn, *Family, Lineage and Civil Society. A Study of Society, Politics and Mentality in the Durham Region, 1500–1640*, Oxford, Clarendon Press, 1974.

Jeggle, Utz, *Kiebingen – eine Heimatgeschichte*, Tübingen, Tübinger Verein für Volkskunde e.V. Schloss, 1977.

Jones, W.J., *Politics and the Bench*, London, George Allen and Unwin, 1971.

Jordan, W.K., *The Development of Religious Toleration in England*, 4 vols., London, George Allen and Unwin, 1932–40.

Kaiser, Gerhard, *Pietismus und Patriotismus im Literarischen Deutschland*, Wiesbaden, Franz Steiner Verlag, 1961.

Kalu, Ogbu, 'Bishops and Puritans in Early Jacobean England: A Perspective on Methodology', *Church History*, 45 (1976), 469–89.

'Continuity in Change: Bishops of London and Religious Dissent in Early Stuart England', *Journal of British Studies*, 18 (1978), 28–45.

Kamen, Henry, *The Rise of Toleration*, London, Weidenfeld and Nicolson, 1967.

Kenyon, J.P., *The Stuart Constitution, 1603–1688. Documents and Commentary*, Cambridge, Cambridge University Press, 1966.

Kiernan, V., 'Communication: Puritanism and the Poor', *Past and Present*, 3 (1953), 45–53.

Kishlansky, Mark, 'The Emergence of Adversary Politics in the Long Parliament', *Journal of Modern History*, 49 (1977), 614–40.

Klepper, Jochen (ed.), *Der Soldatenkönig und die Stillen im Lande. Begegnungen Friedrich Wilhelms I. mit August Herman Francke / August Gotthold Francke / Johann Anastasius Freylinghausen / Nikolaus Ludwig Graf von Zinzendorf*, Berlin–Steglitz, Eckart-Verlag, 1938.

Knappen, M.M., *Tudor Puritanism*, Chicago, University of Chicago Press, 1939, pbk edn 1970.

(ed.), *Two Tudor Puritan Diaries*, Chicago, American Society of Church History, 1933.

Koch, H.W., *A History of Prussia*, London, Longman, 1978.

Koenigsberger, Helmut, 'Dominium Regale or Dominium Politicum et Regale? Monarchies and Parliaments in Early Modern Europe' in Karl Bosl and Karl Möckl (eds.), *Der moderne Parlamentarismus und seine Grundlagen in der ständischen Repräsentation*, Berlin, Duncker und Humblot, 1977.

Estates and Revolutions, Ithaca, Cornell University Press, 1971.

'Revolutionary Conclusions', *History*, 57 (1972), 394–8.

and Lawrence Stone, 'Early Modern Revolutions: An Exchange', *Journal of Modern History*, 46 (1974), 99–110.

Kolb, Christoph, 'Die Anfänge des Pietismus und Separatismus in Württemberg', *Württembergische Vierteljahresheft für Landesgeschichte*, 9 (1900), 33–93, 368–412; 10 (1901), 201–51, 364–88; 11 (1902), 43–78.

'Strenge Handhabung des Edikts von 1743', *Blätter für Württembergische Kirchengeschichte*, 6 (1902), 90–2.

'Zur kirchlichen Geschichte Stuttgarts im 18. Jahrhundert', *Blätter für Württembergische Kirchengeschichte*, 2 (1898), 49–85, 145–63; 3 (1899), 35–42, 160–70.

Kramer, Gustav, *August Hermann Francke. Ein Lebensbild*, Halle, Verlag der Buchhandlung des Waisenhauses, 1880.

(ed.), *Beiträge zur Geschichte August Hermann Franckes. Enthaltend den Briefwechsel Franckes und Speners*, Halle, Verlag der Buchhandlung des Waisenhauses, 1861.

(ed.), *Neue Beiträge zur Geschichte August Hermann Franckes*, Halle, Verlag der Buchhandlung des Waisenhauses, 1875.

von Kruedener, Jürgen, *Die Rolle des Hofes im Absolutismus*, Stuttgart, Gustav Fischer Verlag, 1973.

Kruse, Martin, *Speners Kritik am Landesherrlichen Kirchenregiment und ihre Vorgeschichte*, Witten, Luther-Verlag, 1971.

Lamont, William, 'Debate: Puritanism as History and Historiography: Some Further Thoughts', *Past and Present*, 44 (1969), 133–46.

Godly Rule, London, Macmillan, 1969.

Marginal Prynne, 1600–1669, London, Routledge and Kegan Paul, 1963.

Richard Baxter and the Millennium, London, Croom Helm, 1979.

Larrain, Jorge, *The Concept of Ideology*, London, Hutchinson, 1979.

Laslett, Peter, *The World We Have Lost*, New York, Charles Scribner's Sons, 1965.

Lehmann, Hartmut, 'Der Pietismus im alten Reich', *Historische Zeitschrift*, 214 (1972), 58–95.

Pietismus und Weltliche Ordnung in Württemberg vom 17. bis zum 20. Jahrhundert, Stuttgart, W. Kohlhammer Verlag, 1969.

'Pietismus und Wirtschaft in Calw am Anfang des 18. Jahrhunderts', *Zeitschrift für Württembergische Landesgeschichte*, 31 (1972), 249–77.

'Probleme einer Sozialgeschichte des Württembergischen Pietismus', *Blätter für Württembergische Kirchengeschichte*, 75 (1975), 166–81.

'Die Württembergischen Landstände im 17. und 18. Jahrhundert' in Dietrich Gerhard (ed.), *Ständische Vertretungen in Europa im 17. und 18. Jahrhundert*, Göttingen, Vandenhoek und Ruprecht, 1969.

Das Zeitalter des Absolutismus, Stuttgart, W. Kohlhammer Verlag, 1980.

Lempp, Eduard, 'Philipp Heinrich Weissensee', *Blätter für Württembergische Kirchengeschichte*, 31 (1927), 114–67.

'Weissensees Sturz. Nachtrag zur Biographie Ph. H. Weissensees', *Blätter für Württembergische Kirchengeschichte*, 32 (1928), 234–53.

Leube, Hans, 'Die altlutherische Orthodoxie: ein Forschungsbericht' in D. Blaufuss (ed.), *Orthodoxie und Pietismus*, Bielefeld, Luther-Verlag, 1975.

Kalvinismus und Luthertum, vol. 1, Leipzig, A. Deichertsche Verlagsbuchhandlung D. Werner Scholl, 1928.

Die Reformideen in der Deutschen Lutherischen Kirche zur Zeit der Orthodoxie, Leipzig, Verlag von Dörffling und Franke, 1924.

Leube, Martin, 'Die fremden Ausgaben des altwürttembergischen Kirchenguts', *Blätter für Württembergische Kirchengeschichte*, 29 (1925), 168–99.

Die Geschichte des Tübinger Stifts, 3 vols., Stuttgart, Verlag Chr. Scheufele, 1921–36.

Liebel, Helen P. 'The Bourgeoisie in Southwestern Germany, 1500–1789: A Rising Class?', *International Review of Social History*, 10 (1965), 283–307.

Lieberwirth, Rolf, 'Christian Thomasius und August Hermann Francke in ihrem Verhältnis zum brandenburgisch-preussischen Staat' in *August Hermann Francke: Festreden und Kolloquium*, Halle-Wittenberg, Martin-Luther-Universität, 1964.

Liebing, H., *Zwischen Orthodoxie und Aufklärung. Das philosophische und theologische Denken Georg Bernhard Bilfingers*, Tübingen, J.C.B. Mohr (Paul Siebeck), 1961.

and K. Scholder (eds.), *Geist und Geschichte der Reformation. Festgabe Hanns Rückert*, Berlin, Walter de Gruyter, 1966.

Lindsay, A.D., *The Modern Democratic State*, New York, Oxford University Press, 1962.

Lindt, A., and K. Deppermann (eds.), *Pietismus und Neuzeit*, 2 vols., Bielefeld, Luther-Verlag, 1974–5.

Little, David, *Religion, Order and Law*, Oxford, Basil Blackwell, 1970.

Lives of the Stuart Age, 1603–1714, London, Osprey, 1976.

Lives of the Tudor Age, 1485–1603, London, Osprey, 1977.

Loades, D.M., *Politics and the Nation, 1450–1660*, Glasgow, Fontana, 1979.

Lütge, Friedrich, *Deutsche Sozial- und Wirtschaftsgeschichte*, 2nd edn, Berlin, Springer-Verlag, 1960.

Geschichte der deutschen Agrarverfassung, 2nd edn, Stuttgart, Verlag Eugen Ulmer, 1967.

McAdoo, H.R., *The Spirit of Anglicanism*, London, Adam and Charles Black, 1965.

Maccaffrey, W.T., 'England: The Crown and the New Aristocracy, 1540–1600', *Past and Present*, 30 (1965), 52–64.

MacFarlane, Alan, *Witchcraft in Tudor and Stuart England*, London, Routledge and Kegan Paul, 1970.

(ed.), *The Diary of Ralph Josselin, 1616–1683*, London, Published for the British Academy by Oxford University Press, 1976.

McGinn, D.G., *The Admonition Controversy*, New Brunswick, Rutgers University Press, 1949.

McGrath, Patrick, *Papists and Puritans under Elizabeth I*, London, Blandford Press, 1967.

MacLear, James Fulton, 'Popular Anticlericalism in the Puritan Revolution', *Journal of the History of Ideas*, 18 (1956), 443–70.

McNeil, John T., *Modern Christian Movements*, New York, Harper and Row, 1968.

Mälzer, Gottfried, *Johann Albrecht Bengel: Leben und Werk*, Stuttgart, Calwer Verlag, 1970.

Manning, Brian, *The English People and the English Revolution*, Harmondsworth, Penguin, 1978.

'The Nobles, the People, and the Constitution', *Past and Present*, 9 (1956), 42–64.

(ed.), *Politics, Religion and the English Civil War*, London, Edward Arnold, 1973.

Manning, Roger B., *Religion and Society in Elizabethan Sussex*, Leicester, Leicester University Press, 1969.

Manschrek, Clyde L., *A History of Christianity*, Englewood Cliffs, N.J., Prentice-Hall Inc., 1964.

Mantel, Joachim, *Wildberg. Eine Studie zur wirtschaftlichen und sozialen Entwicklung der Stadt von der Mitte des sechzehnten bis zur Mitte des achtzehnten Jahrhunderts*, Stuttgart, W. Kohlhammer Verlag, 1974.

Marchant, Ronald, *The Church under the Law. Justice, Administration and Discipline in the Diocese of York, 1560–1640*, Cambridge, Cambridge University Press, 1969.

The Puritans and the Church Courts in the Diocese of York, 1560–1642, London, Longman, 1960.

Marshall, Gordon, *In Search of the Spirit of Capitalism*, London, Hutchinson, 1982.

Marx, Karl, 'The Eighteenth Brumaire of Louis Bonaparte' in *Marx and Engels: Selected Works*, London, Lawrence and Wishart, 1970.

Meads, D.M. (ed.), *Diary of Lady Margaret Hoby, 1599–1605*, London, George Routledge and Sons, 1930.

Merton, R.K., *Science, Technology and Society in Seventeenth-Century England*, New York, Howard Fertig, 1970 (orig. 1938).

Miller, Perry, *Errand into the Wilderness*, Cambridge, Mass., Belknap Press of Harvard University Press, 1956.

Moore, Barrington, *Social Origins of Dictatorship and Democracy*, Harmondsworth, Penguin, 1967.

Morgan, Irvonwy, *Prince Charles's Puritan Chaplain*, London, George Allen and Unwin, 1957.

Morrill, J.S., *Cheshire 1630–1660: County Government and Society during the English Revolution*, London, Oxford University Press, 1974.

'The Northern Gentry and the Great Rebellion', *Northern History*, 15 (1979), 66–87.

'Provincial Squires and the "Middling Sorts" in the Great Rebellion', *The Historical Journal*, 20 (1977), 229–36.

The Revolt of the Provinces, London, Longman, 1980.

Morton, A.L., *The World of the Ranters*, London, Lawrence and Wishart, 1970.

Moser, Johann Jacob, *Lebensgeschichte von ihme selbst beschriben*, n.p., 1768.

Mosse, G.L., *The Holy Pretence. Christianity and Reason of State from William Perkins to John Winthrop*, Oxford, Basil Blackwell, 1957.

'Puritan Political Thought and the "Cases of Conscience"', *Church History*, 23 (1954), 109–18.

Mulligan, Lotte, 'Civil War Politics, Religion, and the Royal Society', *Past and Present*, 59 (1973), 92–116.

Myers, A.R., *Parliaments and Estates in Europe to 1789*, London, Thames and Hudson, 1975.

Narr, Dieter, 'Berührung von Aufklärung und Pietismus im Württemberg des 18. Jahrhunderts', *Blätter für Württembergische Kirchengeschichte*, 66/7 (1966–7), 264–77.

'Zur Stellung des Pietismus in der Volkskultur Württembergs', *Württembergisches Jahrbuch für Volkskunde*, 3 (1957–8), 9–33.

Neale, J.E., *Elizabeth I and her Parliaments*, 2 vols., London, Jonathan Cape, 1953–7.

'The Elizabethan Acts of Supremacy and Uniformity', *English Historical Review*, 65 (1950), 304–32.

'Parliament and the Articles of Religion, 1571', *English Historical Review*, 67 (1952), 510–21.

'Peter Wentworth', *English Historical Review*, 39 (1924), 36–54, 175–205.

Queen Elizabeth I. A Biography, New York, Doubleday Anchor, 1957.

Nelson, Walter Henry, *The Soldier Kings*, London, J.M. Dent and Sons Ltd, 1971.

New, J.F.H., *Anglican and Puritan: the Basis of their Opposition, 1558–1640*, London, Adam and Charles Black, 1964.

Nicolai, Friedrich, *Beschreibung einer Reise durch Deutschland und die Schweiz im Jahre 1781. Nebst Bemerkungen über Gelehrsamkeit, Industrie, Religion und Sitten*, vol. 11, Book 3, Section 12: 'Aufenthalt in Tübingen', Berlin und Stettin, 1795.

Nietzki, Albert, *Bilder aus dem evangelischen Pfarrhause Ostpreussens im achtzehnten Jahrhundert*, Königsberg i. Pr., Kommissionsverlag Ferd. Beyers Buchhandlung, Thomas und Oppermann, 1909. (Schriften der Synodalkommission für Ostpreussische Kirchengeschichte, Heft 5.)

Chronik der evangelischen Kirchengemeinde in Mühlhausen, Kreis Pr. Eylau, Königsberg i. Pr., Kommissionsverlag Ferd. Beyers Buchhandlung, Thomas und Oppermann, 1910. (Schriften der Synodalkommission für Ostpreussische Kirchengeschichte, Heft 10.)

D. Johann Jakob Quandt. Generalsuperintendent von Preussen und Oberhofprediger in Königsberg, 1686–1772, Königsberg i. Pr., Kommissionsverlag Ferd. Beyers Buchhandlung, Thomas und Oppermann, 1905. (Schriften der Synodalkommission für Ostpreussische Kirchengeschichte, Heft 3.)

Notestein, Wallace, *The English People on the Eve of Colonisation, 1603–1630*, London, Hamish Hamilton, 1954.

Nuttall, Geoffrey, *Visible Saints*, Oxford, Basil Blackwell, 1957.

Obst, Helmut, *Der Berliner Beichtstuhlstreit*, Witten, Luther-Verlag, 1972.

O'Day, Rosemary, *The English Clergy. The Emergence and Consolidation of a Profession, 1558–1642*, Leicester, Leicester University Press, 1979.

and Felicity Heal (eds.), *Continuity and Change. Personnel and Administration of the Church in England 1500–1642*, Leicester, Leicester University Press, 1976.

Pariset, Georges, *L'État et les Églises en Prusse sous Frédéric-Guillaume Ier (1713–1740)*, Paris, Armand Colin et Cie, 1897.

Parker, Henry, *A Discourse Concerning Puritans*, London, 1641.

Parkin, Frank, *Max Weber*, London, Tavistock Publications, 1982.

A Parte of a Register, contayninge sundrie memorable matters, written by divers godly and learned in our time, which stande for, and desire the reformation of our Church, in Discipline and Ceremonies, accordinge to the pure worde of God, and the Lawe of our Lande, n.p., 1593.

Pearl, Valerie, *London and the Outbreak of the Puritan Revolution*, London, Oxford University Press, 1961.

Pearson, A.F. Scott, *Church and State: Political Aspects of Sixteenth-Century Puritanism*, Cambridge, Cambridge University Press, 1928.

Thomas Cartwright and Elizabethan Puritanism, 1535–1603, Cambridge, Cambridge University Press, 1925.

Pennington, D., and K. Thomas (eds.), *Puritans and Revolutionaries: Essays in Seventeenth-Century History presented to Christopher Hill*, Oxford, Clarendon Press, 1978.

Perkins, William, *A Golden Chaine: Or, the Description of Theologie, containing the Order of the Causes of Saluation and Damnation, according to God's Word*, Cambridge, 1600.

Peschke, Erhard (ed.), *August Hermann Francke: Werke in Auswahl*, Berlin, Evangelische Verlagsanstalt, Luther-Verlag, 1969.

Pfister, Albert, 'Hof und Hoffeste' and 'Militärwesen' in *Herzog Karl Eugen... und seine Zeit*, vol. 1.

Phillips, John, *The Reformation of Images: Destruction of Art in England. 1525–1660*, Berkeley, University of California Press, 1973.

Pinson, Koppel, *Modern Germany*, 2nd edn, New York, Macmillan, 1960.

Pietism as a Factor in the Rise of German Nationalism, New York, Columbia University Press, 1934.

Plum, H.G., *Restoration Puritanism*, Chapel Hill, University of North Carolina Press, 1943.

Poggi, Gianfranco, *The Development of the Modern State*, London, Hutchinson, 1978.

Porter, H.C., *Reformation and Reaction in Tudor Cambridge*, Cambridge, Cambridge University Press, 1958.

(ed.), *Puritanism in Tudor England*, London, Macmillan, 1970.

Prall, Stuart (ed.), *The Puritan Revolution: A Documentary History*, London, Routledge and Kegan Paul, 1968.

Prynne, William, *A Looking-Glasse for all Lordly Prelates...*, 1636.

Anti-Arminianisme..., 2nd edn, 1630.

Rabb, T.K., 'The Role of the Commons', *Past and Present*, 92 (1981), 55–78.

Reiners, Ludwig, *Frederick the Great*, London, Oswald Wolff Ltd, 1960.

Reyscher, A.L. (ed.), *Vollständige, historisch und kritisch bearbeitete Sammlung der Württembergischen Geseze*, vol. 8, Tübingen, Im Commission bei Ludw. Friedr. Fues, 1834.

Richardson, R.C., *The Debate on the English Revolution*, London, Methuen, 1977.

Puritanism in North-West England, Manchester, University of Manchester Press, 1972.

Riedesel, Erich, *Pietismus und Orthodoxie in Ostpreussen*, Königsberg und Berlin, Ost-Europa-Verlag, 1937.

Ritschl, Albrecht, *Geschichte des Pietismus*, 3 vols., Bonn, Adolph Marcus, 1880–6.

Roessle, Julius, *Von Bengel bis Blumhardt*, 2nd edn, Metzingen, Verlag Ernst Franz, 1960.

Roots, Ivan, *The Great Rebellion, 1642–1660*, London, Batsford, 1966.

Rose, Elliot, *Cases of Conscience*, Cambridge, Cambridge University Press, 1975.

Rosenberg, Hans, *Bureaucracy, Aristocracy and Autocracy*, pbk edn, Boston, Beacon Press, 1966.

Rowse, A.L., *The England of Elizabeth: The Structure of Society*, London, Sphere Books, Cardinal edn, 1973.

Rudolph, Martin, *Johann Jakob Brechter (1734–1772): Diakonus in Schwaigern*, Neustadt a. d. Aisch, Verlag Degener and Co., 1969.

Rürup, Reinhard, *Johann Jacob Moser: Pietismus und Reform*, Wiesbaden, Franz Steiner Verlag, 1965.

Russell, Conrad, 'Arguments for Religious Unity in England, 1530–1650', *Journal of Ecclesiastical History*, 18 (1967), 201–26.

The Crisis of Parliaments: English History 1509–1660, London, Oxford University Press, 1971.

'Parliamentary History in Perspective, 1604–1629', *History*, 61 (201) (1976), 1–27.

Parliaments and English Politics, 1621–1629, Oxford, Clarendon Press, 1979.

(ed.), *The Origins of the English Civil War*, London, Macmillan, 1973.

Samuelsson, Kurt, *Religion and Economic Action*, London, Heinemann, 1961.

Sattler, Christian Friedrich, *Geschichte des Herzogthums Würtenberg*, 13. Theil, Ulm, bey Aug. Lebr. Stettin, 1783.

Schall, Julius, 'Zur kirchlichen Lage Württembergs unter Herzog Karl Alexander', *Blätter für Württembergische Kirchengeschichte*, 4 (1900), 123–43.

Scharfe, Martin, 'Pietistische Moral im Industrialisierungsprozess' in B. Gladigow (ed.), *Religion und Moral*, Düsseldorf, Patmos Verlag, 1976.

Die Religion des Volkes: Kleine Kultur- und Sozialgeschichte des Pietismus, Gütersloh, Gütersloher Verlagshaus Gerd Mohn, 1980.

Schattenmann, P., 'Eigenart und Geschichte des deutschen Frühpietismus mit besonderer Berücksichtigung von Württembergisch-Franken', *Blätter für Württembergische Kirchengeschichte*, 40 (1936), 1–32.

Schild, Erich, *Der Preussische Feldprediger*, Part 1, Eisleben, Verlag von Otto Maehnert, 1888; Part 2, Halle, Verlag von Eugen Strien, 1890.

Schlatter, Richard B., *The Social Ideas of Religious Leaders, 1660–1688*, London, Oxford University Press, 1940.

Schlechte, Horst, 'Pietismus und Staatsreform 1762–63 in Kursachsen' in *Archivar und Historiker: Festschrift für H.O.Meisner*, Berlin, Rütten und Loening, 1965.

Schmid, Eugen, 'Aus dem Leben der Württembergischen evangelischen Pfarrer', *Blätter für Württembergische Kirchengeschichte*, 46 (1942), 75–111 and 47 (1943), 21–45.

'Das Volksschulwesen' in *Herzog Karl Eugen... und seine Zeit*, vol. 2.

Schmidt, Martin, 'Christian Hohburg and seventeenth-century mysticism', *Journal of Ecclesiastical History*, 18 (1967), 51–8.

'England und der deutsche Pietismus', *Evangelische Theologie*, 13 (1953), 205–24.

Pietismus, Stuttgart, W. Kohlhammer Verlag, 1972.

and Wilhelm Jannasch (eds.), *Das Zeitalter des Pietismus*, Bremen, Carl Schünemann Verlag, 1965.

Schmoller, G., 'Einleitung. Über Behördenorganisation, Amtswesen und Beamtenthum im Allgemeinen und speciell in Deutschland und Preussen bis zum Jahre 1713', in G. Schmoller and D. Krauske (eds.), *Acta Borussica. Die Behördenorganisation und die allgemeine Staatsverwaltung Preussens im 18. Jahrhundert*, vol. 1, Berlin, Verlag von Paul Parey, 1894.

Schneider, Eugen, 'Regierung' in *Herzog Karl Eugen... und seine Zeit*, vol. 1.

Württembergische Geschichte, Stuttgart, J.B. Metzlersche Verlag, 1896.

Schön, Th., 'Geschichte des Pietismus, Separatismus und Chiliasmus in der Reichstadt Reutlingen', *Blätter für Württembergische Kirchengeschichte*, 13 (1909), 63–81.

Schott, Arthur, 'Wirtschaftliches Leben', in *Herzog Karl Eugen...und seine Zeit*, vol. 1.

Seaver, Paul, *The Puritan Lectureships: The Politics of Religious Dissent, 1560–1662*, Stanford, Stanford University Press, 1970.

Selbmann, E., 'Die Gesellschaftlichen Erscheinungsformen des Pietismus Hallischer Prägung' in *450 Jahre Martin-Luther-Universität Halle–Wittenberg*, vol. 2, Halle–Wittenberg, Selbstverlag der Martin-Luther-Universität Halle–Wittenberg, 1952.

Semler, D. Joh. Salomo, *Lebensbeschreibung von ihm selbst abgefasst*, 2 parts, Halle, 1781–2.

Seybold, David Christian, *Hartmann: Eine Wirtembergische Klostergeschichte*, Leipzig, In der Weygandschen Buchhandlung, 1778.

Sharpe, Kevin (ed.), *Faction and Parliament*, Oxford, Clarendon Press, 1978.

Shipps, Kenneth, 'The "Political Puritan"', *Church History*, 45 (1976), 196–205.

Shriver, Frederick, 'Hampton Court Re-visited: James I and the Puritans', *Journal of Ecclesiastical History*, 33 (1982), 48–71.

Simpson, Alan, *Puritanism in Old and New England*, Chicago, University of Chicago Press, 1955.

'Saints in Arms: English Puritanism as Political Utopianism', *Church History*, 23 (1954), 119–25.

Skocpol, Theda, 'Rentier State and Shi'a Islam in the Iranian Revolution', *Theory and Society*, 11 (3), (1982), 265–83.

States and Social Revolutions, Cambridge, Cambridge University Press, 1979.

(ed.), *Vision and Method in Historical Sociology*, Cambridge, Cambridge University Press, forthcoming.

and Margaret Somers, 'The Uses of Comparative History in Macro-Social Inquiry', *Comparative Studies in Society and History*, 22 (1980), 174–97.

Smith, A. Hassell, *County and Court: Government and Politics in Norfolk, 1558–1603*, Oxford, Clarendon Press, 1974.

Snow, Vernon, 'Essex and the Aristocratic Opposition to the Early Stuarts', *Journal of Modern History*, 32 (1960), 224–33.

Spalding, James C., 'Sermons before Parliament (1640–1649) as a Public Puritan Diary', *Church History*, 36 (1967), 24–35.

Spener, Philipp Jacob, *Pia Desideria: Oder herzliches Verlangen / nach Gottgefälliger Besserung der wahren Evangelischen Kirchen / Sampt einigen dahin einfältig abzweckenden Christlichen Vorschlägen...* Franckfurt am Mayn, in Verlegung Johann David Zunners, 1676.

Spufford, M. *Contrasting Communities: English Villagers in the Sixteenth and Seventeenth Centuries*, Cambridge, Cambridge University Press, 1974.

Stearns, R.P., *The Strenuous Puritan: Hugh Peter, 1598–1660*, Urbana, University of Illinois, 1954.

Stern, Selma, *The Court Jew*, Philadelphia, The Jewish Publication Society of America, 1950.

Stoeffler, F. Ernest, *German Pietism during the Eighteenth Century*, Leiden, E.J. Brill, 1973.

The Rise of Evangelical Pietism, Leiden, E.J. Brill, 1965.

Stolze, Wilhelm, 'Friedrich Wilhelm I. und der Pietismus', *Jahrbuch für Brandenburgische Kirchengeschichte*, 5 (1908), 172–205.

Stone, Lawrence, *The Causes of the English Revolution, 1529–1642*, London, Routledge and Kegan Paul, 1972.

The Crisis of the Aristocracy, 1558–1641, abridged edn, London, Oxford University Press, 1967.

The Family, Sex and Marriage in England, 1500–1800, abridged edn, Harmondsworth, Penguin, 1979.

(ed.), *Social Change and Revolution in England, 1540–1640*, London, Longman, 1965.

et al., 'Stone and anti-Stone: a discussion', *Economic History Review*, 2nd ser., 25 (1972), 114–36.

Strachey, Lytton, *Elizabeth and Essex*, London, Chatto and Windus, 1928.

Tanner, J.R. (ed.), *Constitutional Documents of the Reign of James I, 1603–1625*, Cambridge, Cambridge University Press, 1930.

Tawney, R.H., *Religion and the Rise of Capitalism*, Harmondsworth, Penguin, 1938.

Taylor, A.J.P., *The Course of German History*, London, Methuen, 1961.

Tenbrock, R.H., *A History of Germany*, München, Max Hueber, 1968.

von Thadden, Rudolf, *Die Brandenburgisch-Preussischen Hofprediger im 17. und 18. Jahrhundert*, Berlin, Walter de Gruyter, 1959.

Thomas, Keith, *Religion and the Decline of Magic*, New York, Charles Scribner's Sons, 1971.

Tilly, Charles (ed.), *The Formation of National States in Western Europe*, Princeton, N.J., Princeton University Press, 1975.

Tillyard, E.M.W., *The Elizabethan World Picture*, New York, Random House, n.d.

Toon, Peter, 'Der Englische Puritanismus', *Historische Zeitschrift*, 214 (1972), 30–41.

Trautwein, Joachim, *Religiosität und Sozialstruktur*, Stuttgart, Calwer Verlag, 1972.

Travers, Walter, *A Full and Plaine Declaration of Ecclesiasticall Discipline owt off the Word of God / and off the Declininge off the Churche off England from the same*, 1574.

Trevor-Roper, H.R., *Archbishop Laud, 1573–1645*, 2nd edn, London, Macmillan, 1962 (orig. 1940).

Historical Essays, London, Macmillan, 1957.

Religion, the Reformation, and Social Change, 2nd edn, London, Macmillan, 1972.

Trinterud, L.J., 'The Origins of Puritanism', *Church History*, 20 (1951), 37–57.

Troeltsch, Ernst, *The Social Teaching of the Christian Churches*, vol. 2, New York, Harper Torchbook, 1960 (orig. 1911).

Tyler, Philip, 'The Status of the Elizabethan Parochial Clergy' in G. Cuming (ed.), *Studies in Church History*, vol. 4, Leiden, E.J. Brill, 1967.

Usher, R.G., *The Reconstruction of the English Church*, 2 vols., New York, D. Appleton and Co., 1910.

The Rise and Fall of the High Commission, Oxford, Clarendon Press, 1913.

(ed.), *The Presbyterian Movement in the Reign of Queen Elizabeth as illustrated by the Minute Book of the Dedham Classis, 1582–1589*, London, Offices of the Royal Historical Society, 1905.

Vann, James Allen, *The Swabian Kreis*, Brussels, Studies presented to the International Commission for the History of Representative and Parliamentary Institutions, 53, 1975.

Vann, Richard T., 'Quakers and the Social Structure in the Interregnum', *Past and Present* 43 (1969), 71–91.

The Social Development of English Quakerism, 1655–1755, Cambridge, Mass., Harvard University Press, 1969.

Vierhaus, Rudolf, 'Deutschland im 18. Jahrhundert: Soziales Gefüge, politische Verfassung, geistige Bewegung' in F. Kopitsch (ed.), *Aufklärung, Absolutismus und Bürgertum in Deutschland*, München, Nymphenburger Verlagshandlung, 1976.

Wais, Gustav, 'Samuel Urlspergers Entlassung', *Blätter für Württembergische Kirchengeschichte*, 44 (1940), 4–27.

Walker, D.P., *The Decline of Hell*, London, Routledge and Kegan Paul, 1964.

Wallmann, Johannes, *Philipp Jakob Spener und die Anfänge des Pietismus*, Tübingen, J.C.B. Mohr (Paul Siebeck), 1970.

'Pietismus und Orthodoxie. Überlegungen und Fragen zur Pietismusforschung' in H. Liebing and K. Scholder (eds.), *Geist und Geschichte der Reformation*, Berlin, Walter de Gruyter, 1966.

Walzer, Michael, 'Puritanism as a Revolutionary Ideology' in S.N. Eisenstadt (ed.), *The Protestant Ethic and Modernization*, New York, Basic Books, 1968.

The Revolution of the Saints, New York, Atheneum, 1974.

Watkins, Owen C., *The Puritan Experience*, London, Routledge and Kegan Paul, 1972.

Weber, Max, *Economy and Society*, ed. by Guenther Roth and Claus Wittich, New York, Bedminster Press, 1968.

The Protestant Ethic and the Spirit of Capitalism, London, George Allen and Unwin, 1930.

The Sociology of Religion, Boston, Beacon Press, 1964.

Weckherlin, F.A., *Wirtemberg. Pietismus. Schreiber. Schulen. Und Erziehung und Aufklärung überhaupt*, n.p., 1787.

Weigelt, Horst, 'Interpretations of Pietism in the Research of Contemporary German Church Historians', *Church History*, 39 (1970), 236–41.

Pietismus-Studien. 1. Teil: Der Spener–Hallesche Pietismus, Stuttgart, Calwer Verlag, 1965.

Weller, Karl, 'Geistiges Leben', in *Herzog Karl Eugen...und seine Zeit*, vol. 1.

Württembergische Geschichte, 5th edn, Stuttgart, Silberburg-Verlag, Werner Jäckh, 1963.

Wende, Peter, 'Revolution ohne Vorgeschichte? Neue Literatur zur Geschichte der englischen Parlamente des frühen 17. Jahrhunderts', *Historische Zeitschrift*, 230 (1980), 363–74.

Wendland, Walter, *Siebenhundert Jahre Kirchengeschichte Berlins*, Berlin und Leipzig, Walter de Gruyter, 1930.

Westfall, R.S., *Science and Religion in Seventeenth-Century England*, Ann Arbor, University of Michigan Press, 1973.

Weston, C.C., 'The Theory of Mixed Monarchy under Charles I and After', *English Historical Review*, 75 (1960), 426–43.

Whiting, E., *Studies in English Puritanism, 1660–1688*, London, S.P.C.K., 1931.

Wilson, Charles, *England's Apprenticeship, 1603–1763*, London, Longman, 1965.

Wintterlin, Friedrich, 'Landeshoheit' in *Herzog Karl Eugen... und seine Zeit*, vol. 1.

Wolff, Karl, 'Ist der Glaube Friedrich Wilhelms I. von A.H. Francke beeinflusst?', *Jahrbuch für Brandenburgische Kirchengeschichte*, 33 (1938), 70–102.

Woodhouse, A.S.P., *Puritanism and Liberty*, London, J.M. Dent and Sons Ltd, 1938.

Woolrych, Austin, 'Court, Country and City Revisited', *History*, 65 (1980), 236–45.

Wotschke, Theodor, *Georg Friedrich Rogalls Lebensarbeit nach seinen Briefen*, Königsberg i. Pr., Kommissionsverlag Ferd. Beyers Buchhandlung, Thomas und Oppermann, 1928. (Schriften der Synodalkommission für Ostpreussische Kirchengeschichte, Heft 27.)

Der Pietismus in Königsberg nach Rogalls Tode in Briefen, Königsberg i. Pr., Kommissionsverlag Ferd. Beyers Buchhandlung, Thomas und Oppermann, 1929–30. (Schriften der Synodalkommission für Ostpreussische Kirchengeschichte, Heft 28.)

Wrightson, Keith, *English Society, 1580–1680*, London, Hutchinson, 1982.

and David Levine, *Poverty and Piety in an English Village: Terling 1525–1700*, New York, Academic Press, 1979.

Zagorin, Perez, *The Court and the Country*, London, Routledge and Kegan Paul, 1969.

Index

Note: the German umlaut is taken as an 'e', and the alphabetical order is arranged accordingly.